Jane Martin
Collected Plays Volume II

1996–2001

Jane Martin
Collected Plays Volume II
1996–2001

Edited by Michael Bigelow Dixon

Contemporary Playwrights Series

SK
A Smith and Kraus Book

A Smith and Kraus Book
Published by Smith and Kraus, Inc.

Manufactured in the United States of America
Cover and Text Design by Julia Gignoux, Freedom Hill Design
Cover Photo: *Cementville* with Sally Parrish, Cynthia Carle,
and Peggity Price. Photograph by Richard C. Trigg.

First Edition: December 2001
10 9 8 7 6 5 4 3 2 1

Library of Congress Cataloging-in-Publication Data
Martin, Jane.
    [Plays. Selections.]
    Jane Martin: collected plays, 1996–2001. --1st ed.
        p. cm. --(Contemporary playwrights series)

    ISBN 1-57525-272-4 (v.2)
    I. Title.   II. Series.

    PS3563.A72433A6   1995
    812'.54--dc20
                        95-30492
                         CIP

Contents

Foreword

JANE MARTIN IN CONTEXT

This new collection of plays brings us up-to-date with the preoccupations of Jane Martin — social satirist and purveyor of comedies and dramas that delight in popular culture, scrutinize American politics, and limn the infinite variety in human relationships. Jane Martin's plays mix the virtues of show business — meaty roles for actors, colorful dilemmas, and impassioned confrontations — with the rewards of a formidable intellect. Make no mistake about it, Jane Martin is a lively entertainer with serious intentions. Her plays, be they comic or serious or seriocomic, express a worldview that is at once empathetic and critical, familiar and surprising, endearing and savage. They teeter on a tightrope between outrageous humor and shocking violence, plummeting into both with unexpected results.

The plays anthologized here represent the broad spectrum of subject matter and style in Jane Martin's developing canon. Listed in order of their premiere productions in the Humana Festival of New American Plays at Actors Theatre of Louisville, these recent works include a lampoon of America's most powerful and privileged (*Middle-Aged White Guys*); a foray into the human comedy of modern relationships, which isn't always funny (*Jack and Jill*); an examination of what can happen when one's fear and social conscience collide (*Mr. Bundy*); a satiric valentine to her beloved art form (*Anton in Show Business*); and a parodic genre-bender that creates a comic High Noon with references to "B" Westerns and horror flicks (*Flaming Guns of the Purple Sage*). There are also ten-minute plays and monologues that clearly demonstrate Jane Martin's ability to finesse and distress the defining moment in a character's life.

Since I had the pleasure of working as the production dramaturg on the premieres of these full-length plays by Jane Martin, I thought it might be useful to collect and share my thoughts at the time of each production. The following articles are reprinted from Humana Festival newsletters, 1995 to 2001, and it's my hope that these commentaries provide a context for understanding some of the ideas that informed the first productions of these works by Jane Martin.

· · ·

Middle-Aged White Guys
The Fickle Finger of Forgiveness
(Humana Festival 1995)

Though the 1990s may be remembered as the Age of Disagreement, there remains one plank all parties can stand on — something's gone wrong with America. But what exactly and how to fix it? That's the divisive question. Everyone has a favorite dog to kick and a pint of snake oil to hawk, yet no one dares offer the kind of righteous medicine prescribed in *Middle-Aged White Guys*. Why not? Well, without giving away too much, the recommendations of Jane Martin are unusual, unorthodox, and unabashedly funny!

Jane Martin sets her rogue comedy on a Day of Peculiar Judgment, when three middle-aged brothers from middling America reunite in a garbage dump that sprawls across their old baseball field. These men have gathered to commemorate a wife, a lost lover, and an inspiration — but it's difficult to ignore all the omens. Possums have been acting weird, as have horses, frogs, bats, rats, and a few dangerous people. There's something wonderfully wacky going on in this landfill of dreams. The question is, will it goose the politician, the businessman, the mercenary soldier, or all three?

Seen as a modern-day morality tale with more than a touch of sass, *Middle-Aged White Guys* proposes as a metaphor for America a junkyard that's filled with the refuse of planned obsolescence and the trashing of ideals. Accompanying shards of Barbie, fast food, and Chryslers are distorted images of presidents, family values, and the second Amendment, which is tattered with bullet holes. Emerging Godzilla-like from this heap of kitsch icons, *Middle-Aged White Guys* is, according to director Jon Jory, "a comedy about America's problems and whodunit. This play satirizes behaviors of power and the assigning of blame."

It's interesting to note that *Middle-Aged White Guys* conforms perfectly to the classical rules of satire, "which blends a critical attitude with humor and wit for the purpose of improving human institutions and humanity. True satirists are conscious of the frailty of institutions of human devising and attempt through laughter not so much to tear them down as to inspire a remodeling." In Martin's view, what needs "remodeling" is not the institutions so much as those who run them.

This wild, rambunctious, outlandish new comedy harkens back to the lunacy of past plays by Jane Martin, such as *Cementville* and *Coup/Clucks*. It's also a surprising companion piece to her most recent drama, the award-winning *Keely and Du*. Both plays examine forgiveness in a society bent on retribution and blame. But where *Keely and Du* shows how force can ignite violence, *Middle-Aged White Guys* employs irreverent persuasion to initiate a more peaceful change of heart.

. . .

Jack and Jill
Love's Labors: Lost and Found
(Humana Festival 1996)

Not much is new in the land of love; it is an ancient passion. If we had access to thoughts on romance and relationship from a million years ago, we'd doubtless recognize a theme raised more recently by Jean Giradoux: "The life of a wife and husband who love each other is never at rest." That's the dynamic that fascinates Jane Martin: shifting consciousness, striving for intimacy, the never-ending journey of self-discovery, and the struggle to achieve a level playing field.

Jane Martin's bracing views on love, marriage, and relationship in the 1990s invigorate her latest work, *Jack and Jill*. Subtitled (ironically) "A Romance," this scintillant seriocomedy picks up the amorous scent as two strangers introduce themselves — are their names, reminiscent of the children's nursery rhyme, pure coincidence or fate? Whichever, soon they're tumbling into bed, succumbing to the universal pleasures of love, evoked by William Shakespeare as the "spirit all compact of fire." But can it last?

While many modern love stories emphasize a search for Mr. or Ms. Right, *Jack and Jill* explores what happens after two people find "the fit." That's when the damn hard work begins, according to Jane Martin. Yet who in the 90s is prepared for the real labors of love? Both Jack and Jill are already divorced when they meet, but what have they learned from experience? At most, they seem gun-shy, fearful of a possible fall, wary of repeating the disappointments of their histories.

Martin's fascination with the ins and outs of romance is founded on a basic human truth: Love doesn't often endure. Or as psychotherapist Eric Fromm observed: "There is hardly any activity, any enterprise which is started with such tremendous hopes and expectations, and yet which fails so regularly, as love." Why is that? That's what Jane Martin wants to know. And that's what Jack and Jill must contend with in their long march up the hill.

As far as plot goes, the spine of every romance is a mere complication of getting and losing. The main points of *Jack and Jill* are no different, and yet, what makes love dramatic is not what happens but how. Courting and companionship succeed by style and wit, traits that play into the very strengths of this author. And while *Jack and Jill* varies significantly from Martin's recent works, *Keely and Du* and *Middle-Aged White Guys*, it retains her signature offbeat humor, salty lyricism, fierce passion, and bold theatricality. All of which inspire a series of vivifying encounters with romance as a playground, a battlefield, an X ray, a puzzle, an obsession, and finally, a choice.

．　．　．

Mr. Bundy
(Humana Festival 1998)

You move to a nice neighborhood to raise your child. The house costs more than you can afford, but your child's safety and the quality of the schools seem worth it. Then someone tells you a convicted and released child molester lives next door — and your eight-year-old daughter likes him. What do you do? "Out" him in the press? Out him from your neighborhood? Or leave him be and pray nothing happens to your daughter or anyone else's children? Those are the problems presented by that nice old man living right next door, Mr. Bundy.

In this powerful drama, Jane Martin anatomizes community ethics and personal reactions to sexual offenders. The parents, Robert and Catherine, get torn between potential danger to their daughter and the possible rehabilitation of Mr. Bundy. Two members of a watchdog group, Jimmy Ray and Tianna, advise them to make Mr. Bundy move on. Another neighbor seems to side with the watchdogs. But even if they're right, how do you get him to go — by request, threat, or force? As Robert and Catherine confront their fears along with matters of conscience and constitutional rights, the watchdogs quickly get to the point — get rid of Mr. Bundy *now!*

"I think the play is about two interlocking issues," observes director Jon Jory. "One being the Christian concept of forgiveness and whether it's an active force as a contemporary value. And two, the attempt to stay human — to not allow yourself to participate in violence as a way of solving problems of the culture — and whether that's a naive or useful philosophy."

For Robert and Catherine, the problem of Mr. Bundy is clouded in doubt. Since this sixty-year-old man has already served time for his crime, should the community punish him further? Is there a point where incessant retribution becomes unjustifiable revenge? And, once drawn into this moral morass, is there a choice that's both conscionable and safe? "Our instinct when someone harms us is to harm them in return," acknowledges Jory. "How we respond to violence in others combines both issues of forgiveness and revenge. And is one better than the other?"

In trademark Jane Martin fashion, this explosive new work explores moral dilemmas with theatrical flair and force. Incipient violence underscores many confrontations in the play, as discussion escalates to argument and suggestion turns into threat. In the shadow of these adult issues, there's an eight-year-old girl jumping rope — Cassidy — innocent, unsuspecting, unharmed. How far should we go to protect her against the Mr. Bundys of the world?

. . .

Anton in Show Business
(Humana Festival 2000)

"The backstage comedy" is a wonderful tradition in theater and film. *The Royal Family* by George S. Kaufman and Edna Ferber, for instance, follows the antics of three generations of legendary American actors as they strut their stuff offstage. Noel Coward's *Present Laughter* lampoons the bedroom hijinks of Garry Essendine, a popular and pampered star. In David Mamet's *A Life in the Theatre,* two actors suffer the illusions and realities of their chosen profession amidst hilarious mishaps. And on the screen, *Bullets Over Broadway* executes Woody Allen's wacky scenario of what happens when gangsters dabble in dramaturgy.

Now it's Jane Martin's turn to bring the genre up-to-date for the nonprofit arts scene in America. Like all the comedies listed above, *Anton in Show Business* focuses on the struggle of actors; in this case, three women cast in Anton Chekhov's *The Three Sisters.* Their production is slated for Actors Express in Texas, but first the women must pass muster in New York auditions, which involves having their talents picked apart by an arrogant British director who gets his comeuppance in a surprising tête-á-tête. And so begin the wild adventures of making theater at the turn of the millennium, as we follow three actors down a Texas rabbit hole and into the American Wonderland of "good ideas," power politics, and competing agendas.

On their madcap excursion through this Carrollian universe, the three women try to retain their sense of purpose amidst the clamor of producers, directors, designers, funders, critics, and even the audience. But like Alice, they continually fail in their attempts to connect with or even comprehend the mad tea party that American theater sometimes resembles. Oh, and their failures aren't painless either, but because comedy is an art form based in pain — and because this particular comedy is written by Jane Martin — the actors' traumas and travails are very, very funny.

While *Anton in Show Business* is an equal-opportunity satire of a system running amok, the author's heart is definitely on the side of the artist in America. "This play is interested in the fact that it's hard to feel valuable in this culture if you're an artist because the economics and politics of the theatre shape who artists think they are," suggests director Jon Jory. "And so the artists formed in this crucible lose confidence and direction. This is a comedy about what people in the process confront, and it asks the question, what can the artist do in a culture that doesn't value her?"

As we have come to expect of new plays by Jane Martin, the images here of "putting on a play" in the year 2000 are bounced off some curvaceous fun-house mirrors. There's an homage to Thornton Wilder, for example, from the all-female cast. There are snippets of a performance-within-the-play, and a review-within-the-play, as well. There are directors who fall by the wayside and, of course, a romance or two. But through all the razzle, dazzle, and frazzle, Martin keeps an eye out for her beloved actors: Holly, a television idol who wants to break into film; Casey, the queen of off-off Broadway; and Lisabette, a third-grade teacher with a degree in acting. They're the ones who must run the gauntlet of American theater, only to discover in the process that they share a mission with Chekhov's three sisters — somehow to find a purpose in this work until life's deeper purpose will be revealed.

. . .

Flaming Guns of the Purple Sage
(Humana Festival 2001)

Jane Martin is back with one of her most unruly comedies ever. And that's saying a lot, given the fact that she's already mocked the powerful, the patriarchal, and the naked in *Middle-Aged White Guys* and put a lampoon leg-lock on female wrestlers in *Cementville*. Now Jane Martin roasts the cowboy mentality of writers like Zane Grey, transforming herself into a kind of Inzane Grey for this shoot-'em-up, knock-'em-up, cut-'em-up comic romp through deepest Wyoming.

Flaming Guns of the Purple Sage combines the formulaic elements of classic "B" movie Westerns with the thousand natural shocks that horror flicks are heir to. 'Tis a consummation devoutly to be wished — and laughed at — for this strange brew of genres produces something like an *Addams Family* version of *Gunsmoke* in which the monster Chuckie is terrorized by Chester and Miss Kitty.

At the center of this macabre comedy is one of Jane Martin's earliest creations, Big 8, a character who debuted twenty years ago in the "Rodeo" segment of Martin's award-winning first play, *Talking With*. When we last saw her, Big 8 was in her late twenties, drinking Lone Star beer, working on a piece of tack, and bemoaning the commercialization of American pastimes. She'd recently been fired from the rodeo because, as she explained, she wouldn't "haul my butt through the barrel race done up like Minnie damn Mouse in a tutu." At the time, the fiercely independent Big 8 was understandably bitter, and the years have done nothing to change her.

In *Flaming Guns of the Purple Sage,* we catch up with Big 8 two decades later on her small ranch near Casper, Wyoming. Now in her late forties, Big 8 has fallen behind on her mortgage payments and faces foreclosure. To stave off financial ruin, she grates cheese at the Beatrice Foods plant and augments her income by rehabilitating busted-up rodeo riders at her house. Her current charge is a boy toy named Rob Bob, who's enjoying the full-service "healing" at Big 8's Lourdes for ex-rodeo champs.

One night at 3 A.M., Big 8 and Rob Bob are into some serious drinking and "healing" when a young woman appears. Her body's full of piercings, her hair's the color of "throwed-up strawberry milkshake," and she goes by the name of Shedevil. This colorful stranger quickly steals Rob Bob's heart and Big 8's hidden savings. And if that's not trouble enough for everyone on the ranch, Shedevil's being followed by a Hell's Angel biker from the Ukraine, whose arrival ignites the incendiary events that inspire the title of this bizarrely wild western.

While Jane Martin riffs on the garishness of American pop culture, there is satiric method to her madness. In *Flaming Guns of the Purple Sage* our anonymous author pits the forces of good against evil and discovers a good deal of common ground between the two. This social critique in parodic form raises some interesting questions about the world we live in.

Have good and evil become relative concepts, totally subject to interpretation and defined primarily by the "winners" in a morally ambivalent age?

Seems possible. When every American is armed to the teeth, will our society regress to the violent ways of the Old West? Seems likely. And in our stressed-out universe, is it possible to keep your head on straight while those about you are losing theirs — figuratively and literally? For the answer to that one, you'll have to check out Martin's monster-screwball-comedy. You may laugh your head off, but given the options presented in this play, laughing it off is certainly better than the alternative!

.   .   .

Finally, for those who continue to search for clues to the identity of Jane Martin, my favorite theory is that these plays are written by the seventeenth Earl of Oxford Edward de Vere. If he didn't write Shakespeare's plays, that's probably because he was busy writing these by Jane Martin.

— Michael Bigelow Dixon
Literary Manager, Guthrie Theater

Middle-Aged White Guys

ORIGINAL PRODUCTION

Middle-Aged White Guys was first presented at the 19th Humana Festival of New American Plays at Actors Theatre of Louisville in March 1995. It was directed by Jon Jory with the following cast:

R.V. . . . . Karenjune Sánchez
Roy . . . . John Griesemer
Clem . . . . Bob Burrus
Mona . . . . Karen Grassle
Moon . . . . Leo Burmester
King . . . . Larry Larson
Mrs. Mannering. . . . . Anne Pitoniak

CHARACTERS

ROY: The mayor, 48.

CLEM: The businessman, 47.

MOON: The mercenary, 46.

R.V.: A forerunner, 25.

MONA: A woman in transition, 40.

KING: A messenger.

MRS. MANNERING: Mother to the brothers, 70.

TIME

Present day.

THE PLACE

A dump.

MIDDLE-AGED WHITE GUYS

*A small-town dump and junkyard, its mounds and valleys of debris slightly
steaming in the rose of the sunset. Piles of cans, boxes, barrels, the rusted hulk
of an old car, broken bedsteads, refrigerators, garbage, old signs, mounds of
the unimaginable. The effect created is a dark, eccentric, contemporary hell.*

*On top of the junked car, a young woman in a short, red dress, with a
snake tattoo coiling up her left arm from wrist to shoulder, sits cross-legged.
Heat lightning flashes in the distance. Far away, thunder rolls.*

R.V.: Moon? Yo, Moon, can you hear me down there? Down, down, in that
river of sleep? Down with one foot in the dark continent? You remember that day, Moon? You know the one I mean. Old guy leans over, touches
my tattoo, says, "Hey, Snake, we got a no-hitter goin', woman; we're
workin' a virgin top of the sixth."
(Thunder.)
They say there's an hour in everybody's life where all the luck you shoulda
had comes together like drops on the windshield. You ever hear that? State
championship high school game, and all the luck we'd never have again
just riding your arm through the late afternoon. Roy, he was four for four;
Clem caught that relay bare-handed for the double play. And there you
were, right into the eighth, throwin' smoke and sinkers like Mr. Smooth
in the bigs. And then, just then, some tanked-up dickwad on the third
base side yells out, "Workin' a no-hitter, Moon!" And you froze stiff in
your windup and looked over there like he woke you up from an afternoon nap, and then you shook your head and threw fourteen straight,
fat ones up there, and they put *five* runs on the board. I couldn't believe
it, Moon. *(Thunder nearer; a dog howling.)* Omens and portents. *(She looks
at the sky.)* Read 'em an' weep. *(She knocks on the car top.)* What the hell
were you doin', Moon? How come you threw it away?
*(Roy Mannering, a man in his late 40s, appears over the ridge of the dump.
He is dressed as Abraham Lincoln, including beard and stovepipe hat. Roy
carries two six-packs of beer. He looks down and yells a name, apparently not
noticing R.V.)*
ROY: Clem? You here, Clem? *(To himself.)* What damn color is *that* sky? *(He*

takes a step forward and falls ass-over-teakettle down the dump's incline.) Well, that's just perfect. That's just sweet as hell. Clem?

(The girl has disappeared. He wipes at his clothes with a handkerchief.)

ROY: What is this stuff? Oh, that's perfect. *(He pulls out a portable phone and dials.)* Mona? Mona, it's Roy. What's with the voice, Mona? You're not cryin' again, are you? Well, you better not because I'm sick of it, woman, that's why. Listen, Mona, go to the closet…you got any mascara on your hands? Well, you wash them off, go to the closet, get my gray silk summer suit…gray suit…stop cryin', Mona…run that gray suit up to the July 4th reviewing stand…because I got nasty stuff on the Abe Lincoln suit…Mona, I can't give the Gettysburg Address covered in dog shit. Now give that gray suit to Luellen…my assistant Luellen…I am not sleepin' with Luellen, Mona…she is one year out of high school…what the hell are you cryin' about, I put your Prozac right where you could see it. Now I need that suit, woman; you do what I tell you. *(He cuts her off the phone.)* I can't stand that damn cryin'. *(He dials again.)* Luellen, sweetmeat, it's Long Dong Silver. You got any word where those fireworks are? Well, those damn Chinese don't know what U.P.S. means. Well, we'll shoot what we got. Listen, I'll be there…forty, forty-five minutes, max. *(Feels beard.)* Yeah, I got it on. This stick-on stuff stings like hell. Look, tell Carl keep the high school band a couple extra numbers 'cause we're missin' those Chinese fireworks. Well, you tell him to do it. I'm the damned mayor!

(Puts phone back in pocket. A man appears above. It is Roy's younger brother Clem. He wears overalls and a work shirt, and carries an umbrella.)

CLEM: That you, Roy?

(Roy startles.)

ROY: Damn, Clem.

CLEM: I tried not to scare you.

ROY: *(Scraping at his pants.)* Look at this? What are we doin' in the dump, Clem? What the hell are we doin' here?

CLEM: We promised her, Roy. It's a sacred trust.

ROY: *(Still looking at his clothes.)* A sacred trust.

CLEM: I get it. You're dressed up as a Smith Brothers cough drop.

ROY: This is Abe Lincoln, Clem.

CLEM: Oh, I see.

ROY: Seventy-five dollar rental, and I fell down the hill.

CLEM: Abe Lincoln, sure. We promised R.V. we'd come down here every ten years.

ROY: I know that, Clem.

CLEM: Twenty years ago today. You want some Cheezits?

ROY: *(Another matter.)* Clem, I got to talk to you.

CLEM: It's Mama's birthday, too.

ROY: What?

CLEM: I know, you never like to think of her dead.

ROY: Our beautiful Mama.

CLEM: 'Member how she always called you "Tiny"?

ROY: Mama's birthday! Why did she leave us, Clem?

CLEM: She died, Roy.

ROY: I know she died, goddamnit.

CLEM: Our two beautiful ladies in the heavenly choir.

ROY: I miss you, Mama!

CLEM: Mama and R.V. Makes this a sacred trust.

ROY: Alright, Clem. You hear anything from Moon?

CLEM: Can't make it. Wired R.V. a dozen white roses, just like when we did this in '84.

ROY: Well, I knew little brother wouldn't show. Where was the roses wired at?

CLEM: Liberia.

ROY: Well, brother Moon, he's seen the world. Hasn't *built* a damn thing. Hasn't *been* a damn thing. White roses every ten years. I'm surprised he had the money.

CLEM: R.V. loved him.

ROY: She loved me.

CLEM: Well, Roy, I'd have to say…

ROY: I don't want to hear it! Three brothers, Clem, but everybody thought he was pure gold, didn't they?

CLEM: Oh, they did.

ROY: Well, I'm the gold and you're the gold, an' he's down in Liberia washing out his clothes in a stream full of fecal matter.

CLEM: I miss old Moon. He sure does love to kill people.

ROY: He always killed things. Back in elementary, he'd kill bugs, birds, squirrels, wild dogs…he just grew up, that's all. Clem, I got a time problem…

CLEM: Well, we'll do the toast.

ROY: There's somethin' else, Clem.

CLEM: What, Roy?

ROY: A real bad sign.

CLEM: Bad signs, that's right. You know that palomino horse old Gifford keeps out at four corners? Drivin' over here, seen that horse run mad, goes straight into the barbed wire, tangles himself up, goes to screamin', blood gettin' throwed up into the air, most horrible thing I ever saw, plus everybody's gettin' boils, the creek's turned red, and there's piles a dead frogs right downtown…

ROY: *(Hands him a letter.)* I'm not talkin' about that kind of sign, Clem.

CLEM: There's been three cases of rabid bats…

ROY: Just read the letter, Clem.

(Clem opens it.)

ROY: I'm not worryin' about dead frogs or rabid bats; I'm worryin' about re-election, Clem.

CLEM: *(Referring to the letter.)* So the newspaper guy knows about the chemicals? *(So what?)*

ROY: What chemicals?

CLEM: *(Indicating the barrels stage right.)* Well…these ones.

ROY: They are food additives, Clem, not chemicals.

CLEM: Food additives.

ROY: I got the letter, I went over to the newspaper. Now that pissant editor has a load receipt from Long Island Petrochemical tells him how many barrels of this, how many barrels of that they sent down here.

CLEM: Food additives.

ROY: Food additives, that's right. I explained we have no barrel leakage or groundwater problem on the site. I explained the value of the contract to the city; Hell, it's 37 percent of the municipal income, you'd think a damn moron could understand the economics, but he reads me a state statute says four of these additives—chloroethylene, hexochlorobenzine, polychlorinated biphenyls and…somethin' else—are prohibited from interstate transport. Too much damn government, Clem, that's what that is. Now where do you think he got that load receipt?

CLEM: Well…

ROY: You gave it to him.

CLEM: Well, he goes to our church, Roy.

ROY: You gave it to him.

CLEM: Well, he said, since it got the town so much money, just how many barrels was it? So I gave him the load receipt, and he was real impressed.

ROY: Now we got to go get it back.

CLEM: Why, Roy?

ROY: So he can't put it in the paper.

CLEM: It's just food additives, Roy.

ROY: Uh-huh, that's one thing, plus you and me set up the haulage company. You ever hear of nepotism?

CLEM: That's a positive word around here.

ROY: Never mind, Clem. Luckily you rent him the building he's in, so you got a key.

CLEM: Sure, but...

ROY: I go get the fireworks started. I got to be there 'cause the new poll says it's a real tight race. You go pick up your key...later on, we go on down to the newspaper, get that load receipt.

CLEM: Walk right in?

ROY: Uh-huh.

CLEM: That's not burglary?

ROY: It's fixin' the problem.

CLEM: I see.

ROY: Clem, there is America and there is not-America. America is the light. Not-America is the darkness. America isn't a place, Clem, it's an idea. Right now Clem, America isn't America, Japan is America. The problem is to get America back *in* America. Now, Clem, this is the idea that *is* America: See the problem, fix the problem, that makes a new problem, fix that problem. Whoever does that best *is* America, and right now it's *not* America. Not-America, which right now *is* America, has two damn characteristics. Number one: fools. Fools, Clem, cannot see the problem and cannot fix the problem. These people are Democrats. Number two: idealists. These are fools who fix the wrong problem and tell the people who are fixing the right problem that they are short-sighted. For instance, Clem, let us posit this: The world's greatest bomb defuser is defusing a hydrogen bomb planted by Arabs under the Speaker's platform in the U.S. Senate. This is the only man who can defuse this bomb. He has defused bombs like this for years. Because fixing this problem is stressful, he is a chainsmoker. Not-America number two, the goddamn idealists, Clem, pulls that expert defuser off the job because of the danger to United States senators of secondary smoke, and Washington, D.C. blows up! We are America, Clem—you, me, we fix the problem—but the forces of darkness, the non-America number one and the not-America number two is now America, and these not-Americans are saying the *real* Americans *are* the problem, which of course *is* the problem we, as real Americans, have to fix!

CLEM: We're the real Americans, right?

ROY: That's right.

CLEM: The good ones?

ROY: That's right.

(Clem's face crumples. He pulls out a flask.)

ROY: Don't you dare cry, Clem. You're a big businessman.

CLEM: Then how come Evelyn left me?

ROY: Because you drank her right out of the house.

CLEM: *(Taking a hit.)* I'm a bad person.

ROY: You got a haulin' business, you're into real estate. You run Gunworld, Clem, the biggest handgun retail outfit in a three-state area. You're a big success and you drive a damn Miata, how can you be a bad person?

CLEM: Evelyn still hasn't called, you know. She didn't call you, did she? How the hell am I going to raise those boys? They miss their mama. What kind of woman would run off like that and not even leave a note for those boys? How could she do that?

ROY: *(Handing him his handkerchief.)* She did it because women are a sorry damn lot, Clem. They are neurologically disadvantaged, with the objectivity of a collie dog. They hate all systems, all logic, all authority, and any damn evidence runs contrary to their damn feelings. You take out the sex drive, there isn't one man in a million would stay in a house with 'em for forty-eight hours.

(Clem weeps.)

ROY: Stop cryin', goddamnit.

CLEM: Jimmy Peaslee…

ROY: What?

CLEM: His mama is the daughter of that woman used to run the Cherokee Diner.

ROY: I got the Gettysburg Address in twenty minutes. I got some colored lawyer dead even in the polls…

CLEM: Jimmy Peaslee took a gun to school, tried to shoot his second-grade teacher.

ROY: When?

CLEM: Yesterday. An AK-47. He fired off a burst, but it went wild…

ROY: Down at Lincoln Elementary?

CLEM: Said his teacher was a damn lesbian.

ROY: Was she?

CLEM: I think she just wore a pantsuit.

ROY: We wouldn't have this kind of problem if we had prayer in the schools, Clem. Now let's do the damn toast.

CLEM: *(Heedless.)* That weapon come from Gunworld. It was mine, Roy.

ROY: You sold it to the boy?

CLEM: To the daddy.

ROY: So?

CLEM: I feel real guilty, Roy. *(He weeps.)*

ROY: Clem, I got 1,500, maybe 2,000 people showin' up for my fireworks show, and due to the Chinese I got five, six minutes of fireworks, tops. My wife's on a cryin' jag, I got a little girl on the side is gettin' real pushy, I got to break into the newspaper, I'm runnin' against a damn minority, and my Lincoln suit is covered with dog shit. *You* don't have a problem, Clem. You sold a legal weapon to a legal daddy, and if he is so damn dumb he leaves it where Junior can get it, it sure as hell is not your fault. Democracy honors the individual, Clem, at the cost of givin' him personal responsibility, and if he can't handle the responsibility, the state ought to castrate him so he can't mess up his kid! Plus you don't even know she *wasn't* a lesbian.

CLEM: You explained that real fine, Roy.

ROY: That's right. Now, I got to go to the fireworks. You meet me right after behind the Dairy Freeze. Bring the keys and a ski mask. *(He starts out of the dump.)*

CLEM: What about the sacred trust?

ROY: I don't have time for the sacred trust. *(Starts out.)*

CLEM: She was your wife, Roy.

ROY: That was twenty damn years ago!

CLEM: My wife left me, Roy. *(Weeping.)* My Evelyn left me!
  (Roy stops.)

ROY: Goddamnit Clem, you're gettin' me homicidal. *(Clem weeps.)* If I do the toast, will you stop cryin'?!

CLEM: You'll keep the sacred trust?

ROY: I will keep the goddamn, sonofabitchin' sacred trust. I'm givin' this five minutes, you understand me?

CLEM: You're a prince, Roy. You want some Cheezits?

ROY: Do it! *(He comes back down.)*

CLEM: *(Looking up.)* R.V.? It's me, Clem. I'm here with Roy, in the dump. It's about 8:30. Sky's a real funny color.

ROY: You gonna do a weather report, Clem?

CLEM: Right, right.

ROY: Four minutes.

CLEM: So, R.V., it's Clem. I'm here with Roy in the dump.

ROY: You're drivin' me apeshit.

CLEM: R.V., we're here like we promised. Roy, me...well, Moon, he's tied up with fecal matter. Boy, I miss your shinin' face. You never loved me. Wasn't your fault. I know you loved Moon. I believe you loved Roy here…mainly. I don't know why you killed yourself, but that was just the worst thing ever happened to me. I still wake up cryin'. You asked in that death note would we hoist a beer every ten years on the pitcher's mount where we almost got to be state champs an' you sang the National Anthem. See, they sold the field for a dump site when they combined the high school over to Mayberry.

ROY: One minute.

CLEM: *(Quickly.)* I can still hear your beautiful voice. So clear and high. Sounded like Snow White or Cinderella singin' to the mice. Boy, I miss you, R.V.…it's just a dump now, but it's a world of memories to me. *(He weeps.)*

ROY: Goddamn it, Clem.

(Clem stops.)

ROY: R.V.? You were a damn fine woman with beautiful breasts and a good sense of humor. We shouldn't have got married with you still stuck on Moon, but that's 20-20 hindsight. You knew what a man is, but you didn't throw it in his face. You were mentally unbalanced, but you never let it show up in bed. That's a good woman in my book.

(A middle-aged woman, Roy's wife Mona, wearing only a slip, high heels, and a strand of pearls around her neck, appears on the ridge behind them. She carries a pistol.)

ROY: You are my damn baby, R.V. honey, and any woman since you've gone is just passin' the time.

(At this moment, Mona on the ridge raises the pistol and fires down on Roy. He and Clem scramble. Simultaneously:)

ROY: Hold it.

CLEM: Don't shoot.

MONA: *(Holding Roy's gray suit on a hanger in her other hand.)* You are my nightmare, Roy Mannering! *(She fires again.)* You are a maggot b-b-born in the dung, b-burrowed down in my flesh eating me alive! I hitchhiked out here, so here's your g-g-gray suit! *(She flings it down into the dump.)*

ROY: You hitchhiked in your underwear?

(She fires again.)

ROY: Mona, that's enough now.

CLEM: Jeeminy.

MONA: I c-curse you, Roy. I c-call demons from their d-dank c-caves and crevices the c-creatures of the night to g-give you prostate cancer and Lou G-Gehrig's disease, and make you impotent that one t-time every c-couple of months you can still get it up.

ROY: You've got to relax if you want to stop stuttering, Mona.

(She fires again.)

MONA: Your teenage whore assistant called me up to say you were t-taking her to the Mayor's c-c-c-c-c-conference next week. She said you b-bought her a sapphire and d-d-diamond ring. Said you were divorcing me and m-m-m-m-marrying her. She said you called me a c-c-corpse with jewelry, Roy. Well, I am. I am eaten up with l-l-loathing for m-myself, and you taught m-me that with your fiendish c-c-c-criticism and little jokes and p-patronizing ways. I looked in the mirror t-t-tonight and I saw my b-bleached b-brain an' my d-dead eyes an' I said Mona, what b-became of you? Where are you, Mona?

(The door of the junked car in the lot opens quietly, and Moon, dressed in jeans and a skull T-shirt with an army field jacket over it, boots, and an old kerchief around his head, steps out. He is bearded and in every way piratical.)

MONA: I curse your sons and your sons' sons that they should be b-born without testicles, blind as newts, and they should disinter your corpse and rifle through your pockets for spare change. Now I'm going to shoot your p-puffy head off, and that will make me feel considerably better. *(She raises the gun again.)*

MOON: *(In his left hand, he carries a stubby full automatic as if it were an extension of his arm. As she raises the gun, he speaks consolingly.)* Good evening, ma'am.

(She turns, pointing the gun at him.)

I had a friend used to stutter until his confidence caught up with his heart.

CLEM: Moon.

MOON: How you doin'? Well ma'am, I'd have to agree with you about Roy, untutored as he is, he probably thinks you're a household appliance. He just don't know what a woman is, ma'am, and he's just unteachable as a rooster.

ROY: What the hell, Moon?

MOON: Shut up, Roy. Now ma'am, I'm a brute killer for pay, and they tell me I'm one of the dozen best shots in the world, left-handed or right. May I call you Mona? Mona, what you're holdin' there is a Rossi 518 Tiger Cat Special, accurate up to about 40 feet and, combined with your understandable emotion and inexperience, you most likely won't hit me, whereas, my first couple of rounds will tear off your wrist, leavin' you with one hand for the rest of your life. They tell me the pain's unendurable unless we cauterized it with fire, and by the time we got some kindlin', you'd likely bleed to death. It's strange when you can see right inside your own body like you can when an extremity's gone. We never know what we are because we're covered with skin. Once you find out, you realize we're just walkin' meat. Now I'd feel more comfortable if you'd point that thing at Roy, if you don't mind.

(She does.)

ROY: Damn, Moon.

MOON: Well I feel a whole lot better. Much obliged. Now what can we do for you, ma'am?

MONA: K-K-K-Kill him.

ROY: Moon?

MOON: *(To Roy.)* There's no punishment in death, ma'am. It's over in the blink of an eye. The thing I like least about killin' people is how easy they get off. Hell, he stole your life from you. Wouldn't you say that's the situation?

MONA: I was...I was...I had dreams.

MOON: Sure, I know. You got some place you could go?

MONA: Clem's wife, Evelyn, she called from Arizona.

CLEM: Arizona?

MONA: She says it's n-nice. She l-lives with the Navajos.

CLEM: My Evelyn?

MONA: She said I could c-c-come out there.

MOON: You know what you get out there, ma'am? You get yourself a shadow, so you don't get lonely.

MONA: But I don't have the money. He didn't let me work.

MOON: Well see, he is so small. He is such a small person he could only enlarge himself at your expense.

ROY: Now that's just damned well enough.

MOON: She's going to kill you, Roy, we're lookin' for alternatives.

ROY: She can't hit the side of a barn.

MOON: She isn't stuttering, Roy. Her hand's steady. You ought to hold that with two hands, ma'am. Sort of like this.

(He demonstrates. She changes her grip.)

ROY: Dammit!

MOON: She might get lucky, put one right up your nose.

ROY: I don't know you.

MOON: Ma'am, I believe I'm goin' to take up a collection, how about that? Gimme your wallets, boys.

(They don't respond.)

MOON: I said gimme your goddamn wallets!

(They throw them on the ground.)

MOON: I get real pissed off at myself, the course I've taken. I should have got into robbery, it's just so damn easy. *(Picks them up. He looks.)* You won't mind if your pretty wife goes on a little shoppin' spree, will you, Roy? *(Roy glowers.)*

MOON: So now I'm comin' up there, ma'am. Roy, throw me over your car keys, will you?

ROY: I am not givin' you my car keys.

MOON: What are you drivin' these days?

ROY: No way, No damn way.

MOON: Go ahead, ma'am, shoot him.

    (She fires. Roy hits the ground. She misses.)

ROY: Goddammit to hell. Son of a bitch.

MOON: That was about a foot left, ma'am. And if you wouldn't mind a little advice, I wouldn't go for the head, I'd go for the gut.

ROY: Alright. Alright. I'm gettin' the keys.

MOON: How are you doin', Clem?

CLEM: Well, Evelyn run off.

MOON: Sorry to hear that. You better have a drink.

CLEM: *(Pulling out the flask.)* Okay, Moon.

MOON: There's a case to be made for finishin' the century blind drunk.

CLEM: Care for a dollop?

    (Clem, having taken a hit, passes the flask to Moon.)

MOON: Well, I don't mind. *(Drinks.)* How about you, Mona?

MONA: *(A roar.)* I hate men!

MOON: Me too, ma'am. *(Drinks.)*

ROY: There. *(Tosses the keys.)* This is egregious damn car theft.

MOON: Tell him "Shut up," ma'am.

MONA: Shut up!

MOON: Here I come now. *(Starts up toward Mona.)* Just bringin' the wallets and the car keys. Get you started, you know, before the divorce.

MONA: I was g-good at math.

MOON: Yes ma'am.

MONA: I was better than the boys.

    (He nods.)

MOON: Yes ma'am.

MONA: I could have done r-research on the universe.

MOON: Well, you're still young, ma'am.

MONA: No, I'm not. I'm dried out.

MOON: *(Puts the wallets down near her.)* Well, you look a little chilly. You might like to put this around your shoulders. *(He puts his field jacket down on the ground. He looks off.)* Clem, are you drivin' that Mazda Miata or the Chrysler?

CLEM: I'm the Mazda, Moon.

MOON: Good for you, Roy, you bought American made. Hey, Clem, would she still take 79 South and then 64 West? It's been a long time.

CLEM: 64 to 44, then take Interstate 40 west all the way.

MOON: Down to Arizona?

CLEM: Yes sir, headin' west.

MOON: Nice two-day drive.

MONA: I'm too old, Moon.

MOON: Ma'am, Buddha said a good fire can only be made from seasoned wood. The point isn't to end the journey, the point is to make the journey.

MONA: I made the journey with you, Roy. I thought I would rest easy and you would care for me. I knew I wasn't a beautiful, wild creature like that R.V., but I thought we could make a quiet life, Roy. That's a horse laugh. A woman's just disposable goods to you. I gave myself over an' forgot who I was, but those days are over and gone, Roy. I'm makin' my own movie now, and you're just something in the rearview mirror to me. I let your tropical fish go free in the creek; I burned your Louis L'Amour first editions, and I pushed your satellite dish off the roof. I'm an outlaw now, Roy, no one will ever treat me that way again.

MOON: Louis L'Amour would despise you, Roy. *(To Roy and Clem.)* Take off those belts! Do it!

CLEM: I don't have a belt, Moon.

MOON: Lie down on your stomachs. *(Takes off his own belt and, with Roy's, expertly belts the two brothers' hands behind them.)* It took me four planes, an oxcart, and I forded a river on a man's back to get here, boys. Had to sell the gold teeth I'd been collectin' to get it done. See, I wanted to be here for R.V., do a little business, see my big brothers, and take a little vacation from gettin' people down on the ground and tyin' them up with their belts. I guess it just shows you're a prisoner of your talents. That isn't too tight, is it?

CLEM: It feels real nice, Moon.

MOON: *(Looking over his handiwork.)* Well, okay… *(Up to Mona.)* You might want to get started, ma'am.

MONA: Are you the worst?

MOON: Beg pardon?

MONA: You have raped and pillaged and slaughtered?

MOON: More or less.

MONA: Are you the worst of men? I need a b-benchmark.

MOON: Well I don't know, ma'am. I guess I'm close enough to be competitive.

MONA: Then I'll k-keep the pistol.

MOON: Good idea. Say, you know what they do all over the world?

MONA: Who?

MOON: Those who have prevailed. Those who have brought their enemies to their knees and made them eat the dust of the road. It doesn't matter if it's Medellin or Kumasi or Kuala Lumpur, they fire their weapons in the air. They empty themselves into the universe in celebration. *(He hands her his automatic weapon.)*

ROY: My God, are you deranged?!

MOON: Go ahead, ma'am.

(Mona looks at him and then fires a long burst in the air.)

MOON: Feels good, huh?

MONA: It feels g-g-g-glorious! *(She hands back the automatic, keeping the pistol. She smiles for the first time.)*

MOON: Well, you might want to get goin', ma'am. Keep your mind real empty and close to hand, that'll let it heal up. You might want to put on some clothes, but everybody's got their own way.

MONA: Good-bye, Moon.

MOON: Adios, babe.

MONA: *(She turns to Roy and Clem.)* Good-bye, Clem. Good-bye, Roy. I'm sorry I was such a bad shot. I'm free now. When I'm out in Arizona, I'm going to take this money and raise b-bees. Millions of b-bees. Then with the aphrodisiac of my freedom, I will lure men to hotel rooms. I will tie them to the b-bed with silk scarves for a g-good time. Then I will place the queen b-bee on their penis and when they are completely covered with the swarm, I will leave them there to figure it out. *(She exits.)*

MOON: Nice night, beautiful stars, minimum of snipers. That's what I call perfect conditions.

ROY: Untie me, you bastard.

MOON: How come you're dressed up like an Amish farmer, Roy?

ROY: Do you know what a divorce is goin' to cost me?

MOON: That's just overhead, Roy, it was comin' on anyway, you just have to amortize it.

CLEM: There's ants in my shirt, Moon.

MOON: I'm goin' to smoke me a Cuban cigar, Clem. They roll these babies on the inside of a beautiful woman's thigh. One of the few luxuries left.

CLEM: My wife left me too.

MOON: Everybody's wife leaves, Clem, it's a shit job.

CLEM: How am I goin' to raise my boys?

MOON: Just tell 'em to do the opposite.

CLEM: The opposite?

MOON: I wouldn't worry about it, Clem. *(Moon lights up.)*

ROY: My own brother robbed me.

MOON: You can get on the phone and cancel the cards, they got all-night service.

ROY: I'm talkin' about my car! You stole my car.

MOON: A Chrysler ain't a car, Roy, it's just upholstery on wheels.

(Suddenly the dump is alive with movement. Small black shapes scurry everywhere.)

ROY: My God, what's that?

MOON: Looks like the rats are leavin' the dump, Roy.

ROY: Untie me, goddamnit.

MOON: I once saw rats eat a man alive. They ate him in circles like a corn dog.

CLEM: I'm scared of rats, Moon.

MOON: *(Looks up at the stars.)* You both owe me money. *(Silence falls.)*

ROY: Now Moon, this isn't the time to talk about that. This is a time for three brothers, lost to each other by geography, to take hands, kneel down…

MOON: You owe me for the fishing cabin Pop left me that you sold for me in '86.

ROY: Moon, that cabin was in bad shape.

MOON: How much did you get for it?

ROY: …water damaged, rotted out.

MOON: How much, Roy?

ROY: Maybe $1,300, well, no, a little bit less.

MOON: You sold 1.3 acres down on the river for $1,300?

ROY: Hey little brother, this was eight years ago.

MOON: It was appraised 20 years ago at $7,500.

ROY: Are you accusing me of cheatin' my own damn family?

MOON: Yes.

ROY: There is no bond like blood, Moon, and there is nothing so despicable as to doubt it.

CLEM: Mighta been $5,000, Moon.

MOON: That's good, Clem, and when you started your pawnshop I fronted you $5,000, which was ten percent of the capital.

CLEM: Would you care for some Cheezits, Moon?

MOON: You sure that pawnshop didn't grow into your gun store? Because you would owe me ten cents on every dollar of profit.

CLEM: No. No, the pawnshop and the gun shop, that was two completely different enterprises.

MOON: I see. You still located down on the strip across from the Pentacostal Tabernacle of Simple Faith?

CLEM: Well, no, we kind of shifted over toward the water, when I changed over to family security.

MOON: Uh-huh.

CLEM: Riverfront development, you know.

MOON: It wouldn't be located on 1.3 acres of riverfront property, now would it? *(Pause.)* Would it, Clem?

CLEM: *(Pause.)* Come to think of it, Moon, Roy and me might owe you a small sum, and we'd sure like to settle up. Don't you think so, Roy?

ROY: Well, now that we think of it.

MOON: Sounds good to me, boys, because I'm thinkin' of openin' up a chain of coin laundries over in Albania.

CLEM: Albania.

MOON: Clem, those people really need their clothes done.

CLEM: Sounds like a real opportunity.

MOON: *(Rises.)* Well, boys, I look forward to settlin' up.

ROY: There's nothing' that people of good will can't work out.

MOON: There better not be. *(Moves to untie them.)* Say, Roy, there's some barrels in the dump labeled Phinoethylbarmetholine. Don't they use that stuff in nerve gas?

ROY: *(A beat.)* No, actually it's used in barbecue sauce, stuff like that.

MOON: Sure, that must be where I remembered it from.

ROY: We can work the money out, Moon.

MOON: Okay.

ROY: Well, I got a Fourth of July speech to give.

MOON: So.

ROY: I got to go *now*. Gimme your keys, Clem.

CLEM: We got to finish the sacred trust, Roy.

ROY: Goddammit.

MOON: We got to finish the sacred trust, Roy.

ROY: You can't have your community festivities until the mayor speaks to nail down the significance. That is *democracy* which you two wouldn't know a damn thing about.

MOON: Democracy, sure. Hey, I'm out there killin' people for the free enterprise system.

ROY: You're just out there killin' people.

MOON: When you start a democracy you have to kill a few people, if you know your history.

ROY: You don't know squat about history, Moon.

MOON: I was in Nam, man, I *am* history.

ROY: You're history alright, it was the first damn war we ever lost.

CLEM: Now hold on, Roy.

MOON: Are you mockin' my dead buddies?

CLEM: Now hold on, Moon.

ROY: I been workin' twenty years to fix what you and your buddies screwed up!

MOON: *(Starting for him.)* I'm gonna rip your head off.

CLEM: *(Out of desperation.)* Mama's dead.

(Moon stops in mid-charge.)

MOON: What's that?

CLEM: I didn't know if you knew Mama's dead?

MOON: When?

CLEM: July of '91. We didn't know where you were, Moon. We tried *Soldier of Fortune* magazine.

MOON: How'd Mama go?

CLEM: It was cancer, Moon, it wasn't too bad, she went pretty easy.

MOON: Goddamnit to hell! Was it the cigarettes?

CLEM: I don't know, Moon.

MOON: I told you to get her on to the low tar. I told you to take those Camel cigarettes away from her.

CLEM: I tried, Moon, but...

MOON: Damn! Buried or cremated?

CLEM: Moon, I just don't think...

MOON: Which was it?

CLEM: Cremated.

MOON: Aarrrgh! *(Moon, in a rage, slings trash across the dump.)* A man don't want his mother cremated! You understand that?

ROY: Well, she left instructions.

MOON: Instructions? Piss on the instructions! I want my Mama's grave! Where is she, goddamnit?

CLEM: Scattered.

MOON: *(Sitting down.)* You made bonemeal outta my Mama.

CLEM: Well Moon, she didn't want to be a bother, see. She didn't want us worried about the upkeep. She just wanted to disperse.

MOON: You two morons went and dispersed her?

ROY: Well, we…

MOON: Dispersed her *where*, damnit?

CLEM: Wendy's.

MOON: Wendy's Fast Food?

CLEM: Well, she stopped cookin' with everybody gone and she liked to go down to the Wendy's.

MOON: You spread our Mama out at a fast-food restaurant?

ROY: In the daylily garden.

MOON: I can't kneel down at a fast-food restaurant and ask my Mama what to do.

CLEM: Well you could, Moon.

MOON: Never mind!

CLEM: It's a real busy corner though.

MOON: I don't want to talk about it. *(Throws his head back.)* R.V.!? The world's goin' to hell, R.V. Mama's dispersed. You're dead. Roy and Clem cheated on me. Communism wimped out. My trigger hand shakes. Where the hell are we? What the hell's goin' on?!!

CLEM: I'll get the beer.

MOON: *(A moment. He calms.)* I still remember your smell, R.V., the curve of your thigh. I don't know why you killed yourself, but you're sure as hell well out of it. You could gentle me down, I remember that. We never got to say good-bye, so I'm here to do it. Hell, I'm only twenty years late, that's not too bad. You asked for it, an' I'm doin' it, but I tell you what, R.V., I'm tired of dead people. They're piled up, one on top of the other, everywhere you go on this planet. Damn, I'm tired of *that* smell. You an' me were two crazy sons of bitches, and that always gave me some comfort. I tell you one thing, R.V., I hope wherever you are you still got that red dress and that snake tattoo.

(R.V. appears again on the car behind them.)

Heaven for climate, hell for company. Let's chug these beers.

(They do. R.V. speaks from behind them.)

R.V.: Did you love me, Moon?

(The men turn, startled.)

R.V.: Holy shit, you got old!

(Clem slumps to the ground in a faint.)

MOON: Is that you, R.V.?

R.V.: It's me, Moon.

ROY: *(To Moon.)* You see her, right?

MOON: I see her.

R.V.: I forgot you would get old.

ROY: Go on now, whatever you are. Go on, shoo! Shoo!

R.V.: Hello, Roy.

ROY: Looks just like the day she died.

MOON: What is it you want, R.V.?

R.V.: I bring the messenger to…say, is Clem alright?

ROY: Damn, but she looks real to the touch.

R.V.: Real to the touch?

> *(She walks directly to Moon and involves him in a long kiss. Roy talks through it. Clem moans.)*

ROY: Shut up, Clem. Is she real, Moon? What's she feel like, Moon? I wouldn't do that, Moon. Hell, she could be a vampire.

> *(She steps back from him. Their eyes are locked.)*

MOON: Your lips are cold.

R.V.: I wrote you 1,200 letters in Nam. I got two postcards.

MOON: It was a bad time.

R.V.: How's the Buddha, Moon?

MOON: I lost track.

R.V.: Where'd you go when you left Nam?

MOON: Angola for awhile, Rhodesia, Ghana, Yemen, Burundi, Salvador, Somalia, a little while in the Seychelles, Afghanistan, Azerbaijan, shacked up for a time in Albania, twenty-six days in Cambodia, two years near Zagreb, and I was down around Liberia when this came up.

R.V.: You know I married Roy.

MOON: Damn R.V., what's you do that for?

R.V.: I was having nightmares.

MOON: Were you drunk?

R.V.: Some of the time. Shoot, Moon, back then he was the next best thing.

ROY: Thanks a helluva damn lot.

R.V.: Beggin' your pardon, Roy.

CLEM: *(Reviving.)* Roy! Roy!

ROY: *(Annoyed.)* What is it, Clem?

CLEM: *(Not seeing R.V.)* She was *here*, Roy.

ROY: Clem, damn it…

CLEM: No, no, I saw her. I saw R.V. So help me, no kiddin'. Wearin' the red dress just like the last night. I'm not foolin', Roy.
  (Roy points. Clem looks.)

CLEM: Oh, my God, the graves are opening. It's the last judgment, Roy, it's on us. My God, humble yourself.

ROY: Will you be quiet, Clem?

CLEM: *(Drinks from his flask, sings.)* "Swing lo', sweet char-i-ot, comin' for to carry me home…"

MOON: Clem, knock that off!

R.V.: What's shakin', Clem?

CLEM: Oh my God, oh my God, oh my God, oh my God.

R.V.: *(R.V. touches him on the cheek. He quiets.)* I had Clem one time, too. I had Clem and Roy 'cause you never answered my letters.

MOON: Come on, R.V.!

ROY: Clem!?

CLEM: Oh my God, oh my God.

ROY: You didn't have Clem? Not while we were married, was it?

R.V.: It was just one time, Roy.

ROY: While we were married?

CLEM: It was just one time, Roy.

ROY: *(To Clem.)* You're my own damn blood and you screwed my wife?!

MOON: That's pretty low, R.V.

ROY: It wasn't in my house, was it?

MOON: You said you were waitin' for me.

ROY: You better answer me, Clem!

CLEM: It was in the garden.

ROY: In the garden? It wasn't near Mama's daylilies, was it?

CLEM: Heck no, Roy, it was over in the phlox. You were sleepin'; it didn't mean to happen.

ROY: I just can't believe this!

R.V.: Roy, you and I were hardly makin' love at all.

ROY: Worst case, we always did it once a week.

R.V.: Yeah, Tuesdays.

ROY: It wasn't only on Tuesdays.

CLEM: We didn't do it on a Tuesday, Roy.

ROY: Shut up. Godawful, R.V., ol' Clem puffin' away in the missionary position.

R.V.: Not quite, Roy.

ROY: What do you mean, *not quite?*

CLEM: Well, I'm double-jointed, Roy.

ROY: Goddamnit!

R.V.: He was the only one of you boys ever loved me. Why the hell are you gettin' riled up? I'm dead, for one thing. He'd bring me coffee, get me car parts, roll my joints, remember my damn birthday, and come down every night to hear me sing at the Holiday Inn. He loved me like a dog; why shouldn't he get laid one time?

MOON: Because it's Clem, damn it!

R.V.: Roy was passed out. I couldn't sleep. The moon was real orange over the hills, so I walked out into the garden and there was Clem sittin' on the bench.

ROY: You didn't go out there naked, did you?

R.V.: I went out there naked all the time. It was 3:00 A.M., who cared?

CLEM: I was just out walkin', Roy. I just sat down there for a minute.

ROY: You are a snake in the woodpile.

R.V.: We just sat there on the bench. He told me I looked like a statue in the moonlight. He said he come there some nights when we were asleep, he'd sit there and hope me and him were breathing in and out at the same time. We just sat there, whispering, with our shoulders touching, and after awhile we lay down in the phlox. You did real good, Clem.

CLEM: Thank you, R.V. You want some Cheezits?

R.V.: Sure.

ROY: Why the hell didn't you love me, R.V.? Goddamnit, I'm lovable. I'm a hard worker, ambitious, patriotic; I'm a damn fine provider, like to dance, I got a serious side. Why the hell didn't you love me?

R.V.: You're just too much man, Roy.

ROY: Well, I can't shrivel myself up to win a woman's love. I can't downsize what I am, R.V., I got to let it roll! It's like this country is what it's like. Those pissant third worlds can't stand the sheer magnificent expanse of us. They can't take their eyes off us, but they want to cut us down to size. It's tragic grandeur, that's what I got! Goddamnit, woman, you should have *loved* me!!

R.V.: It's not a function of the will, Roy.

(*A moment.*)

MOON: You're sure you're dead, R.V.?

R.V.: Deader than hell.

CLEM: There was omens, Roy, the Gifford horse, the frogs, the way the sky was. I must have seen fifteen possum in a bunch headin' south on the highway, and a possum he travels alone.

R.V.: How about a beer, boys? A cold one for the road.

ROY: You want a beer?

R.V.: You get pretty dry when you're dead, Roy.

MOON: Get the lady a beer, will you?

ROY: I have got to get over to the…

R.V.: You can't go, Roy, you've been chosen.

ROY: What do you mean, chosen?

R.V.: Chosen, Roy.

> *(Clem hands out the beer.)*

R.V.: How come you were sleeping in the dump, Moon?

MOON: I got in late last night. I can't sleep indoors, it makes me dream.

R.V.: Dream what?

MOON: Things I've done.

ROY: What do you mean chosen?

MOON: Outdoors, I've been dreaming about you.

R.V.: I know. *(She pops the beer and proposes a toast.)* To the white man, God help him.

> *(Clem, Moon, and R.V. drink.)*

ROY: What kind of toast is that?

MOON: Where are you, R.V.?

R.V.: Say what?

MOON: When you're not here?

R.V.: Heaven.

CLEM: Oh my Lord, there is life after death?

R.V.: Well, I'm drinkin' my beer, Clem.

CLEM: Moon, Roy, can you believe this. We're sittin' in the dump, and it's been revealed!

MOON: Take it easy, Clem.

CLEM: What do you do there? What's it like, R.V.?

R.V.: It's pure unadulterated longing. It's like you lost a leg but there's still feeling where the leg used to be. The feeling is for the life you didn't live, and you pass the time until you find some way to make yourself whole.

CLEM: Sure, but what's it like?

R.V.: The one you guys have is a celestial theme park with a thousand T.V. channels, continual sex, and a 5,000 hole golf course.

ROY: Jee-sus!

R.V.: I go over sometimes for the salad bar.

MOON: Are you kiddin', R.V.?

R.V.: Could be.

ROY: I said chosen for what, damnit?

MOON: How you like it up there?

R.V.: Too damn serene.

MOON: Yeah?

R.V.: I tried to kill myself up there, too. Hell, you know, just for variety. Hurled myself down the cloud canyons. Forget it. Once you're immortal, you're immortal.

MOON: Sounds like a tough gig.

R.V.: It's a perception thing, Moon. See, I only got the perception I took up there, and that just doesn't cut it, you know. I took the messenger gig because I figured you could help me out. I'm locked inside twenty-five years, Moon. I only get the heaven twenty-five years can understand. Hell, you must be close to fifty. Tell me what you know.

MOON: Shoot low and shoot first.

R.V.: Goddamnit Moon, I'm not jokin'.

MOON: Who said I was jokin', R.V.?

R.V.: Move me on, Moon, don't leave me where I am.

MOON: Got me a limited perspective.

R.V.: You lived all those years and only got smaller?

MOON: I yam what I yam, babe.

R.V.: Well, damn! *(She kicks something across the dump.)* How come this dump's sittin' on the ball field?

ROY: The dump's the whole point, R.V.

R.V.: What point?

ROY: The point. Town was fallin' apart, R.V. The town, the job pool, the tax base.

CLEM: Dollar movie closed down.

ROY: I said to myself, Roy, what is this country based on? And by God it came to me, it's based on garbage. There is nobody in the world has the garbage we do! *(He pulls stuff out of the dump.)* Blenders, TVs, Lazyboys, syringes! We did a little study showed that within one truck day of this town, two billion tons of garbage produced weekly. Bingo! You know where people want to put their garbage? Somewhere else, that's where. And there is no damn town in this country that is more somewhere else than we are. And I sold that idea, by God, and it saved the town. We got the dump here plus nine other locations. I'm not sayin' I can walk on water, but I'll tell you this here is a damn miracle.

R.V.: So the ball field's down there?

CLEM: Down there somewhere. *(Finishes the flask, throws it away.)*

R.V.: How come you started throwin' those change ups, Moon?

MOON: How come you drove off the bridge?

R.V.: You ever been airborne in a Corvette Stingray on a cool night at 145 miles an hour?

MOON: No ma'am.

R.V.: Hang time, it's a real rush. Damn, I love speed. What was I supposed to do, Moon? Stick around, do hair stylin' at Babettes, work part-time at the Seashell Gift Shop, make chocolate chip cookies down at Suzi's Love Oven?! Blow that crap out your ear, man.

CLEM: You could sing, R.V.

R.V.: Good enough for the Holiday Inn Lounge, huh, Clem?

CLEM: I came every night.

R.V.: Bunch of drunks in bad ties, yellin' out "Moon River." Yeah, I could sing that good.

CLEM: You was pearls before swine.

R.V.: Thanks, baby. Ol' Jimmy Dean an' me, we weren't countin' on tomorrow, see? You think I'm gonna drag a broke life behind me down Main Street, like some old rusty tailpipe kickin' up sparks? Hell with that, man! That night I flew the Corvette, I put on my red dress an' I looked fine! I was wearin' the hell out of that thing, you dig? Figured it was time to go out large, so I just slipped my good lookin' legs into some red rhinestone heels and put the pedal to the metal!

CLEM: We could see you go off the bridge from down at Bob's Big Boy parkin' lot. Slow motion right across the moon.

R.V.: Sure, I could see you boys standin' still lookin' up. Hell, twenty years later you're still there. You look sad, Moon. Is it me or the bridge?

MOON: What bridge?

R.V.: Your bridge.

MOON: What the hell are you talking about?

R.V.: The bridge in Liberia. *(A beat.)*

MOON: How do you know that, R.V.?

R.V.: I keep track, Moon.

MOON: Then why ask me?

R.V.: To see if you have the balls to tell me.

MOON: Just a bridge we held.

R.V.: Yeah?

MOON: Yeah.

R.V.: Just a bridge, huh?

MOON: Only way you could still get over into Sierra Leone. We didn't blow it 'cause we had to run transport through there once the town fell.

R.V.: Go on, Moon.

R.V. AND MOON: *(He is unaware that she speaks with him.)* The bridge stretched out like an old rusty skeleton between two hills…

R.V.: Tell it, Moon.

MOON: Those people…

R.V.: Those people…

MOON: Kept tryin' to come across it.

R.V.: That's right.

MOON: Everybody's snipers up in the hills.

R.V.: *(In sync, she sees it too.)* Man in a big brown coat…

MOON: Midday, somebody tried to run it.

R.V.: Uh-huh.

MOON: Looked like a man in a big coat. I was in the hills…

R.V.: Uh-huh.

MOON: I fired a rifle grenade into the coat…

R.V.: It didn't explode…

MOON: Didn't explode, but the coat opened up and it was a woman…

R.V. AND MOON: …carrying a young child.

MOON: *(Hypnotized now by memory's image.)* That rifle grenade nailed the child to the mother's chest…

R.V.: Down there on the bridge…

MOON AND R.V.: …and they lay, mother and child, nailed together on the bridge for two days…

MOON: See, nobody dared try to go out there and get 'em.

MOON AND R.V.: Lay there screaming…

R.V.: On the bridge…

MOON AND R.V.: Screaming.

MOON: Finally I took a rifle, blew up that grenade on the second shot.

R.V.: Then what, Moon?

MOON: I stayed there another day. Then I walked out, following the river. Took me three weeks.

R.V.: How come?

MOON: I figured I'd try something else.

R.V.: Like my bridge?

MOON: Your bridge?

R.V.: Right across the sky.

MOON: No thanks, R.V.

R.V.: What is it you know, Moon?

MOON: A piece of shit doesn't throw a perfect game.

ROY: You threw the damn game on purpose?

MOON: Shut up, Roy.

R.V.: It's getting late, Moon.

MOON: Could be.

R.V.: You don't have somethin' for me?

MOON: Not a damn thing.

R.V.: Well, it's time to get started, boys. *(She raises her arm, one finger pointing up, and there is a shattering crash of thunder. She raises her other arm.)* Spirits of wind, water, earth, and fire, enwrap me here! *(Thunder, lightning.)* I am appeared before you, sent by the lord of hosts. She who is both the tumult and the eye of the hurricane. She who throweth up continents and maketh men from the fish of the sea. Hear me. Hear me!
(The rain pours down on everyone except R.V. Clem raises his small umbrella. Roy and Moon are drenched.)

R.V.: I come at her behest to be the harbinger of her great messenger. Through him will the blind see, the broken mend, and the heart be made whole. *(A powerful beam of light pours down on her.)* Great spirit, King, right hand of the all-powerful, we welcome thee! Hold onto your seats, boys, he is upon us now!
(A tremendous explosion, as if the stage had been struck in two by a lightning bolt. The rain stops. Smoke, debris, and then sudden silence. Elvis appears. He is dressed in his "suit of lights," the famous white sequined performance suit. A driving guitar riff and final chord surround his entrance. He is the same age as at his death.)

CLEM: My God, who are you?

ELVIS: I'm the King of the White Man, asshole, who are you?

CLEM: Elvis?

ELVIS: The Velvet Rocker, buddy, the Hillbilly Cat, the King of Western Bop.

CLEM: You thinned down, King.

ELVIS: I been dinin' on cumulus nimbus.

ROY: Kinda lost your magnitude.

ELVIS: Well, I'm not dressed up as a Smith Brothers cough drop. I'll tell y'all one thing, boys, there wasn't nobody, nowhere, no time, no way, ever seen a white boy move like me. They couldn't shake it where I shook it or take it where I took it. I was born with a guitar in one hand and the ruination of western civilization in the other. Y'all look a little tight there, boys, so the King's gotta get you ready to party! Heck, have some Dexedrine…

(He scatters hundreds of pills in a multicolored spray from his pockets as if they were coins for the multitudes.) Have some Tuinal, Dilaudid, Quaaludes, and Demerol! Get up, or get down, get wherever you need to be to hear the *word! (Lightning crackles, framing his figure in its flash.)*

CLEM: *(Picking some up.)* Thanks, King.

ELVIS: Uh-huh! Hit it! *(Another crash and sizzle of lightning.)* The Lord, she stood on the rim of the universe, and she did regard the earth, baby. And wherever her gaze did fall there was real bad doody goin' down. There was a sickly caste, a dread pigmentless, soulless, milky pale fungi suckin' the sustenance right out of the world, man, leavin' things undone, done badly, overlooked, overgrazed, snafued, and skimmin' the cream right off the top. And who the hell was in the driver's seat takin' care of business? Buddy, it was a bunch of fat old white men, that's who it was! Greedy ol' farts livin' off the fat of the land while the land fell apart in their hands. They weren't gettin' it there, dudes! You can't rhumba in a sports car, baby. You can't do no Australian crawl in a shot glass. We had it, man, and we pissed it away! Regard me, brethren. I was the most beautiful cat ever rolled into Memphis in a '39 Plymouth. I could sing black boogie and the Mississippi Delta blues. I could shuck and jive like a funky angel. I was the white man triumphant, baby. If I wanted it *now,* I got it *now.* I was the boss, the king, El Presidente Grande, and I ended up fat as a grain-fed hog, down on my knees on the bathroom floor with my head floatin' in a toilet bowl. Hell, you're down in the bowl with me, boys. Y'all had played errorless, no-hit ball goin' into the eighth inning, and you took it from there to the dung heap, poisoned in spirit and your women flee you into the night with whatever they can carry.

CLEM: *(Delighted.)* He's talkin' about us, boys!

ELVIS: She-it, compadres! The last time the Lord saw something like this, she had the game rained out, man but the Lord wouldn't even trust you cats to build an ark! Huh-uh! She was set to hurl the white man into the eternal dark and see what somebody else could do with it. My people were goin' down, baby, the bell was tollin' the midnight hour, cats, so I had the cherubim and seraphim deliver me to the Lord's right hand an' I whipped out my guitar and shucked out a tune, boys.

CLEM: We love you, Elvis!

ELVIS: *(He throws out his hand and an unseen band crashes into a rock and roll riff. Elvis' voice is now amplified.)* I rocked it, baby, laid down a hot lick, turned it every way but loose, like you know I can, and there amongst the beatific host, the Lord, she got down, she got tight, she got right with my music, and she boogied through the day, and a night, and a day and when I sent that last reverb down through the chambers of her immortal heart, she said, "Elvis, I thought I'd seen it all when I saw Lucifer, but the way you're rockin' tonight, I'm gonna give the white man one *(chord)* more *(chord)* chance. *(chord)*" *(The music ends.)* And I said, "Lord, I'm hip and I'm on it, what's the deal?" And she laid her cool hand on my cheek and asked did I remember what my precious mama said to me when I done wrong and lied about it. And I said, "Yes Lord, I do." She said, "Sonny boy, there ain't nothin' done in this old world so debauched and brought low that you can't get right with your God and your mama with just two little words... *(The big finish.)* and listen here now, those two words, those two paradisiacal confections, sweet as plums or summer cherries, those two words are...I'm sorry!" *(A pause. Distant thunder rolls. The words "I'm Sorry" echo through the heavens.)*

MOON: Hey Elvis?

ELVIS: Yeah?

MOON: The Lord God wants us to say we're sorry?

ELVIS: Uh-huh.

MOON: Just "I'm sorry"?

ELVIS: Well, it's kind of a cosmic thing, man. But you got it, yeah. Otherwise she's gonna' send down the white flu, let it blanket the earth, uh-huh, all you white guys sneeze yourself right into eternity inside of two weeks.

CLEM: The white flu!?

ROY: What the hell are we s'posed to have done?

ELVIS: *(His arms wide.)* This.

ROY: Hey, everybody throws things away, okay?

ELVIS: But who was runnin' the store, buddy?

ROY: Well, it wasn't me, big guy.

ELVIS: Well, who the hell was it?

ROY: Hell, you got your media, your cartels, your multinationals, your big government.

ELVIS: And who was runnin' them?

ROY: How the hell am I supposed to know?

ELVIS: Well, let's just say they weren't purple, how about that?

ROY: I'm damn tired of everybody talkin' trash on the white man. Hell, we thought up about 90 percent of civilization. It was twelve of our own kind sat with Christ at his table. If these goddamn minorities shoulda led us somewhere, why didn't they step up to the plate! *(He sneezes explosively.)*

ELVIS: Sounds like you're comin' down with somethin'. Say, R.V., how about some seraphim send us down a milk shake, maybe put an egg in it?

(R.V. snaps her fingers.)

CLEM: Say, King…

ELVIS: Uh-huh?

CLEM: You kinda lost me on the curve, King.

(The milk shake descends from the skies.)

ELVIS: Hell, y'all explain it, R.V., I'm gonna take a load off. (Takes the milk shake and makes himself comfortable.)

R.V.: Hear me, fishermen. (Lightning.) You, before me, of all those assembled, are the chosen. The bellwethers, the forerunners, you hold redemption in the palm of your hand!

ELVIS: She ain't kiddin'.

R.V.: See Clem, the Lord, she asked me did I know any white guys, and I said sure.

CLEM: How come she asked you, R.V.?

R.V.: I was just standin' there. She touched my snake tattoo, filling me with light, saying I should pave the way and we should proclaim the news.

ELVIS: (Drinking his milk shake.) Do it, iridescent one. Attend me, white ones! (Sizzling lightning crash.) The Lord God, the First Cause, the Celestial She, the Big Femina, instructs you here to prepare your hearts and set out on foot from this place to great Washington Monument in the city yclept "D.C." and to carry on that journey of the spirit a sign of apology.

CLEM: Gollee Roy, we could do that!

R.V.: Your garments shall you here divest, and your journey shall be unclothed.

(A pause.)

MOON: Say what?

ELVIS: You got to do it butt-naked, buddy.

ROY: Now just hold on here.

ELVIS: (Holding out the milk shake.) You ever try one with an egg in it?

ROY: You want us to strip down and walk 600 miles from here to D.C. with a sign says "I'm sorry"?

ELVIS: Gonna get a hell of a suntan.

ROY: When hell freezes over, boy! I'm the best damn thing genetics ever come up with, an' that's the American white man, runnin' the most powerful damn nation this world's ever seen, an' we don't strip down for some damn hallucination! (He sneezes.)

ELVIS: Have a Kleenex, Roy.

R.V.: Oh man, repent all and regard thee here thy immortal soul.

ROY: Damnit, Moon, listen to this.

MOON: I'm listenin'.

ROY: Clem?

CLEM: Well...

ROY: Stand up for your own blood, goddamnit!

CLEM: I guess God's my own blood, Roy.

R.V.: Lo, the plague will descend, your bodies be consumed, and your heart sundered.

MOON: I don't have a heart, R.V.

R.V.: You just never turned it on, Moon.

ROY: R.V.?

R.V.: Sinner, save your kind and rejoice, lest you and all your tribe shall perish from the earth.

MOON: You comin', Elvis?

ELVIS: I'll be just above your head, man.

MOON: You sorry?

ELVIS: I failed my precious mama. I can't sleep the eternal sleep when I done like that.

ROY: The white man shouldn't have to take the rap for this!

ELVIS: Tough nuggies, Roy.

ROY: Who the hell has the moral authority to stand here in this dump and tell me I got to take off my underpants?!

ELVIS: I was you, I'd ask your precious mama.

ROY: How the hell am I gonna ask my mama.

MOON: You can't ask her, you damn moron, you dispersed her!

(A heavenly chord; a puff of smoke. Their mother appears on the ridge. She is in her early 70s, wearing a housedress. She has a halo.)

CLEM: Holy smoke!

MRS. MANNERING: Hello, son.

ROY AND MOON: Mama!

MRS. MANNERING: Now you do what Elvis says, Roy. I only hope to goodness you took a shower.

CLEM: It's you, Mama.

MRS. MANNERING: Hello Bootsie. I just cannot believe you let an eight-year-old child get hold of an AK-47.

CLEM: I know, Mama.

MRS. MANNERING: I believe you've been imbibing hard liquor.

CLEM: It's only 80 proof, Mama.

MRS. MANNERING: Well, you had better pull up your bootstraps. Moon Mannering, what is that on your face?

MOON: Facial hair, Mama.

MRS. MANNERING: You got something to be ashamed of hid behind that mess?

MOON: Well, Mama…

MRS. MANNERING: You better not let your father catch you like that. Do you have blood on your hands, son?

MOON: I do, Mama.

MRS. MANNERING: I ought to whip your butt off. Thou shalt not kill, do you hear me? Tiny, what in heaven's name are you got up as?

ROY: Abraham Lincoln, Mama.

MRS. MANNERING: Remember the sin of pride, Tiny. Pride goeth before a fall. Look up sinner.

(Roy does.)

CLEM: Gollee Moses.

ROY: Oh, my God, Mama.

(Clem lets out a long whistle.)

ROY: It's the load receipt printed in fire on the sky.

CLEM: Those letters must be a mile high.

ROY: See what you did, Clem?

CLEM: It's real readable.

ROY: Shut up.

CLEM: *(Trying to make up.)* You want some Cheezits?

ROY: *(Ripping them from his hand. Stomps them.)* Arrrrrrgh!

CLEM: You broke my Cheezits. Those were all the Cheezits I had.

ROY: Shut up!

CLEM: *(Suddenly twisted with rage; the straw that broke the camel's back.)* Don't… you…tell me…to…shut up!! You have…humiliated me…for forty years. *(He reaches down and picks up an iron bar out of the dump.)* If you ever… ever speak to me in that tone of voice…Roy…I will mash you like a potato, tear out your liver and heart and devour them, whole.

MRS. MANNERING: *(Clapping her hands as you do with children.)* Now that is enough, now. You may not eat your brother. That is out of the question.

CLEM: *(Returning to himself.)* Golly, Mama…I didn't mean that.

MRS. MANNERING: Of course you didn't.

MOON: *(Looking at the sky.)* Well, they know what you got in your dump all over North America now, Roy.

MRS. MANNERING: *(With finality.)* People do not eat their own. *(She points up.)* Think of your mama seein' your dirty laundry bein' washed right across the night sky, Roy. You better get right with the deity. *(Roy hangs his head.)* Now have you boys been brushing your teeth?

THE BOYS: Yes Mama.

MRS. MANNERING: Then get undressed.

ROY: I don't want to, Mama.

MRS. MANNERING: It is very, very late.

ROY: I…just can't…Mama.

MRS. MANNERING: Why not, Roy?

ROY: I'm ashamed of the size of my sexual member.

MRS. MANNERING: God gave you that body, there is no reason to be ashamed of it. You think I haven't seen your thing before?

ROY: Yes Mama.

MRS. MANNERING: You have a responsibility to your fellow creatures, Roy Mannering, now I don't want to hear anymore about it. Your sweet Grandpa Abbey, 100 years old, your kind Uncle William always sent five dollars on your birthday, you want them to die of this flu?

THE BOYS: No Mama.

MRS. MANNERING: Well, I would think not. I carried you inside me, boys, and you were, every one of you, breech births. I have cradled your tiny fevered bodies in my arms and sang to you from the opera *Aida* by the immortal Verdi. I watched you grow from beautiful, tiny, tow-headed perfections into big, splotchy, gangly things who masturbated. I paid your car insurance long after it should have been your responsibility. Yes, Jesus, I have suffered! You could see me draining out into you like a bottle emptying. There wasn't a drop, not a scintilla, left for my thoughts or feelings or dreams. I could have been a supply-side economist or the President of the United States. After you were born, your father was afraid to have marital relations with me because you boys never learned to knock. I dreamed of Mr. Presley drenching my body with scented oils and creamy peanut butter and taking his will with me, but none of you would ever drive me to Memphis! I died as I had lived, a housewife, a mother, a cleaning lady and, when that time came, when I did die, when I was no longer your lifelong wet nurse, you irresponsible sons-of-bitches dispersed me to the wrong place!

ROY: Mama!

MRS. MANNERING: I said Hardee's, goddamnit, not Wendy's! Wendy's Big Bacon Classic is pigeon piss compared to Hardee's Frisco-burger! I wanted to be at Hardee's in amongst the begonias, across from the drive-thru!

CLEM: It wasn't Wendy's?

MRS. MANNERING: Never mind! That was then, this is now. You can make it up to me *here, after death*. You can give me what I never had, my dreams, my glory, my *raison d'être*. You three, my spawn, have been chosen by the apogee, the highest of the high, to save the white man! All is forgiven; seize the day, do it for your mama!!

(They stand astounded.)

MRS. MANNERING: Go on, I'm waiting.

(Clem unbuttons his work shirt. Roy and Moon are still. Clem takes off the shirt.)

MRS. MANNERING: Don't make me get the strap, Roy.

(A beat, and then Roy sits and starts taking off his shoes. Moon stands dead still, arms at his side.)

R.V.: Did you ever love me, Moon.

MOON: I did.

R.V.: Then why the hell didn't you write?

MOON: I was ashamed.

R.V.: You damn fool, Moon. Look what became of us.

(He stands for another moment and then starts unbuckling his belt.)

R.V.: Cool.

(She takes a step back.)

MRS. MANNERING: Good night, R.V.

R.V.: Good night, Chlotilda.

MRS. MANNERING: I've still got ironing to do. Good night, Clem.

CLEM: Good night, Mommy.

MRS. MANNERING: Good night, Tiny.

(Roy's hands move instinctively in front of his genitals.)

MRS. MANNERING: Good night, Moon.

(He lifts a hand in farewell. She starts to exit.)

MRS. MANNERING: Everybody sleep tight now.

(Humming a hymn, she disappears. A harmonica, somewhere in the universe, picks up the hymn. R.V. raises one hand and speaks.)

R.V.: And lo, grace descended…

ELVIS: …and they divested themselves, and the harbinger said to them…

R.V.: As you journey, O chosen ones, men where they stand in the fields will lay down the tools of the harvest and join with you…

ELVIS: Yeah, baby…

R.V.: From far off will men hear your righteous tread and stream weeping from the corporate headquarters…

ELVIS: From the condominiums and nouvelle restaurants…

R.V.: From the universities and the oak-paneled boardrooms.

ELVIS: Outta Wall Street and the Silicone Valley.

R.V. AND ELVIS: See them, this multitude of white guys of a certain age…

ELVIS: C.E.O.'s, estate lawyers, congressmen…

R.V.: Pediatric allergists, downsizers, aldermen…

ELVIS: Gettin' on their Harleys and their Swiss Alpine snowmobiles, their longin' palpable…

R.V.: Their eyes regretful, their hands joined.

ELVIS: They are comin', baby!

R.V.: The Catholics, the Jews, the Episcopalians…

ELVIS: The down and dirty Baptists…

R.V. AND ELVIS: And all the lesser faiths!

ELVIS: And Roy, my man, you're in the front, dude.

R.V.: You too, Moon…

ELVIS: And Clem, you swingin' dick, you're drivin' the vanguard forward…

R.V.: Until at last these pale multitudes envelope the Washington Monument, as the muscles surround the heart, and from their throats will spring one single cry…

ELVIS: The cry of sins committed…

R.V.: The cry of sins repented…

ELVIS: The cry of old white guys everywhere…

R.V. AND ELVIS: "I…am…sorry!"

(The word "sorry" echoes through the heavens. Roy's fireworks begin overhead. Three rockets in various colors illuminate those below.)

ROY: Luellen started the show.

(More fireworks.)

R.V.: Oh, boys, you were beautiful that day; your crisp, cream, pin-striped uniforms against that emerald green infield.

(Rocket overhead. The brothers remove their last items of clothing.)

R.V.: You boys, like music box figures, spinnin' and divin'. The endless arching beauty of that final mile-high pop-up.

(Another rocket.)

R.V.: You were gods, boys…

ELVIS: Gods of summer.

R.V.: Think what you might have done?!

(A tattoo of explosions and bursts of color. The brothers are finally naked. They look up at the display. R.V. scribbles on the back of an old "For Rent" sign with her lipstick.)

CLEM: *(A particularly glorious rocket.)* Ooooooo, look at that one!

(A golden light plays down the sequined rope by Elvis. He puts one foot in a loop at the bottom and takes hold of the rope with one hand.)

ELVIS: We've got to get on that resurrection express, boys. *(Making his exit.)* Hail and farewell, buddies. Y'all bring it on home.

(He is gone. A series of sharp explosions. R.V. moves down and hands the sign to Moon.)

R.V.: Let's go, boys.

R.V.: I'd go south on Rural 501 and then east down the turnpike. They'll be comin' that way. Hold it up, Moon. Hold it high, my darlin'!

(He does. It says, "I'm sorry." In the distance the Mayberry High School band strikes up a traditional march, the fireworks redouble. It is the finale of Roy's display. The brothers stare out at us; Moon holds up the sign. R.V., in her red dress, stands on the remains of the car behind them.)

R.V.: Fishers of men! The night is fallen, but the lark yet sings. Oh, you Eurocentric Anglo Saxons, *(They turn front.)* there is still one inning left to play!

(There is a final tattoo of airborne explosions and a dying scutter of fireworks. The Mayberry High School band plays bravely on. The lights fade.)

END OF PLAY

Jack and Jill

A Romance

ORIGINAL PRODUCTION

Jack and Jill was first performed at the 1996 Humana Festival of New American Plays, March, 1996. It was directed by Jon Jory with the following cast:

Jack . . . . John Leonard Thompson
Jill . . . . Pamela Stewart
Dressers. . . . . David A. Baecker, Elizabeth Dwyer,
. . . . Heather LaFace, Sean McNall

and with the following production staff:

Scenic Designer . . . . Paul Owen
Costume Designer . . . . Jeanette deJong
Lighting Designer. . . . . T.J. Gerckens
Sound Designer. . . . . Michael Rasbury
Properties Master. . . . . Mark J. Bissonnette
Movement Director . . . . Gail Benedict
Stage Manager. . . . . Lori M. Doyle
Assistant Stage Manager . . . . Susan M. McCarthy
Dramaturg. . . . . Michael Bigelow Dixon
New York Casting Arrangements . . . . Laura Richin Casting

CHARACTERS

JACK
JILL
DRESSERS

PLACE

Present, in various locations.

DIRECTOR'S NOTE

The stage never goes to black except at the ends of acts. The music is classical, played by small ensembles; perhaps Beethoven in Act I, and Mozart in Act II. To give some sense of pace, Act I runs 48 minutes, Act II runs 52 minutes. The final scene is more painful than romantic. They are old warriors meeting on the road.

GROUND PLAN

The setting is utterly simple. The floor is a deep, shiny maroon. At various times we see four black chairs. There is a mustard-colored table. We see a deep green bed with white sheets and pillows with similarly covered bedside tables. On the tables are maroon lamps with white shades. The chairs are also arranged as other pieces of furniture during the action. The play is performed by one man and one woman in their mid-thirties. There are four stagehand/dressers who assist on- and offstage costume changes, move furniture pieces, and deliver props. They are not characters but regard the actors with grave interest as they go about their duties. They wear clothes in a brown tone that are in the same world as Jack and Jill. The time is now.

Jack and Jill

ACT ONE

A woman sits in a single chair reading a book by Sylvia Plath. A man, sitting and holding several books, stands and crosses toward her. He stops and looks at her for a time. Finally, he speaks.

JACK: Hi.

JILL: Hi.

JACK: Listen, I've been…one minute of your time…sitting over there, and I…no place is safe, right? I'm sorry. By the way, you're reading a poet I admire…in the face of that tragic life, she…wait, wait, I'm backing up here…I was, from over there in the stacks, struck, struck by you…viscerally struck…as if you cared, right? Why, why am I…look, I'm Jack, unpronounceable second name…we could…well, this is fairly mortifying. Let me try to do this without artifice…I'm going to erase this desperate preamble and, uh, say this: I, Jack, would like to meet you, a female person, for…ummm, nonthreatening relating. Why? Because awhile ago I lost some serious relating, and I really miss the feeling. So, severe and transcendent beauty, how about a cup of coffee with me, Jack Stojadinovac? *(Pause)* I have this… intuition…that I am dog meat.

JILL: Jack.

JACK: Yes.

JILL: Jack Stojadinovac.

JACK: That was unbelievably perfect.

JILL: I'm having some problems with men, Jack. On a…yes…lot of levels. I am finding my relating to them is…not to mention the problems implicit here in my name being Jill…relating to men…so to speak, recently is…is like dropping my finite reserves of energy and, umm, insight and empathy down a mine shaft. Doubtless my problem, but…all right, umm, I will seriously relate to you in this way…I will tell you that doing this makes me infinitely lonelier than being alone.

JACK: But…

JILL: Wait, Jack…I'm…listen…I want to say to you…to you…I'm not beautiful, Jack, so…no…well, actually I resent…disdain…no, resent…I don't know, but…your calling me that makes me…very wary…I could think you were a hustler…no-good guy, and I'm…I'm not in the market for the wrong compliment, Jack. What a world, huh? I know. Believe me. How is it possible for a man to approach a woman? I know. Tough. Because I am, I think, unapproachable, I mean now, and for some time before this. So, please, and I mean this, don't take leaving me alone personally…
(He takes a step forward.) …but leave me alone. Bye, Jack.
(He takes a step back indecisively. She speaks gently. Lights change.)

JACK: *(While he speaks to the audience, the dressers re-set the chairs and take books from him and carry them offstage.)* Man. Woman. My mother and father were married for forty years, and they couldn't stand each other. I met a Greek woman on the ferry from Skiros to San Torini; she didn't speak English, I didn't speak Greek. We stood by the rail, shoulders touching, in perfect harmony for nine hours. Naturally I never saw her again. Somebody understands this. I just wondered if by any chance they were here tonight?

(New Scene. The stage is re-set, abstractly, as Jill's apartment. Her living room. He looks out a window. She stands, trying to look comfortable.)

JACK: View, huh? Nice. Nice view. Nice apartment. Ummm…are you nervous? I'm very nervous. Nice apartment though.

JILL: I have scotch and, uh, what? Cheap vodka. This much scotch, actually.

JACK: I don't…

JILL: You don't? I don't either really, that's why…

JACK: Use scotch, drink it.

JILL: Oh, I…

JACK: You know…I…

JILL: Not since…I am nervous.

JACK: Well, this is…

JILL: I guess, if I think about it…I've never been…

JACK: Picked up. Listen…

JILL: Actually I was going to say…

JACK: Not that that's…

JILL: Sounds a little retro…

JACK: This?

JILL: You know…

JACK: Not this.

JILL: How about, "swept me off my feet."

JACK: Pardon?

JILL: Let's say you "swept me off my feet."

JACK: Me?

JILL: What my mother used to say.

JACK: Well, I'd say…

JILL: About my dad. Though I was sitting.

JACK: What?

JILL: When you swept me off my feet. Joke.

JACK: Right. *(Pause.)* Vodka.

JILL: Oh vodka…

JACK: Tonic, straight, whatever.

JILL: I thought you didn't…

JACK: Well, you know…

JILL: Unless you'd like to smoke?

JACK: Actually…

JILL: A joint, but…

JACK: Ummm.

JILL: You don't…?

JACK: What?

JILL: Ganja, weed…

JACK: Oh, hey…

JILL: Reefer, Mary Jane…

JACK: No, really, erase the vodka, I…

JILL: Hang on.
     (Exits.)

JACK: I was married, was married and…

JILL: Can't hear you…

JACK: *(Louder.)* She did no stimulants…with a vengeance.

JILL: Just rolling in here.

JACK: No Coca-Cola, no caffeine…she had her adrenal glands surgically removed.

JILL: Stuff's a little old.

JACK: She was, actually, a person who would have benefited from stimulants.

JILL: Coming.

JACK: Post-divorce, I stayed like…massively whacked out…you know, reacting.

JILL: *(Reappearing with ashtray and joint.)* Have you been married?

JACK: Well, I…

JILL: What's an imagist?

JACK: Well, images…

JILL: I was married.

JACK: Ah.

JILL: Let's not get into that.

JACK: Images are a vocabulary.

JILL: Wait…I'm sorry…one thing…

JACK: What?

JILL: Wait.

JACK: No problem.

JILL: Okay. Wait. If we smoke this, we're going to get involved.

JACK: Involved?

JILL: Historically I'm…susceptible.

JACK: To?

JILL: Physically.

JACK: Am I…

JILL: When I…

JACK: You mean…

JILL: We, Jack. We will get involved physically.

JACK: Us?

JILL: Yes.

JACK: Well…really?

JILL: Really.

JACK: Well…

JILL: Wait…I mean, I didn't mean to interrupt you.

JACK: So you mean…

JILL: But I know myself.

JACK: Sure…well, I mean you would.

JILL: So what are your feelings?

JACK: My feelings?

JILL: About smoking?

JACK: Smoking…ummm…fine.

JILL: Given my susceptibility.

JACK: Susceptibility. Yes.

JILL: But…

JACK: I am… *(Meaning yes.)*

JILL: You mean…

JACK: Sure.

JILL: Okay. Okay, there are some things…

JACK: Absolutely.

JILL: I am completely clean. Vaginally.

JACK: Right…I'm, uh…

JILL: Condoms.

JACK: *(Reaches for wallet.)* I…I…

JILL: I have condoms.

JACK: I…

JILL: You?

JACK: Me?

JILL: You know.

JACK: Oh!

JILL: You know.

JACK: Clean.

JILL: Good. *(They smile.)* Of course, you can't trust anybody.

JACK: I…

JILL: No penetration.

JACK: Me.

JILL: Jack, who ordinarily penetrates?

JACK: Right, I just…

JILL: Agreed?

JACK: Look, we don't have to…
    (Dresser enters with condoms.)

JILL: I want to. I didn't expect to want to, but…I want to.
    (Jill takes condoms from dresser. Dresser exits.)

JACK: Well, I…

JILL: You don't want to? You came on very strong.

JACK: I do…no, I do…only…

JILL: Talk to me.

JACK: Jill, I really do, but…

JILL: You called me Jill.

JACK: Jesus, you're not Jill?

JILL: I am.

JACK: Thank God.

JILL: I liked it. I'm Jill.

JACK: Can I admit to being nervous? Because…

JILL: Would you kiss me.

JACK: Because historically…
    (She kisses him.)

JILL: There.

JACK: Right.

JILL: Contact. One thing…

JACK: There have been times…

JILL: And then, you know, whatever happens…

JACK: Okay.

JILL: Condoms, right? *(He nods.)* Sorry, but…condom, no penetration, then afterwards…

JACK: Then why the condom?

JILL: Not everybody pays attention.

JACK: I promise you…

JILL: And not paying attention is…

JACK: Absolutely…hey…

JILL: Good. Ummm. Listen, do you…can we talk a little bit about oral sex?

JACK: Jill, please…

JILL: Which is to say that, I know, stupid but…

JACK: Too much structure, and I…

JILL: Otherwise…

JACK: My turn, my turn…

JILL: Nothing bad, nothing bad, I just thought…

JACK: Jill…

JILL: Yes?

JACK: Jill…

JILL: What?

JACK: Close your eyes.

JILL: Why?

JACK: Because I can't say this to open eyes.

JILL: My eyes are closed.

JACK: Oh, God. I have, you know, sometimes in the past, had uh, okay, something I'm…still working on, not even, not even a pattern…

JILL: Problems with functioning.

JACK: Well, umm, you know…yes. Maybe stress or…

JILL: Jack…

JACK: Sometimes months at a time, whoosh, smooth sailing, but uh…but uh…

JILL: Jack?

JACK: What?

JILL: It's perfect. It fits right in with no penetration. It's good.

JACK: Yeah, but later…

JILL: We're not anywhere near later, we're trying to do now.

JACK: Thanks.

JILL: Can I light this joint?

(Jack removes jacket and hangs over chair back.)

JACK: You were married?

JILL: A disaster.

JACK: Long?

JILL: Long.

JACK: *(Points to himself.)* Of moderate length.

JILL: Here. *(Hands him joint.)*

JACK: Every mistake…I made that mistake. One time…I don't know if you…should I go into this?

JILL: Unbutton my blouse.

JACK: *(Pause.)* You're sure?

JILL: Sure of what?

JACK: This is all right?

JILL: Please. *(He reaches out.)* One thing…

JACK: Okay, but only one…

JILL: You can't stay over.

JACK: Could we please not…

JILL: Sorry, that's the deal.

(While he responds, she unbuttons and takes off her blouse.)

JACK: But see…I, uh…this staying over thing…see, I have this, reaction…you know, to…this is, um, embarrassing…I can never go back to sleep, my God, you're beautiful! *(Last line said as one sentence.)*

JILL: And don't ever call me beautiful.

(She kisses him. Lights change. Jack and Jill walk into separate spots while the chairs are shifted and a table is added. Each speaks while putting on a sweater given to them by separate dressers.)

JACK: Feeling. I don't know…overloaded.

JILL: Feelings.

JACK: To feel. Oh boy. Why?

JILL: Unlooked for.

JACK: Pretty dismaying.

(Lights change. New Scene. Dresser hands Jill roses. She moves to Jack.)

JILL: *(She hands him a dozen roses.)* For you.

JACK: You're kidding.

JILL: *(She shakes her head.)* You look like someone who never got flowers, Jack.

JACK: No, I never got flowers. I never expected to get flowers.

JILL: Well, you should have.

(Jack stands looking at the flowers, then hands them to a dresser.)
(Lights change. New Scene. His place. They move to the table and sit.)

JACK: Okay, okay, if this was a negotiation…

JILL: It's not a negotiation…

JACK: If it was…

JILL: I said…

JACK: Jill, Jill, don't go off on me…if it was…

JILL: I'm not moving to California…

JACK: I didn't tell you…

JILL: "N" …"O."

JACK: Wait…

JILL: No, negative…it's not…

JACK: Five minutes of logic, okay?
     (A beat.)

JILL: Are you patronizing me?

JACK: Umm, no…I hope not…I'm saying…

JILL: Like you represent cool, lucid…

JACK: Oh boy…

JILL: Objective process…

JACK: No…

JILL: And I…

JACK: Back up…

JILL: Untamed, misty…

JACK: Hold it…

JILL: Intuition mixed with P.M.S.?

JACK: Your job can move…you're laughing?

JILL: Well…move my job…I am laughing…don't you…my job to accommodate your career opportunity…

JACK: No…

JILL: And you don't see…

JACK: You have topped out, Jill, that's what I'm saying…

JILL: No…

JACK: You already manage…wait…a nine-person office for an orthopedic surgeon…

JILL: Like, "Throw her on the wagon, boys, we're movin' west!"

JACK: Okay, point, good point, but…

JILL: I know you don't…

JACK: Unless you go to medical school…

JILL: You're saying I couldn't?

JACK: ...but unless you do...

JILL: But are you saying I couldn't?

JACK: Jill, objectively aside...listen, let's not react for a second...

JILL: But are you saying I couldn't?

JACK: Jill, stop reacting and listen...

JILL: Don't give me your "I'm dealing with a barely rational creature" voice. It's demeaning.

JACK: As a woman?

JILL: As a woman, yes.

JACK: Great.

JILL: What?

JACK: Is every waking conversation a male/female issue?

JILL: Is this a good-natured question?

JACK: Do we have any aspirin?

JILL: Male/female issue? Do you know what culture you're living in?

JACK: Jill.

JILL: How could you...

JACK: Jill, do you love me?

JILL: I...bathroom.

JACK: What?

JILL: Aspirin. *(Jack exits.)* Listen, don't confuse love with leverage.

JACK: Bullshit.

JILL: Sure, right, you say that to me from, see, another room. I would like to have one companion...

JACK: This is Advil...

JILL: Who would stay in the room while we...you're all wusses.

JACK: Oh boy...

(Jack enters with a bottle of Advil and a glass of water.)

JILL: You got me to move in with that hustle about you...you did...having two bedrooms.

JACK: I stay in the room.

JILL: You just went...

JACK: I have a splitting...

JILL: And you have two bedrooms...

JACK: Don't start...

JILL: ...because of basic inequalities in the...

JACK AND JILL: Pay scale.

JACK: But it makes sense, given our...

JILL: Yes, it made sense, and the sense it made…

JACK: More work space, we agreed…

(Jack exits with Advil and glass.)

JILL: Because males, from infancy, get more space…

JACK: What? I had a split-level crib?

JILL: And if I want more space…

(Jack enters empty-handed.)

JACK: You got more space…you're in more space…

JILL: At the price of giving up my space and…

JACK: Practicality, puh-leeze, isn't a feminist issue…

JILL: Cook for you.

JACK: I said I would cook.

JILL: You eat out of cans, Jack. You know how to grill three kinds of horrible meat…good, you're laughing.

JACK: California.

JILL: So?

JACK: Think about it, I do images for a living. Where is image everything?

JILL: I understand why it is advantageous for…

JACK: And they will snap you up. You will be able to walk to the beach over the supplicant backs of orthopedic surgeons.

JILL: Jack…

JACK: What?

JILL: I must not do this again.

JACK: It's not…

JILL: I really must not. Build a life around somebody else…

JACK: With.

JILL: It's bad for me, it's bad for you…

JACK: With, not "around."

JILL: It's identity, Jack.

JACK: Marry me.

(A pause.)

JILL: That's kind of blockheaded, given the moment.

JACK: I mean it.

JILL: You mean to be blockheaded?

JACK: You say that to me when I'm asking you to be my wife?

JILL: You just heard me say it was a question of identity.

JACK: It's a question of commitment…

JILL: I have to get some stuff straight…

JACK: Don't start…

JILL: Because until then…

JACK: Jill…

JILL: What do I bring?

JACK: Don't start!

JILL: Don't yell at me!

JACK: I love you.

JILL: There's no such thing.

JACK: I love you!

JILL: There's no such thing!

JACK: What, then?

JILL: Companions.

JACK: Yes.

JILL: Meaning…

JACK: Yes?

JILL: Equal voice.

JACK: My God, you make 90 percent…

JILL: Of the completely peripheral…

JACK: Of the…not peripheral…all the decisions…

JILL: I'm not talking about movies or restaurants…

JACK: I am talking about every…

JILL: Forget it.

JACK: No, I won't forget it, I…

(Jill gets coin from purse.)

JILL: I'll flip you for it.

JACK: Will you stick to the…

JILL: Heads it's California, tails it's here.

JACK: You're kidding?

JILL: Huh-uh.

JACK: We can't make this decision based on…

JILL: Why not?

(Beat.)

JACK: Did you hear me propose to you?

JILL: No.

JACK: No?

JILL: I'm proposing to you. *(He breaks into frustrated laughter.)* I'm serious.

JACK: I just…

JILL: But first, the prenuptial agreement.

JACK: This is your idea of romance?

JILL: Don't beat me up with "romance."

JACK: I love you!!

JILL: There's no such thing. Now, heads we go, tails we stay.

JACK: I can't get the work here.

JILL: And Dr. Lake can't get me into medical school there.

(A pause.)

JACK: Medical school?

JILL: Yes.

JACK: That's seven years or something.

JILL: Yes. Will you marry me, yes or no?

JACK: I asked you!!

JILL: You dismissed the prenuptial agreement!

JACK: You are…really…flip the goddamn coin.

JILL: That would be premature.

JACK: All right, I'll marry you!

JILL: Was that so hard?

(She flips.)

JACK: What is it?

JILL: Let's not look yet.

JACK: Jill…

JILL: Tell me ten reasons you love me. Good reasons. If I think they're good, I'll show you the prenuptial agreement.

JACK: If they're good.

JILL: Yeah. Then we go to dinner…you pick the restaurant, then we go to bed.

JACK: Does this include penetration?

JILL: It demands it. Then you get up and grill me some meat, and we look at the coin, which is binding.

JACK: What if there are problems with the agreement?

JILL: We only look at the coin when we're clear.

JACK: That could take…

JILL: Coins wait. Now what's the first reason?

JACK: Reason for what?

JILL: That you love me, remember?

JACK: You are an implacable hard-ass.

JILL: That is very, very good. What's number two?

(Lights change. Jill exits to do fast change into traditional wedding dress over swimsuit. During his monologue, Jack first removes his sweater, hands it to a dresser. He later removes his shirt, hands it to a dresser. He is wearing a

long-sleeved T-shirt and looks disheveled. During monologue, dressers also strike the table and chairs.)

JACK: You get, you know, married…time passes…you get, you know, divorced. "A" leads to "B." Yin/Yang. Why is this? Let's see. Well, up to that point… getting married…the only, you know, long-term relationship most, um, people have had is with their parents. And, of course, you blew that. Plus, naturally, in most cases, different sexes are involved, mainly, sort of like mating antelopes and tigers. Plus, some sexes are smarter than other sexes… and some sexes earn more money. How could this ever work out? And, of course, it doesn't.

(A dresser hands him a beer bottle, and he takes a swig.)

So, why would you get married in the first place…why?…why would you do that? My God, why would you do that!?

(Lights change. New Scene. He knocks on the air; we hear the knock.)

JILL'S VOICE: Who is it?

JACK: Me, Jack.

JILL'S VOICE: You can't come in.

JACK: I have to come in.

JILL'S VOICE: It would be bad luck.

JACK: I have a problem.

JILL'S VOICE: What, Jack?

JACK: I can't get married.

(Jill appears in a traditional white wedding dress. She is radiantly beautiful.)

JILL: Don't fuck with me, Jack.

JACK: You're wearing white…

JILL: Yes…

JACK: But…

JILL: Jack, the first time, I didn't wear white as a protest against, who knows… traditional values. This time I'm wearing white, okay?

JACK: Sure.

JILL: What, Jack?

JACK: I can't marry you, I'm a bad person.

JILL: I see.

JACK: I have a very bad track record, Jill. While involved with one person, I have had, you know, sexual congress with others. More than once. I am…

secretive by nature. Hell, I don't really know myself. I pretend to be nice, but I'm not nice. I'm very self-centered. I feel…I do…women should take care of me. I should be their, you know, priority. I will share the house-work, yes, but secretly I will hate the housework and whoever made me do it. I think I think, when I really examine it, that men are better. And, believing that, the long and the short of it is, I believe I'm a shit.

JILL: I see.

JACK: So I wanted to tell you, you know, while we could…still turn back.

JILL: First of all, Jack, you look very handsome.

JACK: Thank you, but I'm a shit.

JILL: Doubt's okay. Thanks for coming to tell me. Nobody likes housework. It is not only men who have affairs. I think women are better, but I don't want to marry one. I know I drive you crazy, Jack, with all my doubts and regrets and sexual politics and questionable karma and tragedies of the past and unresolved this's and half understood that's, but you're the only one…the only one who has ever seemed to love me, doubts, luggage, feroc-ity and all, and that is incredibly meaningful to me, Jack, and…uh…I'm a bride, Jack, see…all dressed in white, and I am…full of feeling, and umm…full of hope…and…

JACK: Shhhh.

JILL:…and I would like to marry you and cherish and be cherished, I really would. I really, really would. So please marry me. I would like to try.

JACK: *(A pause, then simply.)* Okay.

JILL: I love you…or something.

(Lights change. Jack goes offstage where he changes into swim trunks. Jill stays and, as she speaks, the dressers remove her shoes, veil, and wedding dress, reveal-ing her swimsuit. Both add wedding rings.)

JILL: I have always felt, ummm, alone. Sort of like I was, well, alone. Not…look, I responded, related…sure, I kept up my end…absolutely…even mistaken for outgoing, but…okay, okay, the watchamacallit…water sport…on TV, c'mon head…synchronized swimming. In sync. Two people…effortless, frictionless…completely…as if grace descended and what's outside the "sync," outside the two of you, seems…infinitely clumsier…alienated, divided…*(Two dressers spread towels on the stage.)* I mean we all experi-ence that…for…for brief periods…you have…"in sync." That's proba-bly the paradise they speak of.

(Lights change. New Scene. They lie down on towels. They are bathed in sunset.)

JILL: Incredible. God, can you…it's, oh…

JACK: *(The sky.)* Overwhelming.

JILL: Like we're inside the sunset.

JACK: Amazing…

JILL: Amazing grace. *(A pause.)* Why doesn't everybody live here?

JACK: Fear of perfection.

JILL: Yeah. *(A moment.)* Right. Tell me I don't have to go back.

JACK: You don't have to go back.

JILL: *(A moment.)* Jack?

JACK: What?

JILL: Tickle me.

JACK: Really?

JILL: Yeah.

JACK: You want me to tickle you?

JILL: I do. Gimme, gimme, gimme.

> *(He leaps on her and tickles her unmercifully. Cries of "Wait," "Jack!," "Not there," "Not so hard," "You bastard," "No more, no more, no more!" etc. After complete wrestling hysteria, he just as suddenly leaps off. She regards him gravely.)*

JILL: Thank you.

JACK: *(Just as gravely.)* Please, think nothing of it.

> *(A moment. He begins kissing her chin and kisses slowly to her toes.)*

JILL: *(Somewhere in the process.)* Sometimes, Jack, I think…

JACK: Shhhhhh.

JILL: I think we are like…

JACK: *(Still involved.)* Skin. *(He kisses.)* What?

JILL: More kissing. *(He does.)* Incredible weather…a complex conjunction of…

JACK: Not weather…

JILL: Unprecedented, but it could pass through and…

JACK: An amalgam…

JILL: No, really…

JACK: You make aluminum…

JILL: Change is the precondition, so…

JACK: It stays aluminum.

JILL: This could change.

JACK: No. *(Jack finishes kissing.)* That's looking for trouble…

JILL: I want, God, I want to be in sync, deeply…with you, but I don't…look at me…don't want to lose myself in you, Jack, and you shouldn't either.

JACK: I am lost in you.

JILL: I don't think that works, Jack, when I've done that before...

JACK: This isn't before...

JILL: No, but...

JACK: Hold me.

JILL: Jack...

JACK: C'mon.

(They hug.)

JILL: *(Not unkindly.)* I can't reassure you every...

JACK: This isn't...

JILL: Just saying...

JACK: Okay...

(They break embrace. He stands.)

JILL: We need to keep some resources outside...

JACK: *(More seriously.)* Stop.

JILL: Outside this. That's all I'm saying.

(A moment.)

JACK: I understand that.

(They take hands and lie down. She withdraws. A moment.)

JILL: *(Wiping her eyes.)* Faith. Got to keep the faith. Help me keep the faith, Jack. Maybe I'm just petrified of my good fortune. *(She sits up.)* Oh, my God...

JACK: What?

JILL: Look at that big dead fish.

(Lights change. He exits and changes to khakis, boat shoes, T-shirt, design shirt, and sports coat. During Jill's monologue, dressers enter and assist her as she puts on slacks and matching jacket, long-sleeved shirt and low-heeled pumps. Other dressers set two chairs and strike the towels.)

JILL: So weird, the feelings...who's in here feeling this? To be clear, so hard to be clear...if you had a child and...would you...at this point...what would you teach this child? Would you...for instance, teach her...obedience, respect, diligence, propriety, cotillion, S.A.T. skills...I mean, given the way things are...you know, the way they're going...in the paper...or...given how those...virtues...what they've made...what we...maybe you should teach her disobedience, disrespect, impropriety, pagan rituals, carpentry, and see if that works out...better.

(Lights change. New Scene. Jack enters. They are dressed. Jill sits in a chair. Jack sits across from her.)

JACK: Whew. Damn. Long day. Whew. How about you?
    (She doesn't answer. During the following exchange, the dressers set the stage for a future scene, a table piled with dishes in another area of the stage. We're talking at least eighteen plates and two stacks of three bowls each.)

JILL: I started taking the pill again.

JACK: What?

JILL: The pill, I'm on it.

JACK: *(Pause.)* Well…Jesus, Jill.

JILL: I don't…I don't want a baby now.

JACK: What about what I want?

JILL: Ummm…okay, you have a baby.

JACK: Don't…we, hey, talked about this, I…

JILL: Since we talked about it…

JACK: Said that…

JILL: You hardly come near me.

JACK: Last night…

JILL: You pulled out before you came, how…

JACK: That wasn't…

JILL: Wasn't what?

JACK: Okay, all right, mixed feelings for a second…

JILL: Should we have a baby with mixed feelings?

JACK: That was…we're not so young, Jill, you…

JILL: Hey, I have mixed feelings, so…

JACK: Yes. Okay. You could have asked.

JILL: I did. You didn't tell me, don't…okay so I'm asking. I need you to tell me, Jack. *(A pause. He exhales.)* No baby, Jack. Not right now, right? Don't you think? Talk to me. *(Pause.)* So, how was your day?

(Lights change. New Scene. They rise. She removes her jacket and exchanges it for a dustbuster with a dresser. The dustbuster is on, and she vacuums invisible drapes. Another dresser hands Jack a slip of paper. Other dressers remove the chairs.)

JACK: What is this?

JILL: It's a phone message.

JACK: It's a guy's name and you…did you draw these hearts?

JILL: What!? Yes.

JACK: So who is he?

JILL: I was doodling, Jack.

JACK: Who is he?!

(Jill turns dustbuster off.)

JILL: Are you kidding?

JACK: No, I'm not kidding, I…I'm sick of this, do you understand me, I go to these, yes, hospital parties these guys…

JILL: If you…

JACK: Are all over you, they…

JILL: These are…

JACK: You leave me standing there…

JILL: Are my colleagues, they…

JACK: I don't like it, do you hear me?

(Jill hands dustbuster to dresser.)

JILL: I hear you, but…

JACK: I am…last week, you go bowling with, wait…a bunch of these…on the one night…

JILL: They are my friends, you said…

JACK: What am I supposed to say?

JILL: We needed to blow off some…

JACK: Who is this guy, Marty indecipherable, with hearts?

JILL: I can't believe this.

JACK: Who, goddamnit, is he?!

JILL: *(Pause.)* He has been assigned to me. I am his secret Valentine. I'm supposed to send him jelly beans and a card at a total cost of less than two dollars.

JACK: Yeah?

JILL: Yeah. Anonymously.

JACK: *(A moment.)* Well, I don't like it. I don't like this stuff. Do you hear me clearly?

JILL: *(A pause. Levelly.)* Will you stop?

(A moment. Lights change. New Scene. She goes to the dishes and begins breaking three of them. Jack exits and puts on sports coat. Then he enters when she's broken three dishes.)

JACK: Hi.

JILL: *(Smash.)* Hi.

JACK: You uh…I guess you aren't…

JILL: Don't say anything stupid, Jack.

(Smash.)

JACK: Bad day at work.

JILL: Bad day at work.

(Smash.)

JACK: Listen, I understand…

JILL: You don't understand. Just…just…

JACK: The amount of stress…

JILL: Do not explain this to me!

JACK: I am on your side!

JILL: Great.

(Smash.)

JACK: I know what you're feeling.

JILL: Goddamnit! Does everything I feel have to…to pass through you to exist? Why? Why, Jack? What is your…I don't know…compulsion…as if… compulsion to translate for me as if I didn't…

JACK: I'm not…

JILL: Like I have no feelings unless you define them.

(Smash.)

JACK: You tell me all the time to relate, damn it, I'm relating.

JILL: Well, I don't want to relate, I want to break the dishes.

(Crash.)

JACK: I understand it's…valuable to…to get the feelings…

JILL: And don't patronize me.

(Crash.)

JACK: You're patronizing me.

JILL: Jack, aren't you…something else…aren't you cataloguing images or something?

JACK: While you…

JILL: Don't you have something else to do, Jack?

(Crash.)

JACK: Oh, I should alphabetize slides…

JILL: Good…

(Crash.)

JACK: While you destroy the house?

JILL: I don't want…

JACK: Or what, what?

JILL: I'm saying I don't want to be…

JACK: Be what?

JILL: Interpreted.

(Crash.)

JACK: This is a marriage, what you do…

JILL: You want to fix it, right?

JACK: Don't start with that, Jill…

JILL: It's like having a plumber for my feelings.

JACK: And I…

JILL: You can't fix me, do you understand?
  (Crash.)

JACK: This is stress because of your residency.

JILL: My God, I can't shut you out, you're like the ocean, you're all-enveloping.

JACK: I am your companion, I love you, this is our house.

JILL: I am your companion. This has nothing to do with you. I'm not mad at you. I don't mean to hurt your feelings. I don't need to be placated. I just want to break these dishes.

JACK: Let's go out and grab a beer.

JILL: I don't want a beer.

JACK: Coffee, tea, cheesecake, a movie…

JILL: I was enjoying breaking the dishes…

JACK: It doesn't make any sense…

JILL: I'm not making sense, Jack, I'm breaking the dishes.
  (She shoves a stack of bowls onto the floor.)

JACK: Goddamnit, stop that!

JILL: Don't worry, I'll pay you for them.

JACK: That is really cheap, Jill.

JILL: Oh, it wasn't in your mind?

JACK: It was in my mind that it's wasteful.

JILL: Well, you can make a big point of replacing them.
  (Crash.)

JACK: You mean I'm financially brutalizing you?

JILL: Tell me you don't trade on my dependence?

JACK: I don't even think about it.

JILL: Bullshit.

JACK: Don't tell me what I think.

JILL: You know you like it.

JACK: It is incredibly temporary…

JILL: But it's a hold.

JACK: As a physician, you'll make…

JILL: So it's not merely supportive?

JACK: I'm not supportive?

JILL: Financially, yes.

JACK: That's the only way you find me supportive?

JILL: Don't give me the martyred look.

JACK: If that's your perception, I can fix it.

JILL: Fix it?

JACK: What is it that's wanted here, anger?

JILL: Will you…Jack…listen to yourself, "What is it that's wanted here." Jesus!

JACK: Yes?

JILL: That's not an emotion, that's a preface.

JACK: The question, damnit, precedes the answer.

JILL: Jack, you start with a question and then, worse, worse, you immediately try…

JACK: Fix it. I try to fix it. Yes, right, I know my sins. God forbid we should try to do anything about anything…*(Smash.)*…we should, we should experience it…or something, imbibe it, embody it, swim in it or some goddamn…

JILL: I want you to leave the room.

JACK: What?

JILL: You asked what I want, I want you to leave the room.

JACK: This room…

JILL: Is your room…

JACK: I never said…

JILL: Your room, your apartment…

JACK: Goddamnit!

JILL: …your life, your agenda, your wife.
    (Smash.)

JACK: You are my wife, yes. And I…

JILL: Jesus, I wish I was out of here…

JACK: You are in the middle of a residency…

JILL: Why did I ever think…

JACK: The hours are horrendous, the sleep deprivation is brutal, you have no time to yourself…

JILL: Because every second I have, you're there.

JACK: We have no time…

JILL: I don't need "we" time, I need…

JACK: I need "we" time.

JILL: I don't.

JACK: How can you say…

JILL: I want to be alone, Jack. I know…believe me…it's a terrible failing… I'm…
anti-social or something…there are times…yesterday, all day, I thought
about you, but you never tell me I irritate you…don't I irritate you? You
irritate me. For one thing, you can't do anything, Jack…don't get martyred…it's just the way you were raised, but it's…it's oppressive, so…what,
what are you doing?

(Jack begins pushing fragments into piles with feet.)

JACK: It is very indulgent.

JILL: What?

JACK: Breaking things. Being anti-social. Showing off your emotions. Pretending
who has what money or whatever is the point here. It is very, very, very
indulgent. Now, let's stick with one problem and fix it.

JILL: Jack, you can't fix a toilet, you can't cope with…

JACK: Here we go…

JILL: Okay, it's not easy…the insurance…

JACK: I can cope with…

JILL: Canceled.

JACK: One time.

JILL: They turned off the phone.

JACK: One time.

JILL: The car registration.

JACK: All right, Jesus, I get the point.

JILL: And I'm not saying…

JACK: And they didn't turn off the phone.

JILL: That you're not generous, because you are, you are so generous it's like
water torture.

JACK: Jill, I love you. My heart…this life, it's richer, more…more various, just
better.

JILL: Wait…

JACK: No. You give value…you change me.

JILL: It's sweet, it's…vague. I don't recognize…I wish, I really do…recognize
me, Jill, as that person, Jack…that value-adding person…you are making up, and that's generous, too, this person who…I am selfish, I am ambitious, I am…oh, yes…unpleasant, angry, I-don't-know-what person…it's
a burden…really…I'm sorry it's this way…but, Jesus, feeling like a shit
all the time because I'm not…that! That stuff you make up to sustain this.
Honestly say to me that you don't see…

JACK: I want connection, and you…

JILL: I want…

JACK: To be, see...one with you and...

JILL: Baloney.

JACK: To be one...

JILL: This is nice, Jack.

JACK: Nice?

JILL: Nice, yes, this is something somebody would want to hear...

JACK: But I mean it.

JILL: Which is nice, which is your specialty.

JACK: Nice is?

JILL: Yes.

JACK: I want this central, but...

JILL: But disingenuous.

JACK: I am not...

JILL: Disingenuous. You obsess on my stimulus...

JACK: I wouldn't...wait...

JILL: Stir things up...keep you...

JACK: No, I want to share...

JILL: But you don't share. I don't know what you're feeling...

JACK: What?

JILL: Right now, now I don't...you just...Jack, you say a bunch of stuff just to...to restore order...to reduce people to calm...you don't care what you say...you'd say anything.

JACK: Right now?

JILL: Yes.

JACK: I am pissed off.

JILL: At what?

JACK: At what?

JILL: At what?

JACK: This, this conversation. The...the dishes, you know, to mention one...the tone...all of it.

JILL: And your feelings?

JACK: My feelings?

JILL: Yes, Jack, your feelings.

JACK: My feelings are...damn, Jill...what are these endless...endless feelings... c'mon Jill, these goddamn whatevers...right?...that you say I'm not having?

JILL: You want me to tell you about your feelings?

JACK: No, as a matter of fact, I know my feelings, actually, I'm having them.

JILL: And?

JACK: And what?

JILL: They are?

JACK: This is ridiculous, you know my feelings!

JILL: Say them!

JACK: I'm upset, this is upsetting.

JILL: What is?

JACK: You say you're leaving.

JILL: When in this conversation did I…

JACK: About being alone…treating you…wanting to be alone.

JILL: I only want to be alone because I'm already alone with you.

JACK: How can you say that? How dare you say that?

JILL: What-are-you-feeling-Jack?!

JACK: I don't give a shit what I'm feeling!

JILL: And that's why I'm alone!

> *(She starts out.)*

JACK: Don't walk out on this!

JILL: *(Simply.)* What are you feeling, Jack?

> *(She waits. He is at a complete impasse. She goes and adds a vest and uses scarf to tie ponytail.)*

JACK: *(Another moment.)* Goddamnit! Goddamnit!!

(He shoves the rest of the dishes and bowls to the floor. Lights change. During monologue, Jack removes sports coat and tosses it offstage. Later, he removes shirt and tosses it offstage. Also during monologue, two dressers sweep broken dishes into a large circle, inside which the last scene is played. Other dressers strike the table and spread books and empty boxes on the floor within the circle.)

JACK: Nice, right? Nice. Okay. One second. One second. This nice we are talking about here…"Don't be nice, Jack." This "nice" has a bad name…to say the goddamn least. Women, to generalize, hate nice…no, no, they like it in clerks, they like it in auto mechanics…but…nice guys finish last, right? Why? Because "nice" is essentially thought to lack complexity, mystery. "Nice" just…has no sex appeal…it just doesn't understand the situation. Women distrust "nice" because, given the cultural context, they themselves can't possibly be nice. How can the powerless be "nice." What good is nice to the "exploited"? So women loathe nice because they see, they know what a phony mask it is in their own lives, so when they perceive it in a man it just pisses them off. What they prefer are abusive qualities moderated by charm, because they are already abused personalities, given the culture. I'm not kidding. Hey, I don't buy it because there is another "nice," a hard-won, complex, covered-with-blood-and-gore "nice." An existential, steel-willed, utterly crucial and necessary "nice" that says to the skags in the motorcycle gang, "Fuck you and the hogs you rode in on. I exemplify hope and reason and concern." See, I raise the fallen banner high, Jill, so satirize me, shoot me, stab me, dismiss me, go screw the Four Horsemen of the Apocalypse if that's what turns you on, I'm nice!! *(He slowly turns back into himself. Jill enters and sits by stack of books.)* Sorry, I didn't, uh…don't know how I got into that…just "nice," you know… well, anyway, sorry.

(Lights change. New Scene. He turns back and is now involved in dividing books with Jill.)

JILL: Are all the Joyce Carol Oates…

JACK: All yours.

JILL: Not all.

JACK: Just take them!

JILL: We can't divide them if you won't divide.

JACK: Goddamnit, you divide them!

JILL: So you can criticize how I do it?

JACK: *(Looking away.)* Bitch.

JILL: God, Jack…

JACK: Let's just do the books.

JILL: You called me a "bitch."

JACK: I did, yes.

JILL: You don't think that's sad?

JACK: Get off it!

JILL: *(Calm, not sarcastic.)* Do you mean "bitch" in the sense that I told you something you didn't want to hear? Or that I'm "uppity" and don't do what I'm told…

JACK: Just shut up, okay?

JILL:…or remind you of Bette Davis or have assumed the male role…

JACK: I'm warning you…

JILL: Warning me?

JACK: Do the books, Jill.

JILL: Or is it just a lot simpler, and you mean "bitch" as a kind of catch-all general category for a woman who is truly, really sick of trying to laugh off your endlessly passive-aggressive behavior?

JACK: I want you out of here! Out of this space. Out of my life. Out of my nervous system. Out of here!

JILL: Why can't we…

JACK: Because we can't.

JILL: Close this out with some sense we were right to try.

JACK: *(Packing.)* Because we obviously weren't.

JILL: Since it's a failure, why can't it be a useful failure?

JACK: Dostoevski, mine. Dr. Doolittle, mine. Toni Morrison, yours.

JILL: This is just another version of you walking out of the room.

JACK: Don't start with me. Goddamnit! What I would like is to finish this up and walk out of here without punching you out!

JILL: Whoa??

JACK: You want to know what I think? I think you can't feel anything but an extreme. I think the middle ground is without sensation for you. You drive too fast, you love the unknown, you love extremes. I think I was your last experiment in the ordinary, and it didn't have enough tingle, so you blew it off.

JILL: You don't think punching me out would be an extreme?

JACK: I think punching people out is the final, frustrated expression of the ordinary mind. I think you would like me to hit you so this would be all my fault. It is the only stupid, vulgar, debasing male idiocy you haven't been able to pry out of me, but you uh…you'll never know how…do you have any sense how close…this close…to nailing you…yes, there…happy now?

JILL: I'm supposed to feel sorry for you because you wanted to hit me?

JACK: I was making…

JILL: Well, I do. I am sorry.

JACK: You are, huh?

JILL: Really sorry.

JACK: Have I ever hit you?

JILL: Not the point.

JACK: Then why are we talking about this?

JILL: Jack…

JACK: No.

JILL: Jack. *(A moment.)* I think marriage is like the cockpit of a commercial airliner…you know…all those switches…and they all…all 200…have to be in…the right positions, only in aviation they know what those are, and in marriage you never do, so the odds…the odds are astronomical you won't…stay in the air. So I don't think we're bad people, Jack, I think we are disgruntled victims…of the odds.

JACK: But you always thought…

JILL: I thought they were long…the odds, yes, I did.

JACK: So we're a self-fulfilling prophecy.

(They look at each other.)

JILL: We don't have the switches in the right places…so…it won't stay…up. *The Age of Reason?*

JACK: Mine.

JILL: *Anna Karenina.*

JACK: Yours.

JILL: *Co-Dependence in Contemporary Marriage?*

JACK: Mine.

JILL: *The Hardy Boys.*

JACK: Very funny.

(A pause.)

JILL: Hey, Jack?

JACK: What?!

JILL: Come kiss me good-bye. *(He stops packing but doesn't look at her.)* Come on, Jack, be my pal. *(He looks at her but doesn't move.)* Okay, I'll come over there.

(She goes and wraps her arms around him. Finally, he raises his arms and puts them around her.)

JACK: Bye, Jill.

JILL: Bye, Jack.

(They sit holding each other. The lights go out.)

END OF ACT ONE

ACT TWO

The scene begins in the dark. Jack and Jill are in bed.

JILL: *(A dream.)* No!

JACK: Ow. What?…Ow!

JILL: Wait…what?…wait.

JACK: Right in the…

JILL: Oh no…

JACK: It's okay. Ow.

JILL: Jack?

JACK: Your elbow…

JILL: Jack.

JACK: Jack, yes. I don't think it's broken.

JILL: I had no…

JACK: That hurt…

JILL:…idea, not a clue.

JACK: What idea?

JILL: Who you were…
 (Switches light on.)

JACK: No!
 (She switches light off.)

JILL: You're bleeding.

JACK: Nothing…it's just a…

JILL: Get you a Kleenex.

JACK: Forget it.

JILL: Really sorry…here. *(Switches light on. Hands him Kleenex.)* It's been years…

JACK: Thanks. Please…
 (She switches light off.)

JILL: I'm so used to being…

JACK: Time thing…
 (Referring to a glowing clock face.)

JILL:…alone. So you touching me…

JACK: Clock?

JILL: It just startled…
 (He turns on the light on his side.)

JACK: Three A.M.

JILL: God…

JACK: You've been alone?

JILL: Look, we're on different sides.

JACK: Where?

JILL: Of the bed.

JACK: Who changed?

JILL: I did. Oh, my God…

JACK: What?

JILL: Three A.M. Once I'm up…

JACK: Me neither. You look great, Doctor.

JILL: Your poor nose…

JACK: About this alone.

JILL: I'd really rather…

JACK: Are you?

JILL: Jack…

JACK: What?

JILL: Knock it off.

JACK: I'd call this…

JILL: Please…

JACK: Chemistry.

JILL: Nostalgia.

JACK: We pass on two moving stairways in an airport…

JILL: Dopey.

JACK: Cinematic.

JILL: So…

JACK: So…

JILL: Maybe you should go back to the hotel.

JACK: Huh-uh.

JILL: We should leave it at this.

JACK: That's just anxiety.

JILL: Just?

JACK: Normal two-years-divorced, pass-in-the-airport, cancel-a-plane, take-a-taxi, rip-off-our-clothes anxiety.

JILL: This was fine, but…

JACK: Really?

JILL: All right, good then…

JACK: Objectively.

JILL: I don't mean I didn't like it.

JACK: You liked it.

JILL: Don't tell me what I liked.

JACK: Sorry.

JILL: You blew it.

JACK: I meant I liked it.

JILL: Okay, but…*(He turns out the light.)* I don't want…

JACK: One minute.

JILL: No, Jack…

JACK: Thirty seconds.

JILL: When I say no…

JACK: Please. Please. Just…please. *(Silence in the dark.)* Oh, God…

JILL: Jack?

JACK: This is…better. Much, much…better.

JILL: This wasn't…

JACK: Shhhhhhhhhh.

    (A silence.)

JILL: What are we doing?

JACK: We're restoring.

JILL: That feels good.

JACK: Sometimes things fall into disrepair and then if you care about them, you restore them.

JILL: Not what is restoring, restoring what?

JACK: Us.

JILL: *(Turns on his light.)* You really need to go back to your hotel.

JACK: *(Turns off light.)* I'm serious, Jill.

JILL: Turn on the light.

JACK: Listen…

JILL: Turn it on.

JACK: No.

JILL: No?

JACK: Just…

JILL: You say "no" in my bed? No in my house? You have no authority in my universe.

    (She hits him.)

JACK: Ow.

JILL: You cannot restore me to someone you can say "no" to.

    (She hits him again.)

JACK: Ow.

JILL: Do you get it?

JACK: What would you call this if I was hitting you?

JILL: I would call this not being listened to.

JACK: So don't do it again.

JILL: I am turning on the light.

> *(She does. A dresser helps her into a robe.)*

JACK: I want this.

JILL: If people, once, you know, were what we were…

JACK: Don't put on the robe.

JILL: At the center, central…no Jack…then realistically there's a residue…

JACK: Beautiful.

JILL: Stop it. A residue…

JACK: And don't tell me…

JILL: That can be played on…

JACK: That isn't…

JILL: In certain situations…

JACK: Going on here.

JILL: What?

JACK: We are.

JILL: Residue can flare up briefly…stop looking at me.

JACK: You like it.

JILL: I am turning out the light.

> *(She does.)*

JACK: Fine.

> *(Jill turns light back on.)*

JILL: Which doesn't mean…

JACK: Fine.

> *(She turns it out.)*

JILL: Because I want to say this undistracted…

JACK: Where are you?

JILL: I loved you, and…

JACK: And I…

JILL: Shhhh. But it malfunctioned…

JACK: Take my hand.

JILL: Jack, I was…ill defined…I…you defined me…

JACK: But…

JILL: Shhh.

JACK: My hand…

JILL: Okay. And you were, without, um, question, perfect to be ill defined with, really…because nobody, no-body beats you for reassurance, Jack…you were nicer to be nobody with than anybody, hands down, but when I…and you supported…sustained, sympathized…all the S's, and I got…really, you were wonderful…when I started defining…separating from your…reassurance…

well, you…you were still back there with the S's…you…redoubled your efforts because…why not? You were way, way better suited to support me than to acknowledge me, and you were, meaning no harm, plain fucking oppressive, Jack. Sorry, but…so I'm, well, whatever I am now, but it's alone, I'm afraid, barring a little…screwing around…and that's just…my old friend…*(Turns on her light.)* Just the way I like it. Amen.

JACK: My turn…

JILL: Look, Jack…

JACK: My turn. My turn. *(He turns on his light.)* To really support…really support someone is acknowledgment, okay? Plus, plus…when you…okay… were busy defining, separating…look, no offense, self-realizing, would there were another word, Jill, that's important, no doubt about it, but I give it a six on degree of difficulty, keeping something going between two humans, that's what you, I know you're going to hate this, you grow up for. That's a grown-up's job. *(A pause.)* Okay, okay, I had to say it.

JILL: Jack…

JACK: What?

JILL: Hotel.

JACK: Let me…

JILL: The end. With empathy.

JACK: What are you feeling?

JILL: You asked me what I'm feeling.

JACK: Yes.

JILL: You said the word, "feeling."

JACK: Yes.

JILL: Wow. Well, freed up…or…

JACK: For what?

JILL: Unpatterned, maybe.

JACK: Because free to do what?

JILL: In the sense of not…

JACK: Because free…

JILL: Banging up against somebody's borders.

JACK: Because freedom's just another word for nothing left to lose.

JILL: I know.

JACK: Which is why I got off the moving stairway…

JILL: The freedom doesn't oppress me, Jack.

JACK: Look, I'll fit in around the edges.

JILL: Oh, Jack…

JACK: I'm a little confused.

JILL: Who wouldn't be?

JACK: I don't want to go back to the hotel.

JILL: I don't want somebody around the edges…

JACK: It would feel truly terrible…

JILL: It would.

JACK: At the hotel.

JILL: Oh.

JACK: I'm sincerely feeling…

JILL: What's happened to you?

JACK: You, at the airport.

> *(Pause)*

JILL: Okay, Jack, but no more…only sleeping.

JACK: Only sleeping.

> *(He turns off his light.)*

JILL: For auld lang syne.

JACK: For auld lang syne.

JILL: *(Pointing at him.)* Don't mess with me. *(She turns off her light.)* No touching. *(A pause.)* No touching. *(A pause.)* Oh, to hell with it.

> *(Silence. An alarm rings; it's morning. Lights change. New Scene. Jack dresses in the clothes he has left on the floor: dress slacks, button-down shirt, shoes and socks. Jill exits and dresses in her business suit for the hospital: matching skirt and blazer, silk blouse and pumps.)*

JACK: *(Dressing. To Jill, who is offstage, rather than to the audience.)* So I…California…very uh…image collages for, uh, big-time screenwriters…weighty paychecks but, you know, uh…uh…severe loss of anything resembling meaning and…dates, I would date…

JILL: *(From offstage.)* No???!!

JACK: …that didn't…I don't know…go too well because…absence of you…like a hole in my chest…this size…and nothing I could stuff in there, things, people, sex, drugs, travel, Stephen King books, cappuccino…nothing filled it up…*(Jill enters, putting up her hair.)*…massage therapy…nothing…that's the God's truth, cross my heart…and I don't…there is, still is such a thing as love…call me stupid…no co-dependency, not paternal-uh-Jill-ism… not the self-help library…c'mon, there has to be…the fit…the fit…don't you think there has to be the fit? Heloise and Abelard, you know. Love which is…love between, you know, man and woman…or, of course, other combinations, but anyway…

(They are dressed. A dresser brings on Jack's suit coat. By now, the dressers have cleared away the bed and side tables.)

JILL: I have to go, Jack...wait, your collar...

JACK: Could we...

JILL: I don't think so.

JACK: Just...

JILL: Cat hair, oh God, look...

JACK: Brunch.

JILL: I'm at the hospital till...

JACK: Lunch.

JILL: Jack, don't get me confused...

JACK: Goddamn you...

JILL: Hey...

JACK: This isn't...this won't come again, don't you understand that?

(A dresser hands Jill a lint brush, which she uses on Jack's coat.)

JILL: Jack, the Industrial Revolution is over. It doesn't take two people to live a life. We don't till the soil. One person is plenty...that's what Lean Cuisine is for. You are sweet and...fulsome...I don't want to step on those feelings...your idea is beautiful...really...*(Jill returns lint brush to dresser.)*...in fifty years maybe, on some new basis, umm, romantic love, God bless it, will make a comeback. Try me again in the nursing home. *(Kisses him lightly.)* I have to go.

JACK: Lunch.

JILL: Lunch I run, you know, running.

JACK: Okay.

JILL: Yi, yi, yi. Five miles.

JACK: Okay.

JILL: You don't have any...

JACK: I'll get some.

JILL: Couldn't we just be...

JACK: I can run five miles.

JILL: You can?

JACK: Yeah.

JILL: *(A moment.)* You know what?

JACK: What?

JILL: Never mind.

JACK: Okay.

JILL: This is confusing, Jack.

JACK: What "this?"

JILL: You…here…so pleasurably, densely…familiar. It is…it is comfortable. You are a complex damn comfort, Jack. Boy. I am still often scared, Jack, and you are masterfully…familiar.

JACK: Somebody asked once what I saw in you…and I said you never, never told me anything I already know, which quality excels agreement.

JILL: You are…a serious person. No kidding. And they are…in short supply.

JACK: And?

JILL: Is that a dare, Jack?

JACK: What?

(She studies him.)

JILL: I'm wavering. Yes, I am.

JACK: Great.

JILL: I'm a sucker for a dare, Jack. *(A moment.)* Okay, let's go to the airport.

JACK: Jill?

JILL: Get a flight. Prague. Sao Paulo. Go out the door, go down the steps and do that. We could do it. Get a cab. Right now. Right now. *(A moment.)* But we would have to do it in the next fifteen seconds, because…*(A moment.)* We could.

JACK: *(A slight nervous laugh.)* Jill, you…I have a camera crew over on…hey, really, come on…you won't do lunch, but you'll do Prague? We need time now…absolutely…yes…I'm clear in March…I can clear March…are you…

JILL: Never mind, just…just kidding, I…what time is it?

JACK: Hey, it's just I have a crew…

JILL: *(Dresser enters and hands Jill her watch.)* Oh, boy. Hey, I'm a hospital administrator, Jack. Did I tell you that? No more hands-on. I live by the clock. I have five meetings, two committees. Anyway, listen, this was good, I never…I told a date last week that if I had to choose between great sex and a good executive secretary, I would…

JACK: I can be a secretary…

JILL: *(Laughing.)* Jack…

JACK: Plus…

JILL: Okay.

JACK: I now cook like an angel, I even took a pastry class…I can do tarts. I know wines, I can fold origami napkins, I can do flower arrangements.

JILL: You win. You win. Lunch.

JACK: Lunch. Good. What about March?

JILL: Lunch.

JACK: Okay. *(She starts to go.)* Maybe we could make that three miles.

(Lights change. The dressers now begin to dress both people into running gear; Jill onstage, Jack off. Dresser enters with a chair and her clothes. Jill removes shoes, skirt and coat and pulls on jogging sweatpants. She then removes blouse and puts on sleeveless T-shirt. Then she sits and puts on shoes and socks—all during monologue.)

JILL: What is this battlefield upon which we are engaged? Who has done what to whom? You know as I get the power, men…the money and the power men used to…well that they essentially had as their own province…now I don't like admitting this…I feel less. Yeah, diminished…bound in… where I existed in a universe of feelings, intuitions…now, they're receding. They don't get the same workout in money and power land…oh-oh…I wake up halfway through a day in the…well, great American marketplace and I say, "Hey, Jill," literally, "I know what you're doing, but what the hell are you feeling?" Because, and this scares the shit out of me, if my feelings are not functional, if they atrophy in the marketplace, then just who and what is being sold here? *(She stands and ties sweat jacket around her waist. A dresser enters and strikes clothing and chair.)* I want…

(Lights change. New Scene. Jack enters and begins running with her. For stage purposes, they run in place throughout most of the scene. He is wearing a bright orange jogging outfit and very white sneakers and socks that he bought that morning.)

JILL: *(Referring to his outfit.)* You are very orange.
JACK: Yeah. They had sold all the blue and dark green ones.
JILL: Well, the hunters won't get you.
JACK: Whew. Wow. You do this every day?
JILL: Every day. Jack?
JACK: Yeah, what?
JILL: Breathe.
JACK: Right.
JILL: Find a rhythm.
JACK: What rhythm?
JILL: Your rhythm.
JACK: A perspective.
JILL: Yes.
JACK: Other men?
JILL: Yes.

JACK: Are they like me?

JILL: No, they have giant dicks and wild untamed emotions.

JACK: I thought so.

JILL: And blue running suits.

JACK: Ah. Are they such, these men, that you could love them?

JILL: No.

JACK: Why?

JILL: Because I don't want to.

JACK: Stop.

JILL: Jack…

JACK: Stop.

JILL: Damnit.

> *(They do.)*

JACK: Tell me what you want.

JILL: What I want? Look out! *(They jump to one side.)* We are standing…Look out! *(They jump the other way.)* Jack…

JACK: You want?

JILL: I want a control in my life that is still full of feeling. I want to be…I don't know…powerful and amazed. This is ridiculous…

JACK: Are you okay?

JILL: Run.

> *(They run in place.)*

JACK: But you're sad.

JILL: No.

JACK: But you are.

JILL: Will you shut up?

JACK: I am.

JILL: Well, you're a melancholy baby, Jack.

JACK: Are you?

JILL: *(She points.)* See the guy with the sores, urinating on the street? *(They run.)* In the morning paper was a picture of a six-month-old baby who got hit with shrapnel and had her leg amputated. And here we are, I don't know, getting aerobic on a lunch date. *(They stop running.)* Okay, you want the straight dope, Jack? I can't possibly be sad because I am too goddamn privileged. Now, let's run.

> *(They do, taking one full lap around the stage.)*

JACK: The problem isn't…

JILL: You can't fix it, Jack.

JACK: The problem is…

JILL: Breathe.

JACK: Satisfaction.

JILL: Pick it up.

JACK: And how we, whew, how we get it?

JILL: We don't. I can't…unbelievable…*(They stop running.)* I can't believe you are doing this to my run.

JACK: Seriously.

JILL: Okay, seriously. We won't get satisfaction because the culture isn't based on satisfaction. They only fabricate the idea of satisfaction so we'll keep buying things. The bad news, Jack, is there is no satisfaction.

JACK: Except this.

JILL: What?

JACK: This.

JILL: Come on, Jack…

JACK: Being sad in your company. That is elegantly satisfying. And I am really very sad.

JILL: *(She looks at him.)* Oh, boy. *(She wipes his brow with her hand.)* You're an okay guy, Jack. You want a Kleenex?

JACK: Where would you keep a Kleenex?

JILL: Viola. *(She hands him one.)*

JACK: Thanks. *(Wipes eyes.)* What are you doing tonight?

JILL: You give no quarter.

JACK: I find I can't.

JILL: I am attending, God help me, a charity ball.

JACK: Should I wear a tux?

JILL: I have a date.

JACK: Ah.

> *(A long pause. They look at each other.)*

JILL: But I will call and tell him I have Legionnaire's Disease.

JACK: Thank you…very, very much.

JILL: But then, oh avid one, I go on with my life.

JACK: Sure.

JILL: Hotel Gaulitier.

> *(She jogs to the other side of the stage.)*

JACK: Right.

JILL: Nine o'clock. *(He nods and starts off.)* Jack?

JACK: What?

JILL: You don't dance.

JACK: I dance like the wind. My feet are like thistledown.

JILL: Really.

JACK: Lessons every Wednesday from Fred Astaire.

(He exits. She runs two more laps. Lights change. A dresser enters with a chair. Jill sits and removes sneakers and socks. Two dressers enter with evening gown, shawl, slip, and heels.)

JILL: *(As she's changing.)* It should…I think so…be mandated…three years alone… this is as an adult…no companion, no significant other…both sexes. And uh, after that, barring children…two hours a day. A room, a chair and… you. See without that, and who gets it, you? Me? Him? No. You never, absolutely never…cannot process this life. Cannot take it in. What are you making of it, you know, what? You can…can do this living and… incredibly…never be introduced to…to yourself, actually…you can live eighty years…whatever…and your consciousness, your sense of the event… well, there's damn little difference, none really, between you and a lab rat. *(Jill has finished change, and dressers strike chair and jogging clothes.)* The unexamined life, followed by cancer and the life-support system. Of course, not you, not me, I speak, naturally, of the others.

(The dance band plays. Lights change. New Scene. Jack, in a truly tacky tux moves directly into Jill's arms, and they dance.)

JACK: Only one they had.

JILL: Elvis, you came.

JACK: I did.

JILL: He cooks, he dances…

JACK: He plumbs, as in plumbing.

JILL: No.

JACK: Yeah, adult education.

JILL: What possessed you, Jack?

JACK: I wanted to be able to fix something. To fix the toilet, this is power.

JILL: Dead on.

JACK: Napoleon could feel no more.

JILL: Jack?

JACK: Yes.

JILL: Who is all this for?

JACK: Ah, a trick question.

JILL: Well…

JACK: You thought I'd say, "for you."

JILL: I did.

JACK: And then you'd say…

JILL: Wrong answer…

JACK AND JILL: It should have been for yourself.

JILL: A little obvious, but…

JACK: Relevant. Listen…

JILL: Yes?

JACK: Where can we meet?

JILL: You mean…

JACK: In this life?

JILL: Ah.

JACK:…on level ground.

JILL: Let's just be here, okay?

JACK: And?

JILL: Let's just be here, Jack.

(The music ends.)

JACK: Dumb orchestra.

JILL: It is not desirable they should overshadow the gowns.

JACK: I will go where you go. I will be your friend, your…more importantly… plumber.

JILL: You turned down Prague, Jack.

JACK: That was a fantasy.

JILL: Because you say so?

JACK: We have jobs, we have responsibilities, we have mortgages that are no fantasy. We couldn't do that. We could do this.

(New music begins. Mirror ball goes on.)

JILL: What "this?"

JACK: This!

(They dance again.)

JILL: *(Pause.)* You know what I don't want to be?

JACK: Pursued.

JILL: You don't really want to catch me, Jack.

JACK: What the hell are you…

JILL: You don't want me, you want…

JACK: How can I…

JILL: An "object of desire."

JACK:…make clear to you…

JILL: Hey, Jack. I think you have changed in some ways. I think you have worked hard at it. But I don't know that we change essentially, Jack. You know, after a certain age. You always touch me because you are…of good will. You are a good person in a bad tux, Jack. I should love you, there's no doubt about that. I should. You deserve that. But something in me is in revolt. Something warns me about you. It whispers to me, you are making me up.

JACK: I love you.

JILL: What don't you like?

JACK: Excuse me.

JILL: About me, Jack?

JACK: We're dancing.

JILL: You never tell me.

JACK: I don't?

JILL: Never.

JACK: Ummm…

JILL: Let's assume I have a downside.

JACK: *(Laughing.)* Not now.

JILL: *(Dead serious.)* It's hard to love somebody who's afraid of you, Jack.

JACK: Okay.

JILL: Good.

JACK: Judged for accuracy?

JILL: Judged for insight.
      (They stop dancing.)

JACK: You're a bully.

JILL: A hit.

JACK: You isolate yourself to maintain control and then make other people responsible for your isolation.

JILL: A palpable hit.
      (Music and mirror ball end.)

JACK: You're a snob. You mask a lot of self-loathing. You need to win, and you'll raise the stakes until you do. You're judgmental, you're manipulative, you sweat the small stuff, you tease with an edge, you hate holidays, you have no empathy for insecurity, and you make no leap of faith.

JILL: But am I pretty?

JACK: You're a real babe. *(A moment.)* Why did you make me say all that stuff?

JILL: Because you don't.

JACK: But how was my analysis?

JILL: Rudimentary…but painful. And with an interesting hint of malice.

JACK: And me?

(New music begins.)

JILL: My criticism of you? You're a nice man, Jack. It's how you control everybody…usually.

(A pause.)

JACK: One more dance.

JILL: One more.

JACK: But you lead.

JILL: I can do that.

(They whirl away. Lights change. New Scene. They turn to face each other; they are at her place, in the middle of a conversation.)

JACK: No, really…

JILL: Jack, come on…

JACK: Really, seriously.

JILL: No…

JACK: Jack and Jill went up the hill to fetch a pail of water; Jack fell down and…
   (Dresser enters with two beers and hands them to Jill.)

JILL: How did I know we would get to this?

JACK: "Went up the hill?" The search, the need for intimacy…fetch water… they sought meaning together…

JILL: I have to get up early.

JACK: Listen, listen. He didn't have the tools, he fell down…

JILL: So did she, Jack…

JACK: Yes, yes. Their destinies are entwined.

JILL: Where is it written?

JACK: It's implied. They both climbed…

JILL: They both fell…

JACK: Then what happened?

JILL: No second verse, Jack. Kiss me and go home.
   (He pulls her into a serious kiss. She responds. She pulls back.)

JACK: I think because…

JILL: I didn't…I mean…to let you come home with me…last night, fine…two nights…

JACK: …does not live by bread alone.

JILL: Man. Man doesn't. A woman with any sense…

JACK: Why do the first climb over? Why do that?

JILL: *(She sits in chair and removes her heels and shawl.)* What time is it, Jack?

JACK: Three A.M.

JILL: It is always three A.M. between us. Why is that? What does that say to you?

JACK: It says it's too late to do over. We've carved each other like glaciers, for God's sake. *(Jill takes Jack's beer from him and hands it to dresser.)* What the hell is different about you? Something's gone. Something's...I don't know, I'm scared for you...*(She moves to him and removes his jacket.)* What?

JILL: I'm taking off your jacket.

JACK: I feel it's...Jesus, Jill, it was so...

JILL: Painful.

JACK: Really painful...but...we could, you know, skip a grade...move on...not take the same...

JILL: *(She points at his waist.)* Pray you, undo this button.

JACK: *(He does and unzips his fly.)*...the same fall, you know, because history...*(She begins removing his pants.)* God, let's believe...

JILL: Sit down.

(He does.)

JACK: History, between people...*(She kneels and removes his shoes.)* Goddamnit, it has to be worth something...it has to be the basis...some way to...what are you doing?

JILL: *(She pulls his pants off, pulling them by the cuffs.)* I'm paying you a compliment.

JACK: Because one way or another...you know this...you'll hook up...make connection...so why not...why pick some...some guy when...why not...

JILL: *(Her dress.)* Unzip this.

JACK: *(He does.)*...because the pain was for something...give the pain some respect, it was for something.

JILL: *(She is in a slip. He is in a tux shirt, vest, tie, underwear, and socks.)* Be quiet. *(She kisses him. They get involved.)* Jack. *(He's busy with her neck.)* Jack.

JACK: Sorry.

JILL: We're going to...obviously...I want you here tonight...and I...you know I do, appreciate the...the history.

JACK: Missing the point...

JILL: I am ever so glad you came, Jack. Truly. Deeply. Truly. I want you to eat me alive. And tomorrow...

JACK: Right...

JILL: I have to be alone and do stuff.

JACK: In the morning?

JILL: Forever. Now if that's understood...

JACK: It's not understood...

JILL: Well, it has to be. Because that's the way it is. New ways with new people. I want…I'm sorry, I want, for now, no history. *(He looks at her.)* I'm just all out of romance, Jack. Not in a bad way. I'm good. I think you're, you're good. See, we can go on.

JACK: What a waste.

JILL: We were never a waste, God, Jack…whatever you…you can't have, you want to wipe off the map. Whoa. No. Listen, we'll…we'll talk, Jack, but… but all that is tomorrow. Some other universe, but…in this moment… surely I don't have to explain this moment to you?

JACK: Fuck you.

(He picks up his clothes and exits. Lights change.)

JILL: …he said, and he left. Well, you know, stuff…stuff has to end some way. I mean the end wasn't what it was. What it was, was… *(She shakes her head, at a loss.)*…'Bye, Jack.

(A moment. A dresser enters and helps Jill into a silk robe. Dresser strikes chair and exits. Another dresser enters and strikes ballgown, her beer, and her heels.)

JILL: My dog died. I was little, seven, I don't know, six…my dog died and I, well, I was hysterical, hysterical for days because I couldn't feel sad, wasn't devastated…cried, wept, rocked myself in my room because I couldn't cry for my dog. I grieved I couldn't grieve. I mourned I couldn't mourn…it was that way with Jack. I missed Jack, but…hey, I was a mess for two weeks because I wasn't a mess…and then…then I realized…the decks are clear…really, really clear. I could…I was mine. At the wheel of my own ship…or something. Time passes, my time passes, and I'm…you know… medically empowered…have some authority…no one dictates…very few at this level, gender issues…well, some, but…I have stocks, I have bonds, my car turns heads, I have a vacation…cabin. You know, doctor stuff. I feel good. I feel calm. Have some control. So the deal now is…the deal…in most situations…well I could, at the very least, negotiate. Very least. The question being…with whom?

(Lights change. New Scene. A dresser hands Jill a cell phone. A phone rings. Jack enters on opposite side of stage, carrying a phone. He picks it up. He's wearing a robe over clothes for the next scene: dark khakis, button-down shirt, pullover sweater, and socks.)

JILL: Hi.

JACK: Hello. *(A pause.)* Jack Stojadinovac.

JILL: Happy birthday.

JACK: Who is this? Hello? Who is this?

JILL: I'm not bad, how are you?

JACK: Jill? Is this Jill?

JILL: Am I interrupting?

JACK: No…no.

(A pause.)

JILL: Well, this seems like a bad idea.

(A pause.)

JACK: Listen…ummm…where are you? Are you okay?

JILL: I'm well, Jack.

JACK: Great. Really. Really great.

JILL: Happy birthday, Jack.

JACK: Thanks. It's, uh, it's tomorrow actually.

JILL: It is tomorrow.

JACK: God, what time is it?

JILL: Three A.M. *(A pause.)* Hey, Jack, remember you asked me what was gone? I didn't…couldn't say, but…I'm not angry anymore, Jack. Not you, it's not specific, I…I must have left the window open, the door, and it just let go. I didn't know it. It was always just…right there…below…underneath every other feeling…but I don't have it anymore, isn't that weird, I just sloughed it off or…just wore it out…and it had always been there, but…I just realized and I didn't have…nobody to celebrate with…no one who knew what it was…so I…happy birthday, Jack. *(He can't answer.)* Jack? *(He doesn't answer.)* Talk to me. *(A moment.)* Jack, damnit.

(No answer. He clicks off. Lights change. Jill exits and changes offstage. A moment. He hands off the phone to a dresser. Then he removes his robe and hands same to dresser.)

JACK: Okay. That's it. Done. I can…handle that. I can tear out that root system because if you can't…take mortality, you know, for example…if you can't handle loss…the idea…the ideal is self-reliance, and you better…I better…any instant could leave you alone…a cancer cell…a brake lining…the wrong time in the wrong place, and in a finger snap, man…so protect some part of yourself…don't give yourself away…*(A dresser enters with Jack's loafers. He steps into them.)*…build up some callus on your heart, some deep remove, because…we know this…you and I…because any dependence is an affront to chaos…and when…when riled, that chaos will eat your lunch. The temptation to leave someone who really…powerfully…profoundly wants your company is just too delicious…and a person who wants to know herself…themselves…well, my conclusion is she couldn't resist it. *(A dresser enters and helps him on with raincoat and hands him an umbrella.)* It was a cosmic dare. Well, I have had that need arterioscopically removed. I'm the ice man. There is some part of me you couldn't touch with all your need and skill. No way. *(He opens umbrella.)* I'm there.

(Lights change. Thunder and lightning. New Scene. Jill enters, dressed in dress, lace-up boots, long raincoat, and carrying open umbrella. Jack and Jill walk by each other.)

JILL: Jack?

JACK: What? Oh.

JILL: My God…

JACK: Geez.

JILL: I'm just…I can't believe this.

JACK: In town?

JILL: In town.

JACK: Wow.

JILL: So…um…speechless.

JACK: Fine.

JILL: Fine?

JACK: What? You didn't ask how I was?

JILL: Did I?

JACK: Sorry I'm…

JILL: Listen…

JACK: Gosh, I have to…

JILL: Now?

JACK: Yeah…one o'clock.

JILL: *(Checking watch.)* Yeah.

JACK: Sorry…

JILL: No, I just…

JACK: On business?

JILL: My sister…

JACK: She's…?

JILL: Fine…she just…complicated…she's fine.

JACK: Right…look…it's, uh…how's, uh…?

JILL: Sure. You know…nice to…

JACK: Absolutely…you look…

JILL: Don't ask.

JACK: Ummm.

JILL: Damn.

JACK: Well…oh, this was funny…

JILL: Yeah?

JACK: Last, uh, Wednesday…no, Thursday…last week I was…the movies, um-mm…on this, uh, date…no big deal, but we, uh, my date, we sit down… terrible film with, uh, what's her name? The blond…married to the writer.

JILL: Oh, the writer.

(During the next speech, they notice the rain has stopped and close their umbrellas.)

JACK: Never mind…and she…we sit down and…get this…umm, incredible… next to her, Laura, the date, where we sat…crowded completely…was, uh, her ex-husband…unbelievable…

JILL: …ex-husband…

JACK: And he is with this, umm, woman she, Laura, roomed with in, uh, college, really…I mean the odds…

JILL: Right.

JACK: So everybody talks, you know…the guy's Wilson…little confusing but later, post-film, the four of us, Laura, Wilson, the ex-husband, Laura and Wilson, yattata, yattata, yattata…they leave together…can you…you know, great…together and I'm there, you know, the other one, hair out to here…the college friend…so, hey, what could I do…I offer, you know… anyway we go outside, maybe a drink later…on the street, Laura and Wilson, locked in combat, screaming and slapping…so it ends up… wait, before that…Laura, earlier…oh, oh, I met this guy…the one…where am I, I am completely…

JILL: Coincidence. Big one.

JACK: Exactly. Unbelievable.

(Pause.)

JILL: So is this sad or what?

JACK: *(Looks at his watch.)* Actually…

JILL: Ten of…

JACK: Downtown. 20th.

JILL: 20th.

JACK: Gotta go. *(Jack starts to go, then returns.)* Oh, Jessica Lange.

JILL: Right.

(He exits. Lights change. Jill stands. Finally, she takes in the audience and speaks to them.)

JILL: I have a friend with a three-year-old, and I had borrowed…five-year-old, too…anyway, I brought it back about eight at night, and she opened the door and involuntarily, I kind of blanched, and she said, "I look like *Night of the Living Dead,* right?" And I said, "God, you look exhausted." And she said, "The five-year-old has chicken pox, the three-year-old is in my closet peeing on my shoes, plus I haven't cleaned up the legos or the Play-Doh or the crayons and the Barbie parts, not to mention, God help me, the orange marker all over the sofa." So I asked, "What's the good part?" And she said, "How can you ask me that?" *(A pause. A dresser enters, and Jill removes raincoat and hands coat and umbrella to dresser, who exits.)* When I come home, my house is neat. The lights automatically turn on. I eat what I want. I stay up late. I see who I please. I'm in charge of my environment. My book is book-marked. My TV guide is underlined. My bed is hard but with slight surface give. My pre-cooked meals are ready. I'm not too tired. My mind is clear. I have no desire to go out. I think I'm in deep shit.

(Lights change. New Scene. Two dressers enter and set chairs. Same library as ACT I, Scene 1. Jack enters and sits, reading Mother Goose.)

JILL: Hi. *(He looks at her. He is amazed.)* Listen, I've been…been over in the stacks watching you…you care for a, uh…no place is safe, huh? That, by the way, is a poet I admire…so…look…I am…I'm Jill, medical dominatrix, who would…would like to meet you, Jack Stojadinovac, because… well…some years ago I lost…mislaid…mislaid is better…some serious relating…umm… serious relating, and I find now…in my heart…I would like to meet you, severe and conflicted beauty…for…at a time you found conducive, ummm, such as now or…well, shortly after now. *(Pause.)* Or if you…I have the feeling…well, what the hell, never hurts to roll the dice. Jill, by the way. *(Pause.)* Your turn.

JACK: Fuck.

JILL: Yeah, who knows, maybe after coffee…but, you know, right here in the reading room…?

JACK: To what, Jill, do I owe this honor?

JILL: I miss you.

JACK: You miss me?

JILL: I miss you, Jack.

JACK: *(Pounding his forehead.)* How…is…this…possible?

JILL: First I was alone. Then you came, and I wasn't. Then I needed to know I could be. Now I can, and I don't need to. And to a person who doesn't need to be alone, you were the first person who came to mind. So, anyway, I thought I'd check in.

JACK: I just…can't you see what it feels like to…I just got you…out…off…but to do that…to do that…as if, really, I plunged my hand into my chest, tore out my heart, ripped you off it, put it back in, closed it up…came in out of the goddamn rain…now I turn around…what in hell are you doing here!

JILL: I needed…

JACK: You needed!? Well, it's a little late for what you needed, wouldn't you say? People whose needs don't get met over and over again are bloody likely not to meet the needs of the people they needed when those people show up with their needs! I practically begged you, in case you don't remember, saying I would, I don't know, fit in around the edges, turn into a plumber and pastry chef, turn myself inside out, only to be told to give you a try in the nursing home! *(Jack rises, rounding on someone in the library.)* Don't tell me to be quiet so you can read *Cosmopolitan!* *(Back to Jill.)* I may not have known how to love you but I loved you unendurably, whether or not love exists, and if you had invested in what I felt, we could have shaped it any way that would have worked for both of us, but you were in such a narcissistic fit of self-realization you wouldn't have known if a perfect union walked up and bit you in the ass.

JILL: Thank you.

JACK: Thank me?

JILL: For saying what you feel, Jack.

JACK: Forget it…

JILL: Don't cut me off!

JACK: What I'm feeling? I am feeling that there is the possible and the impossible, and this is impossible!

JILL: *(Topping him.)* Just because it isn't possible doesn't mean it isn't necessary! *(Aware of the other people in the library.)* Sorry.

JACK: Really sorry.

JILL: Sorry. *(They focus back on each other.)* Oh, Jack. I alone have…escaped…to bring you…stuff. Being fully and capable alone, Jack, maybe in the end that is…that is the one thing you have to fix.

JACK: Why me?

JILL: You know why.

JACK: I swear to God I don't.

JILL: Because I don't know if there is anything called love, Jack, but there is "being known," which I've done without and done without, and I see now the time is getting short, and I plain old can't afford to do without, and I see now, given the lovers I'm meeting and the lovers I knew, that you were the one who wanted to know me…really, really wanted to know.

JACK: I wanted to know you.

JILL: Well, I want to be known.

JACK: I think the time came and went, Jill.

JILL: Are you sure?

JACK: How the hell would I be sure?

JILL: Well, because some of us are not what we used to be, we could take what we are feeling now and put it in a room, and we could talk.

JACK: *(Looking down. To himself.)* Bloody hell. *(To Jill.)* No.

JILL: Jack…

JACK: No…huh-uh…no. Listen, I am really…we just shouldn't, you know what I mean?

JILL: I don't. No.

JACK: I need…somebody…somebody softer.

JILL: There's nobody softer than me, Jack. Not when you come right down to it. I will support every good thing in you. I will kill anybody who messes with you. We'll have a kid. We will work. I will take no shit. I will be your mate. How about it? *(A pause.)* Jack?

JACK: No.

JILL: Okay. *(A pause.)* Really no?

JACK: Yes.

JILL: Oh, Jack…

JACK: I can't.

JILL: *(A pause.)* Okay. I took the Red Eye. I hate the Red Eye. Could I possibly have a hug?

JACK: *(Looking directly at her.)* No.

JILL: Because I'm a bitch? Because this is payback? Because timing is everything? I do have bad timing. I do.

JACK: You were wrong about change.

JILL: What did I say?

JACK: It doesn't matter.

JILL: Tell me. *(He doesn't answer.)* Anything? *(He doesn't answer.)* So, anyway… *(They stand in silence. Finally, she turns and starts to go.)*

JACK: Maybe.

    (She turns.)

JILL: *(Wary.)* Did you say "maybe"?

JACK: *(A pause.)* Maybe.

JILL: As opposed to "no"? *(He doesn't answer.)* Okay then. *(Accepting it doesn't have to be clear.)* Okay, Jack.

    (They stand looking at each other, not moving.)

END OF PLAY

Mr. Bundy

ORIGINAL PRODUCTION

Mr. Bundy premiered at the Humana Festival of New American Plays in March 1998. It was directed by Jon Jory with the following cast:

Cassidy Ferreby. . . . . Margaret Streeter
Robert Ferreby . . . . Mark Schulte
Catherine Ferreby . . . . Stephanie Zimbalist
Jimmy Ray Bosun . . . . Norman Maxwell
Mr. Bundy. . . . . William Cain
Tianna Bosun . . . . Peggity Price
Mrs. McGuigan . . . . Adale O'Brien

and with the following production staff:

Scenic Designer . . . . Paul Owen
Costume Designer. . . . . Nanzi Adzima
Lighting Designer . . . . Amy Appleyard
Sound Designer . . . . Martin R. Desjardins
Properties Designer . . . . Ron Riall
Fight Director. . . . . Steve Rankin
Production Stage Manager. . . . . Debra Acquavella
Assistant Stage Manager . . . . Heather Fields
Dramaturgs . . . Michael Bigelow Dixon, Val Smith, & Megan Shultz
Casting . . . . Laura Richin Casting

CHARACTERS

CATHERINE FERREBY: A woman of thirty-six. Well educated. A child psychologist.

ROBERT FERREBY: Her husband. Age forty. Works in an advertising agency. Volunteers weekends for AA.

CASSIDY FERREBY: Their daughter. Eight or nine years old.

MR. BUNDY: Their next-door neighbor. A man in his mid-to-late 60s. A retired teacher.

JIMMY RAY BOSUN: A truck driver in his mid forties.

TIANNA BOSUN: His wife. A woman in her early forties. A southerner.

MRS. McGUIGAN: A neighbor. Sixty years old. She is raising her grandson whose parents passed away.

TIME and PLACE

Various locations in the middle of the country. The time is the present.

AUTHOR'S NOTE

The play is performed without an intermission.

MR. BUNDY

The play takes place on an empty stage surrounded, if possible, by a cyclorama. Into this space emblematic pieces of furniture are brought for each location. There are no walls and no complete rooms, though there might be a use for a free-standing rolling door. There is no attempt to hide the moving on and moving off of furniture during the monologues that bridge the scenes. Props are mimed except for a select few, central to the narrative. We begin with a chair, a television set, and a bottle of cream soda beside the chair. The rolling door defines the front door. Catherine, a woman in her mid-to-late thirties, is discovered standing, in a freeze, holding the handle of her luggage-cart suitcase. Robert, her husband, a little older, stands several feet away looking at her. Cassidy, eight years old, is jumping rope in front of her parents' tableau.

CASSIDY: Don't listen to him sing;
　　　　don't heed his call.
　　　　It's the oogey-boogey monster
　　　　over the wall.
　　　　Don't throw him pennies,
　　　　or feed him sweets,
　　　　'cause you're just what
　　　　the oogey-boogey eats.
　　　　Don't open the cupboard
　　　　if you need a cup,
　　　　'cause the oogey-boogey's in there,
　　　　and he'll eat you up!

(Cassie emphasizes the last line with a double or crossover jump. Then she runs off as the light emphasizes her parents and they break out of their tableau.)

ROBERT: *(After a pause.)* Oh boy.
CATHERINE: Hi.
ROBERT: Hello, Catherine. *(A pause.)* Can I hug you?
CATHERINE: Not yet, okay?
ROBERT: *(Nods.)* I am really, really glad. I am…really glad.
CATHERINE: Cassie's great. Wait'll you see her haircut. *(He smiles and nods. A*

pause. He walks over and embraces her. She stands with her hands at her sides. Finally she embraces him. They hold each other. They let go. She reaches up and takes him by the ears.) Robert, you are such a jerk.

ROBERT: I know.

CATHERINE: *(Punches him in the chest.)* Don't be a jerk anymore.

ROBERT: I won't.

CATHERINE: *(Warningly.)* I don't forgive you. *(He nods.)* But I brought you some Switzers licorice. *(He takes it ruefully.)* And your new glasses are okay. *(Awkwardness sets in.)* I want to, uh…want to get this stuff put away before, uh, I pick up Cassidy at school.

(She moves past him with the suitcase. He stands for a moment and then speaks to us. She exits.)

ROBERT: What's forgivable and what's not and what's the difference? I was a jerk. "The quality of mercy is…" something, something. I don't even know if you can earn it? Maybe it just happens…like spontaneous combustion.

(He goes and sits down. The lights change. He is watching television. There is a bottle of cream soda by his chair. A doorbell rings.)

ROBERT: *(Surprised.)* Who is it?

JIMMY RAY: *(Offstage.)* Mr. Ferreby?

ROBERT: Who is it, please?

JIMMY RAY: You don't know me, Mr. Ferreby. I'm Jimmy Ray Bosun.

ROBERT: What is it you want?

JIMMY RAY: Got some info for you.

ROBERT: Who are you?

JIMMY RAY: It's about your little girl.

ROBERT: My little girl?

JIMMY RAY: Yeah.

ROBERT: Look, it's after nine at night. I'm in the book. Call me in the morning.

JIMMY RAY: I drive truck, buddy. I'll be three states away in the morning.

ROBERT: *(A pause. He opens the door.)* All right, state your business.

JIMMY RAY: *(Indicating it would be best if he came in.)* You got a convicted child molester livin' next door, pal. *(A moment.)* You want the info?

ROBERT: *(A moment.)* All right, come in.

JIMMY RAY: Nice place. I used to renovate.

ROBERT: So what's the deal, Mr....

JIMMY RAY: Bosun. You got a beer or somethin'? I been hitting it pretty hard.

ROBERT: No, I don't have a...

JIMMY RAY: What's that by your chair?

ROBERT: Cream soda. What is it you have to tell me?

JIMMY RAY: You got an abuser next door.

ROBERT: How do you know that?

JIMMY RAY: Well, I make it my business to know it. Lemme give you a card. *(Gets out wallet, hands him a card.)* You'll be glad I came down here, tell you that.

ROBERT: *(Looks at card.)* I thought you drove truck?

JIMMY RAY: Drive truck for my family, Mr. Ferreby. I do this for your family.

ROBERT: "Watch Dog."

JIMMY RAY: Yeah. Guys travelin' the country in the line of their work. Loose knit.

ROBERT: *(Indicating the card.)* The cross.

JIMMY RAY: Yeah. Christian guys.

ROBERT: And?

JIMMY RAY: We're gonna like stand here? *(Robert nods.)* Okay, whatever, so...sex abuser notification...so you should know these guys are on your block, right? Thing is, it varies real wide how effective that is. Some states, California, they get the work out real good, some places, they're real remiss. Buncha states actually draggin' their feet on it, if you can believe that. Okay, sometimes these scumbags move around a lot, hard to keep track on 'em. *(Points at the card Robert holds.)* "Watch Dog," we uh...we try to help out...notification, that falls down a lot.

ROBERT: You track sex abusers?

JIMMY RAY: Track 'em? Yeah, we kind of track 'em. You might say that.

ROBERT: And you're sure, absolutely, there's such a person in this neighborhood?

JIMMY RAY: Yeah, we got verification. We don't go off half-cocked or nothin' like that. He's out there waterin' his lawn, buddy, big as life you want to take a look. *(A moment.)* I saw a bike out front, how old is she?

ROBERT: Eight.

JIMMY RAY: Got three boys. Had a girl too.

ROBERT: What is he accused of?

JIMMY RAY: No sir, he's not accused, been convicted and served time.

ROBERT: For?

JIMMY RAY: Not likin' me too much, huh buddy?

ROBERT: I never said that.

JIMMY RAY: Ol' redneck rig guy. Feel a little out of place in the 'burbs. Folks, they usually figure out I'm here to help. Doesn't end up I'm standing out in the hall beggin' for a beer.

ROBERT: What, exactly, was he convicted of?

JIMMY RAY: Buddy, I think what you'll want to be doin' is get your neighbors in on this. They'd be real pleased you let them know. Best way's you put together a little neighborhood meeting, you know what I mean? We'll get this citizen moved along you catch my drift.

ROBERT: And tell them what for God's sake?

JIMMY RAY: It would be a real favor to me, buddy, if we didn't take the Lord's name in vain while we were talkin' this over.

ROBERT: Listen, I would like you to step back out on the porch, Mr. Bosman.

JIMMY RAY: Bosun.

ROBERT: Mr. Bosun. I'm going to give you my business card here… *(He gets it out.)* And if you have…hard documentation of your charges I would be extremely glad to see it. At which point I would make my own decisions about how to proceed. Thank you very much for your trouble.

JIMMY RAY: Wouldn't want to move too fast, right? Abrogate the scumbag's civil rights, somethin' like that? He was a high school teacher down at St. Alphonsus, Illinois, and what he would do is bring kids home, give 'em ice cream, videos, get 'em to play dress-up, Mr. Ferreby. Dress those boys up in girls' clothes, underwear, put lipstick on 'em, you know, have a little harmless fun such as that. Little later on he got picked up parked on a country road havin' oral sex with a kid and this whole thing, his whole modus operandi, well it came right out. Second offense, matter of fact. Down in New Mexico before that up to his tricks. Did three years, got out, went to movin' around, lo and behold he's out there right next door, big as you please.

ROBERT: But his offenses were with boys?

JIMMY RAY: Dressed 'em up as girls, see? Just a little hard to know which way his pin is bent, if you're on my wavelength here.

ROBERT: And you are suggesting?

JIMMY RAY: What's your line of work, Mr. Ferreby?

ROBERT: Marketing, why?

JIMMY RAY: You an' me, we're two different breed of cats you might say.

ROBERT: Meaning?

JIMMY RAY: Meaning, I'd cut his sorry balls off an' take him around to schools in a cage. Be real educational, but we live in what they call a civilized society. Don't they call it that? So, what you can do, buddy, is get your neighbors goin', your local TV goin', your Christian churches goin', run this guy right on off, 'cause I figure you love your kid, right?

ROBERT: Loving my child isn't the only issue here.

JIMMY RAY: Uh huh. Buddy, I travel the country on behalf of the Lord's innocent children who are given to us to guide and care for, and they are the only issue, my friend, far as I'm concerned. See, your beautiful little girl will not be harmed on my watch, that's not gonna happen, and if you take a good look at me, Mr. Ferreby, you will see that's not gonna happen.

ROBERT: Look…

JIMMY RAY: Now, buddy, I'm gonna send you down the documentation you lookin' for, along with a Watch Dog action sheet tells you one, two, three how to get this problem solved. When the time is right, or you run into a hitch, you give Jimmy Ray a call and we'll bring this to a *satisfactory* conclusion for all concerned. To a satisfactory conclusion is what I'm sayin' here. *(Looks at his watch.)* Gotta get back on the pedal. Like they don't pay me for what don't get delivered, right? Not in this lifetime. Thank you for hangin' with me on this thing. My wife Tianna would say I'm a better person for you not givin' me that beer.

ROBERT: I'm a recovering alcoholic, Mr. Bosun.

JIMMY RAY: Well who the heck isn't, buddy, I don't cast the first stone. *(He slaps Robert on the shoulder.)* God's will be done.

(He exits. Robert stands for a moment then looks at the card Jimmy Ray gave him. Lights change. Jimmy Ray moves downstage. Behind him the furniture is changed to a kitchen table and four chairs, representing the Ferrebys' kitchen. Mr. Bundy, a man in his sixties dressed in gardening clothes, sits drinking coffee. Catherine, Robert's wife, nicely dressed, sits with him as does their daughter Cassidy. It is a Saturday morning in the fall. They maintain a tableau until the end of Jimmy Ray's monologue.)

JIMMY RAY: Trouble is people don't seem to know the difference between talkin' and doin' anymore. I got a little land, not enough to amount to nothin', keep a few sheep. Guy down the road had this airedale dog he don't restrain. Dog got in with my sheep, you know, chased 'em around, one of 'em died right there like a heart attack. I told him restrain that dog…he's like some retired accountant. Happens another time, bites a couple sheep. I go down there, told him I told him twice that was all I was goin' to tell him. Next time I shot the dog dead, walked down there with the dog in my arms, ring the bell, he opens up, I hand him the dog. Just said, "I believe this is your dog." Dog he's got now, he restrains that dog. My idea is, you got to know when to stop talkin'.

(Light fades on Jimmy Ray. We are now in the Ferreby kitchen with Catherine, Cassidy, and Mr. Bundy.)

CATHERINE: *(To Mr. Bundy.)* Coffee? More?

MR. BUNDY: Fine.

CATHERINE: Did you read today about that man who shot into the schoolyard in Kansas? *(He nods.)* Killed three children? Fifth graders. And then he said…he said he had sent them to heaven? As if, really, he had done them a favor? I mean I really think the world is a madhouse, and we're in a completely open area with the inmates. *(Picking up a nearly empty Pepsi can. She calls.)* Cassie!

CASSIDY: *(Off.)* What?

CATHERINE: Cassidy, how many Pepsis is that?

CASSIDY: *(Off.)* One.

CATHERINE: You didn't have one earlier?

CASSIDY: No.

CATHERINE: Then why is there an empty Pepsi in the garbage?

CASSIDY: *(Appearing. She is eight years old.)* It was in the fridge with one sip in it.

CATHERINE: You know the rules. What's that?

CASSIDY: Dad gave it to me.

CATHERINE: You've been eating that terrible white chocolate? That's why you're in a bad mood. What time is it, Mr. Bundy?

MR. BUNDY: Twelve forty.

CATHERINE: If you want something sweet, have a fig.

CASSIDY: I don't want a fig.

CATHERINE: Then forget the whole thing and read a book.

CASSIDY: I hate books.

CATHERINE: Was it this way when you grew up, Mr. Bundy?

MR. BUNDY: *(Reaches out and tickles Cassidy.)* You don't hate books.
(She jumps away.)

CASSIDY: Can I work on the train at Mr. Bundy's?

CATHERINE: *(An answer.)* Gymnastics. I don't know where Robert is, Mr. Bundy. You could go down in the basement and see if you could find the drill bits. You know where the closet is.

MR. BUNDY: I can…I can wait.

CASSIDY: Well, if Daddy isn't here, can't Mr. Bundy and I…

CATHERINE: Cassie…

CASSIDY: We're making a train with wheels that move and the smoke coming out has the house number.

CATHERINE: Well, Mr. Bundy is an incredible craftsman.

MR. BUNDY: *(Pleased.)* Not so much.

CATHERINE: Your house number signs are so charming. You should take a booth at the summer fairs.

MR. BUNDY: Not everybody likes such things.

CATHERINE: *(Seeing her nibble chocolate.)* Okay, pears and berries when we get back.

CASSIDY: Please let me stay at Mr. Bundy's. Gymnastics is horrible.

CATHERINE: It's just the new teacher…

CASSIDY: She's yucky.

MR. BUNDY: *(Patting her hand.)* Come over after dinner.

CASSIDY: Now.

CATHERINE: Whoa, honey.

CASSIDY: Please Mommy. Then you wouldn't have to drive, and you could do stuff. You always say you don't have time to do stuff. Mr. Bundy can watch me.

CATHERINE: We take advantage of Mr. Bundy. *(To Mr. Bundy.)* Honestly. Without you I couldn't have kept any of my caseload.

MR. BUNDY: No one takes advantage.

CATHERINE: *(Looking out window.)* Thank God, here's your father. How late are we? *(Looks at Mr. Bundy's watch.)* Late. *(Checks her dress.)* Now what have I stained myself with? Cassie, go up and put your gym stuff on.

CASSIDY: The teacher is hopeless. You can't understand a word she says!

CATHERINE: *(To Mr. Bundy.)* She's from Bosnia, or Croatia. An ex-Olympian, I think.

CASSIDY: She goes like blah, blah, blah.

CATHERINE: That's an accent, go get your stuff.

CASSIDY: And she's got pimples.

ROBERT: *(Offstage.)* Catherine—

CATHERINE: We're in the kitchen. *(To Cassidy.)* Go on, Cassie, upstairs, he can take you. *(Cassidy exits.)*

ROBERT: *(Entering.)* Mea culpa, mea culpa, mea double culpa. *(He sees Mr. Bundy and stops.)*

MR. BUNDY: Afternoon.

CATHERINE: Are you all right?

ROBERT: Yeah but, first of all they gave me the wrong address…Oak Avenue. Not Oak Street, a little ten-mile differential, then this guy, a complete… oh, man, ummm, never mind…*(Hands her flowers.)* I know I am way late.

CATHERINE: No, okay, Cassie's getting…where did you get these?

ROBERT: From our front yard. *(Catherine laughs. To Cassidy.)* Cassie, do you have your stuff?

CASSIDY: *(Offstage.)* No.

ROBERT: Well get it, sweetie, we're late. *(To Catherine.)* The guy was…I couldn't walk out.

CATHERINE: He counsels for AA on the weekend.

ROBERT: Completely nuts.

CATHERINE: *(To Mr. Bundy.)* Alcoholics Anonymous.

MR. BUNDY: Oh, sure.

(Robert stares at him.)

CATHERINE: *(Not understanding his look.)* Robert?

ROBERT: Listen, Catherine…*(To Cassidy.)* Upstairs now. *(Pushing her toward the door.)*

CASSIDY: Daddy…

ROBERT: Don't Daddy me, get the stuff.

CATHERINE: So?

ROBERT: Honey, they don't…don't have the people to pick up my hours, they…they lost…they're kind of in a bind…*(To Cassidy.)* Run, do not walk. *(She exits.)* Look, Mr. Bundy…

CATHERINE: Robert's hoping to cut down his weekend hours…

ROBERT: *(Overlapping.)* I, uh, listen…

CATHERINE: Lest we fail to recognize each other when we pass in the hall.

ROBERT: *(A look at Bundy. Back to Catherine.)* Look, could we get ten minutes?

CATHERINE: Honey, Cassie is…listen, thanks for the flowers. *(She smiles.)* Mr. Bundy wants drill bits.

ROBERT: What?

MR. BUNDY: Snapped a number nine.

ROBERT: Ummm…

CATHERINE: Could you look?

ROBERT: *(Looks at his watch.)* If I'm going to take…

CATHERINE: Cassie's still dressing.

ROBERT: *(Looks at Catherine, realizes it's not the time.)* Sure, okay, drill bits. *(Turns to go.)*

MR. BUNDY: I can do without.

ROBERT: No, no…hurry up, Cassie! I'll just…no problem…white box. *(He exits.)*

MR. BUNDY: Hard to find stuff.

CATHERINE: Well…your workshop is so well-organized.

MR. BUNDY: He uh…

CATHERINE: It's no bother.

MR. BUNDY: But uh…

CATHERINE: He's just frazzled. Cassidy! Now I'm going to have to run out… dumb stuff.

MR. BUNDY: *(Quickly rising.)* Oh sure.

CATHERINE: No, finish your coffee.

ROBERT: *(Re-enters.)* Drill bits. They don't uh…they don't have numbers on them.

MR. BUNDY: *(Looking.)* These are…sure, these are good.

ROBERT: Okay…great. So, uh, what, uh…Cassie!

CASSIDY: *(Offstage.)* Coming.

ROBERT: *(To Mr. Bundy.)* Look, we should…should talk.

CASSIDY: *(Offstage.)* Mom, where are my shoes?

CATHERINE: I am going to commit shoe-icide. Look in the bathroom! I need the advice of a child psychologist and I am a child psychologist. So we'll see you later, Mr. Bundy.

MR. BUNDY: Oh. Sure. *(He rises.)* These are just the thing. *(Starts to go.)* Tell Cassie after dinner.

ROBERT: After dinner what?

MR. BUNDY: Come over…if uh…

ROBERT: Cassie's busy after dinner.

CATHERINE: She is?

ROBERT: Yeah.

CATHERINE: *(To Mr. Bundy.)* Well, anyway, we'll see what's going on. And thanks for this morning.

MR. BUNDY: Oh, sure. *(To Robert.)* I'll get these back.

ROBERT: Right.

MR. BUNDY: These are the old ones.

ROBERT: Yeah.

MR. BUNDY: Good old ones. Can't find these. *(Awkwardly touches Robert's arm. Robert freezes. They stand there.)*

CASSIDY: *(Offstage.)* Found 'em.

CATHERINE: What time is it? That teacher is going to have a fit. Cassie! Bye,

bye, Mr. Bundy. Cassie! *(Calling off.)* Come on, honey. *(To Mr. Bundy.)* Thanks. *(He goes, to Robert.)* What on earth?

ROBERT: What the hell is that guy doing over here?

CATHERINE: Shhh.

ROBERT: What do you mean, "Thanks for the morning"?

CATHERINE: Cassie loves him.

ROBERT: Yeah, well…

CATHERINE: The babysitter had hives. I had to do fruit-for-a-million for Cassie's school, he was nice enough…

ROBERT: Okay. I just don't think…

CATHERINE: *You* weren't here.

ROBERT: No…right, but…forget it. Later.

CATHERINE: Later what?

ROBERT: Okay, Catherine.

(A pause.)

CATHERINE: What's your deal?

ROBERT: I said okay. I'm just uncomfortable with him.

CATHERINE: In what way?

ROBERT: Catherine, I can't do this in…how about we skip gymnastics?

CATHERINE: We made a big thing about her going.

ROBERT: Okay, never mind, tonight.

CATHERINE: I just…we…you said you were going to tell them today, what…

ROBERT: They have nobody to replace me.

CATHERINE: *(Attempting a light tone.)* Hey, neither do we.

ROBERT: I want to be here. I do. But I have an obligation, they saved my life.

CATHERINE: I know. Robert, they saved you for us. They'll understand. Robert, please, please don't take this as a…as a threat, but…you know this. Swearing you would open up your weekends is one reason I came back.

ROBERT: I'll talk to them again.

CATHERINE: You have to tell them, not talk to them. You have to make up your mind it's important, otherwise…

ROBERT: I told you I'd go back to him, just lay off it.

CASSIDY: Are you fighting?

CATHERINE: No, honey.

CASSIDY: Then why is Daddy mad?

ROBERT: I'm not mad, honey.

CASSIDY: You are too.

CATHERINE: We're discussing, honey, sometimes that gets almost like mad.

CASSIDY: Do I have to go to gymnastics?

ROBERT: Yes, you are going to gymnastics.

CASSIDY: I want to finish the lawn train at Mr. Bundy's.

ROBERT: No. We're going. Let's go.

CASSIDY: No.

ROBERT: I don't like that tone of voice.

CATHERINE: Robert, if she really…

ROBERT: Come on, Cassie, it'll be fun. We can look in the Disney store afterwards.

CASSIDY: I'm not going. Mommy said I didn't have to.

ROBERT: We are going, Cassie.

CASSIDY: No!!

ROBERT: *(Picking her up.)* We're already late. *(She fights him.)* Ow.

CASSIDY: I don't want to. No!

ROBERT: Stop it.

CASSIDY: I won't stop it. I'm not going with you. You're poopy. You're a poopy daddy. Stop it!

ROBERT: We're going!

CASSIDY: You're hurting me! Let go of me! I want to get down!!

CATHERINE: Robert, for God's sake!

CASSIDY: Ow.

(*Robert puts her down. Cassidy runs into her mother's arms.*)

CATHERINE: That's not right, Robert.

CASSIDY: That teacher is jerky. I won't!

CATHERINE: *(To Robert.)* What were you thinking?

ROBERT: I didn't hurt her.

CATHERINE: *(Stroking Cassidy in her arms.)* It's okay, Cassie.

(*Scene ends. We now go to Mr. Bundy's workshop, probably located in his garage. The kitchen table and chairs are moved off by scene changers. A workbench is moved on. Cassidy sits on a crate nearby. During the scene change, Catherine talks to the audience.*)

CATHERINE: Shaky. Look at that. *(A prayer without trimmings.)* Dear God, it's me, Catherine, and would you mind sending me a little equilibrium, because…ummm…I've been off-balance so long, it's hard to remember what balance is. *(A moment.)* Last week I saw a bumper sticker, it said "Harm not," and I thought, oh yeah, exactly, that's my ambition now…not to suffer harm and not to do it. Because I'm shaky. I can't handle it. And I want to be okay. Amen.

(She exits, and we are into the scene between Mr. Bundy and Cassidy.)

CASSIDY: Okay, "I'm looking over a four-leaf clover."

MR. BUNDY: You want sanding or you want singing?

CASSIDY: *(Begins the song.)* "I'm looking over a four-leaf clover that I overlooked before."

MR. BUNDY and CASSIDY: "The first leaf is sunshine, the second is rain, third is the lady who lives down the lane."

CASSIDY: Then what?

MR. BUNDY: "Someone that I adore."

CASSIDY: No, that's later.

MR. BUNDY: "No use complaining…" I don't know. Maybe rhymes with raining.

CASSIDY: Why do people only know the first part of songs?

MR. BUNDY: If they know the first part. No more singing, just working.

(A pause. They work.)

CASSIDY: Knock, knock.

MR. BUNDY: Who's there?

CASSIDY: Old lady.

MR. BUNDY: Old lady who?

CASSIDY: I didn't know you could yodel. *(Mr. Bundy chuckles.)*

MR. BUNDY: *(Repeating.)* Old lady who.

CASSIDY: I want to do something.

MR. BUNDY: We sand, then we paint. Sand.

CASSIDY: I don't want to sand. I'll stand on your feet and you dance me.

MR. BUNDY: *(Working.)* No dancing.

CASSIDY: Can I get the dress-up box?

MR. BUNDY: Are we working here?

CASSIDY: Please!

MR. BUNDY: All right, all right.

CASSIDY: Yea! *(She goes to get it.)*

MR. BUNDY: For peace and quiet.

CASSIDY: *(Starts dragging a box.)* No, I did this box. Where's the other box?

MR. BUNDY: *(Points.)* Junk.

CASSIDY: *(Pulling other box over.)* I love this junk!

MR. BUNDY: You get fleas, it's your fault.

CASSIDY: I love fleas. *(She holds up a garment.)* What's this one?

MR. BUNDY: My grandfather's vest.

CASSIDY: *(Another one.)* This one?

MR. BUNDY: My mother's.

CASSIDY: It's too small.

MR. BUNDY: When she was a child.

CASSIDY: It's old.

MR. BUNDY: World War I maybe.

CASSIDY: What was that war about?

MR. BUNDY: Money.

CASSIDY: I have twelve dollars.

MR. BUNDY: Twelve? That's good.

CASSIDY: What's this?

MR. BUNDY: A barber's strop.

CASSIDY: Can I put this on?

MR. BUNDY: It's old and rotten.

CASSIDY: I'll be careful.

MR. BUNDY: It's just junk. *(He nods.)* Sure.

    (She immediately takes off her T-shirt but leaves her play shorts.)

CASSIDY: Don't look.

MR. BUNDY: I won't look.

CASSIDY: You're still looking.

MR. BUNDY: I was thinking. *(He sands.)*

CASSIDY: Was she rich?

MR. BUNDY: She lived in downtown Los Angeles. If we had that land, we'd be rich.

CASSIDY: Was she pretty?

MR. BUNDY: She was ugly as a stone.

CASSIDY: She was not.

MR. BUNDY: She was. Her grandfather had horses. She teased them with a broom, she got kicked in the face. Many, many bones broke like that. *(He snaps his fingers.)* In those times they couldn't fix it. She always wore a veil, even when she would cook. One time the veil caught fire. I didn't care if she was ugly. Nobody cared except her.

CASSIDY: Was she nice?

MR. BUNDY: My mother? *(A slight laugh. The only time we see him laugh.)* Sure, she was nice sometimes. Everybody is nice sometimes. Even me.

CASSIDY: *(Finished, it's big on her.)* You can look. Am I pretty?

MR. BUNDY: Very pretty.

CASSIDY: No, really?

MR. BUNDY: Okay, okay.

CASSIDY: I can't reach. Button me.

MR. BUNDY: Come over here. *(She does.)* Turn around.

(She stands in front of him, facing out as he buttons the dress. The lights fade. As the scene is changed back to the breakfast table, a blond woman in a showy summer dress enters and talks to the audience during the change. She is Tianna, Jimmy Ray's wife.)

TIANNA: Oh yes, honey, I got the hair, you know I got the hair. That's right. Those bad diet pills kickin' in, suitcases out from under my eyes, shoot, darlin', look me over! Hey, I was at death's door, no kiddin'. Flat out I was, I'm tellin' you the truth. I tried to kill myself three times. I was that bad off, yes ma'am. But now even Jimmy Ray says I'm lookin' prime, and you don't get a compliment from Jimmy Ray that easy. Ladies, you know why I'm here. I lost a child just like every one of you here tonight, God bless us an' God help us, but I'm back an' I'm standin' here up front in my shiny hibiscus lipstick, an' you wanna know how the pieces got put back together, right? Well, my three sweet boys, sure. Jimmy Ray, my rock, my anchor, sure. My Lord and Savior, for dead sure. But what really brought me back was just how, pardon my French, pissed off I really was. See, I figured out I had a right to be angry, and a right to do somethin' about it. That rage is how I patched up my broken heart, and it's how you're goin' to start on yours tonight. Hey, I know what you've suffered, I know the loss sits in your heart like a stone, but listen to me, you got to take your personal tragedy an' turn it into your life's work, because there is such a thing as blessed revenge, honey, an' I'm gonna pass out some instructions right here on how to get it.

(We are now back in the kitchen with the Ferrebys who are in the midst of heated discussion.)

CATHERINE: This is…awful. This is awful.
ROBERT: I know.
CATHERINE: We don't need this.
ROBERT: What should we do?
CATHERINE: Cassidy…
ROBERT: Right.
CATHERINE: I don't see any…do you? In her?
ROBERT: No.
CATHERINE: It's not in her behavior, not in her drawings, not in her moods.

ROBERT: Okay.

CATHERINE: What are we going to do? I can…okay, I can watch Cassidy…I can…we don't know the guy who brought this. You never saw him before in your life, and we have no idea what his real agenda is!

ROBERT: Right.

CATHERINE: Can we buy this? I can't buy this. In terms of Cassidy, this is…okay, it's high school boys…when was it…can you read this date? This is a mess…

ROBERT: But he's next door…

CATHERINE: Yes, Mr. Bundy has been next door for two years. Nothing has happened, nobody has complained, he's been making lawn ornaments.

ROBERT: I think you're defensive because you let her go over there…

CATHERINE: No…

ROBERT: You didn't know, we lost our two best babysitters in one month, he seemed harmless, we're under…you know…stress…

CATHERINE: What I thought was…

ROBERT: We didn't think.

CATHERINE: I certainly did.

ROBERT: We had no reason to think…an hour here, an hour there, hey…

CATHERINE: What is your point?

ROBERT: Catherine, no matter what goes on between us, I have never, for the briefest moment, imagined Cassie wasn't your priority. Never, never, never. But there is a guy next door now who has harmed children…done them grievous harm, Catherine, we have to satisfy ourselves that no hint of this is in the wind here.

CATHERINE: If I thought…

ROBERT: Exactly. I don't think there has been harm, but I am going to watch my daughter's face while she tells me there hasn't. Better still, because I trust you absolutely, you are going to watch and I know you could see a flicker, or the flicker of a flicker. And then we are both going to know that there has been no harm. Then we are going to lay down some ground rules and then we can stop.

CATHERINE: *(Lifts documents.)* And open up what, Robert?

ROBERT: Catherine…

CATHERINE: All right, let's do it.

(He goes. Catherine sits. Mr. Bundy moves down into a solo light while we wait for Robert to return with Cassidy.)

MR. BUNDY: *(He holds a lawn sign jigsawed out of plywood in the shape of a loco-motive with the word "Ferrebys" on it and the house number "42.")* I do a… a locomotive, this one…and uh…I do kitties, puppies, the kids like those, they…tugboats, lions…the manes on the lions, they're uh…oh, pretty hard on a jigsaw. I like the lions though. I uh…I give…guess you'd call those lawn signs…I give 'em to people, I don't sell 'em. Tell the truth, I do it to have the kids around. I've lived several places, always ends up the kids, they uh…when I'm doing my lawn signs. You know, makes me… makes me feel good. I taught kids. I understand kids…well, they uh, they pep you up late in life. *(Wipes eyes with a handkerchief.)* Got a…watcha-callit…tear duct problem. Lot of old folks, they get that. But a…but a… nice thing about kids, you make a mistake, something like that, with kids, well say, they forget about it. Next day it's like it never happened…what-ever it was, all forgiven. Grown-up people, well in my experience that's not a quality they have.

(A pause.)

So a…that's…that's my lawn signs…kids they like 'em real well. Couldn't get along without the kids…I guess that's it.

(He exits as Robert re-enters with a sleepy Cassidy in his arms.)

ROBERT: We are very marginally awake.

CATHERINE: Hi, Cassie.

CASSIDY: Hi, Mommy.

ROBERT: *(Putting her on Catherine's lap.)* Here, sit with your mom.

CASSIDY: What's wrong?

CATHERINE: Nothing's wrong, sweetheart.

CASSIDY: Is it a tornado?

ROBERT: No, it's not a tornado. Do you want some juice? *(Cassidy shakes her head.)* Fruit loops?

CATHERINE: Daddy is joking.

CASSIDY: I want to go to sleep.

CATHERINE: Me too.

ROBERT: I have to ask you a couple of questions, honey, just for a minute.

CASSIDY: In the night?

CATHERINE: You know Daddy.

CASSIDY: Okay, juice.

(Robert goes to get it.)

CATHERINE: How is your spider bite?

CASSIDY: Itchy.

CATHERINE: You want something on it?
   (Cassidy shakes her head no.)

ROBERT: *(Returning.)* Juice, honey.

CASSIDY: What questions?

ROBERT: Quick ones.

CASSIDY: What ones?

ROBERT: Have you ever hurt yourself at Mr. Bundy's?

CASSIDY: *("Are you kidding?")* Daddy?

ROBERT: Mr. Bundy ever hurt you, honey?

CASSIDY: I hurt myself on the glue gun once.

ROBERT: But he never hurt you?

CASSIDY: Why would he hurt me?

CATHERINE: He wouldn't.

CASSIDY: Can I go back to bed?

CATHERINE: In one second. *(She looks to Robert.)*

ROBERT: *(To Cassidy.)* Honey, ummm, while you were over there, has umm…over with Mr. Bundy…was there…nothing ever scared you?

CATHERINE: *(Seeing that Cassidy is confused.)* Has he ever touched you anywhere private, honey?

CASSIDY: You mean down there?

CATHERINE: Anywhere private?

CASSIDY: This is stupid. No, he hasn't.

ROBERT: Hugging or…just physical…physical stuff.

CATHERINE: Robert…

CASSIDY: *(Squirming out of her mother's arms.)* This is yucky. It's dark. *(Robert reaches out for her.)* No.

ROBERT: Come here, sweetie.

CASSIDY: Has he ever touched you?

CATHERINE: Cassie, it's fine. You said no.

CASSIDY: That's so stupid. I want my bed. *(Starts to go.)*

ROBERT: Can I have a hug.

CASSIDY: He didn't. That's yucky. *(And she's gone.)*

ROBERT: She may not go over there.

CATHERINE: Stop, Robert. Agreed. I'm going up.

CASSIDY: *(Offstage.)* Mommy?

CATHERINE: Coming honey.

(She goes. The lights change. The tables and chairs are cleared leaving a bare stage. During the change, Robert speaks.)

ROBERT: I haven't had a drink in twelve years. Before Catherine. I was a bad drunk, a mean drunk. I woke up once in some motel with a gun, .22 pistol, on the nightstand. No idea where I was or…where it came from. I was a…was a graphic artist at that time. TV was on…religious cable or something…Evangelicals…shoot, it was Falwell, Jerry Falwell, and I…I stayed there and watched that for ten hours. Took that in. Long time. Some spirit entered me. Then I ordered pizza and uh…called AA, and they came and got me. Since then I have to be careful to assign meaning, to make things important enough to me to stay sober. I have to remember to like my work. I have to remember that I love Catherine. Sometimes things, they still lose meaning. I know I love Cassie though. That's always clear. I tell some of the drunks that if there's one thing you're really clear about, you'll be okay. Telling them, that makes me remember.

(We're now in a mall parking lot, maybe there's a section of yellow parking lines on the floor. Catherine enters with shopping bags. Someone calls to her from offstage. It is Tianna.)

TIANNA: *(Offstage.)* Mrs. Ferreby? *(Catherine looks, she doesn't see anyone.)* Mrs. Ferreby, honey? *(Tianna appears.)* Oh my goodness, it's warm… *(Touches her forehead with a handkerchief.)* I'd have to say this isn't glow, this is plain ol' sweat.

CATHERINE: It's warm.

TIANNA: Looks like you shopped up a storm, darlin'. Oh, I do too. But I got to tell you I'm in recovery from shoppin'. I just got to keep my grabby little hands out of the malls by main force 'cause I'm a shopping fool and no kiddin'.

CATHERINE: I'm not sure we've met.

TIANNA: 'Cause you'd remember me, huh? Well I got my own style…even I don't like it sometimes. Well, hi, I'm Tianna Longest. Like a long man's tie, Tianna. I think my bad-boy husband Jimbo's friends with your Robert. I'm right, it's Robert? *(Catherine nods yes.)* I think they're workin' on a little project. You want a wet wipe? I think I got wet wipes.

CATHERINE: No thank you, I think I'm all right.

TIANNA: And you're Cathy, ain'tcha? Ooooh, pretend I didn't say that. I'm on a campaign with that word…and I've been doing good since last summer, I have.

CATHERINE: Yes, I'm Catherine.

TIANNA: Well, I know what you are goin' through on this next door thing, and there is nobody in this world can sympathize like I can.

CATHERINE: I'm sorry, you said your name was Longest?

TIANNA: Married name's Bosun, but I use my own name for my consultin' business.

CATHERINE: Was there something you wanted to talk to me about…or…I'm about to…*(Looks at watch.)*…pick up my little girl at a birthday party.

TIANNA: You're kiddin', it's her birthday.

CATHERINE: No, a little friend's.

TIANNA: That is always so cute! You slipped out, huh? I always slip out too. Get a few precious minutes on my own.

CATHERINE: *(Looks at watch again.)* I might even be a little late.

TIANNA: Well, I could ride along if you wanted…of course I don't know if you're comin' back by here?

CATHERINE: What is it you want?

TIANNA: Oooh, that's chilly. Don't be chilly, darlin', don't do that.

CATHERINE: I'm sorry but…

TIANNA: Now, you're going to think this sounds crazy, but I'm here to save your life, honey. Make precautions for savin' it. See, Cathy, you can't tell it by lookin' at me, but there's…somethin' dead somewhere in here…inside here…an' I don't want you feelin' what I feel, darlin'. I don't want you to feel this. *(Catherine looks at her for a moment and then turns to move to her car.)* My little girl was raped. She was five years old. Raped, sodomized, then he killed her, darlin', wrapped her up in a dry cleaner bag, he…he was a convicted abuser they let out to live down the road from me. *(Catherine turns back.)* My bad-boy Jimmy Ray an' me hadn't heard from you, we were gettin' real worried.

CATHERINE: Oh my God.

TIANNA: Oh sweetie, there's no use sympathizin' with me. There's just no use in it. There just isn't any kind of Band-Aid you can put on it you know what I mean.

CATHERINE: When did it happen?

TIANNA: Pretty near nine years now comin' up.

CATHERINE: I'm so sorry.

TIANNA: An' he's still there on death row. Yeah, still goin' on. He's workin' on some advanced correspondence degree from the University of Calfornia but Jimmy Ray an' me we think we'll get him executed pretty soon now.

CATHERINE: What was her name?

TIANNA: Cathy, honey, if I tell you her name I'm gonna cry all over this parking lot an' ruin my real nice makeup.

CATHERINE: I didn't mean...

TIANNA: Don't you worry. We got to go on come what may. Now the thing is we got to put our pretty heads together on your little problem, don't we now?

CATHERINE: You're talking about Mr. Bundy?

TIANNA: Mr. Bundy, uh-huh, I sure am.

CATHERINE: Well it's...it's taken care of really.

TIANNA: Well, how is that?

CATHERINE: Cassidy's not spending time there anymore. We took that step.

TIANNA: *(Encouraging.)* Well that's so good! Good for you!

CATHERINE: Robert felt...

TIANNA: That's a real good start, but we were wonderin' if you'd got the neighbors together, anything like that?

CATHERINE: Mrs. Bosun, we didn't think it was necessary to...

TIANNA: Tianna.

CATHERINE: Tianna...Mr. Bundy's...transgression, according to the things...documents your husband sent were quite long ago. Years ago. And they weren't violent...they were sex crimes but there seems to have been no repetition...

TIANNA: Uh-huh.

CATHERINE: And his...interest...never seems to have been little girls. I believe teenaged boys were involved.

TIANNA: Oh, you never know but, am I wrong, doesn't the neighbor on the other side of...Mr. Bundy...have a teenage boy? Am I mixed up?

CATHERINE: Well...

TIANNA: Then there's those two twin boys further down, the Kellerman boys, I believe they're in seventh grade and, of course, that boy won State High School Golf, but that must be, oh, two blocks or so, I guess.

CATHERINE: How do you know that?

TIANNA: Oh, darlin', we got to be real...thorough...we take up this burden.

CATHERINE: Then why come to us?

TIANNA: Well it would be safest to start next door we thought...see, directly concerned.

CATHERINE: He's an older man now, Mrs. Bosun, Tianna, he's in his sixties and he apparently, from your materials, has been, you know, completely straight arrow since his prison term thirteen years ago.

TIANNA: Honey, you're talkin' all about him an' just nothin' about your little girl.

CATHERINE: You know that is, uh, we don't really know each other, certainly not well enough to make judgments or uh, or accusations…

TIANNA: Oh, now, you got me all…

CATHERINE: I love her, Mrs. Bosun. I love her and I want her safe, but when she is safe I want her to learn people can change, people can make mistakes, and people can be forgiven.

TIANNA: Uh-huh. Well, there's just so many views on a thing like this. An' I bet your feelin', like mine, is where many are affected, all should have a voice. You know, a democratic kind of thing. 'Course too, it's a big old country, there's a lot of places Mr. Bundy could go to. Move along if he felt like it.

CATHERINE: Move along?

TIANNA: Just move, honey.

CATHERINE: Whether or not he's dangerous?

TIANNA: Well, why would he want to be where he's not wanted?

CATHERINE: Who has said that?

TIANNA: Nobody's had the opportunity, darlin'. Plus I believe he's…well, gone to movin' around in the past.

CATHERINE: Look, Tianna, I am…or I was a, you know, child psychologist, and, uh, there was a young boy, my client, and uh, it was uh…clear…he shouldn't be released back to his parents' "care," and so…representing the State I fought that…hard…in court, and the parents, the parents…sometimes this boy had to be restrained…claimed I had, struck the boy during our sessions…and I had not…had not…and this, uh, went on for… endlessly for…eighteen months…in hearings…before it was decided in my favor. So I am sensitized…to these charges.

TIANNA: But, see, honey, you didn't hit the boy.

CATHERINE: I did not hit him, no.

TIANNA: Darlin', I don't believe you did. But it brings up the point that people get concerned, rightfully concerned, I can tell you that. With my little girl, I have asked a thousand times down on my knees why somebody didn't let me know there was danger, darlin'. And I've come to believe that is not a question for my Lord, it's a plain ol' question for my local police. Now the lady on the other side, Mrs. McGuigan, Jimmy Ray let her know and I would call her concerned.

CATHERINE: Other people know? I think that is…Tianna, I can't even begin to imagine what you have suffered and are suffering. I think you are an amazing person. I could never be so strong, I know I couldn't. And that you are…take the time to…devote yourself to this cause…well, I see many admirable things in that but, and please don't take this as…any lack of respect, but I think Robert and I can handle this…speak to Mrs. McGuigan privately…be on the lookout for any…anything. I guess what I'm trying to say is that this is, we feel, a neighborhood matter to be handled by people in the neighborhood.

TIANNA: Lucy. That was her name.

CATHERINE: Your daughter?

TIANNA: From "Lucy in the Sky with Diamonds." You remember that? *(Catherine nods.)* She was…I miss her every day of my life. I miss her right this minute. An' my belief, darlin', is that the "neighborhood" is all the little girls and boys…all of them…so I help out there in that neighborhood. I promised my Lucy I'd do that. *(Dabs at her eyes.)* Cry me a river! Lordy, I have given these eyes a workout! I'm surprised I still got 'em. My, oh my. *(Pulls together.)* My own fault. So Cathy darlin', your sweet little girl she's probably the last one left at that party, an' you can blame it on me.

CATHERINE: *(Looking at her watch.)* I completely lost track.

TIANNA: Honey, she's just eatin' too much cake.

CATHERINE: I should…I can call on the cell phone.

TIANNA: Well, good then…listen, Jimmy Ray an' me, we'd like to come down Wednesday, nothin' formal, nothin' big, meet with you two and Mrs. McGuigan, she's real nice, try to get all this ironed out so we can get out of your business.

CATHERINE: I don't even understand why we're part of your equation. If you're bound and determined to do this, why don't you and your husband go ahead and do it?

TIANNA: Honey, we just can't be everywhere. We can't. An' Jimmy Ray, he says he's a bad one to do it 'cause he's just way too angry, poor man, an' he knows, an' he'll say this isn't an act of revenge, darlin', it's a precaution people have to take for their children. All I'm askin' is would you be kind enough to let me have my say on Lucy's behalf. Just an hour of your time, that's all I'm askin'.

CATHERINE: Well I…

TIANNA: Five thirty be real good for Jimmy Ray an' that darned truck, which might as well be his wife if you want to know the truth.

CATHERINE: I suppose we could try.

TIANNA: Well, you try *real* hard, you cute thing, 'cause we're gonna be here with bells on, an' it's real close to a nine-hour drive with my motion sickness. Lord have mercy! Now you trust me it's going to be for the best, honey. There's not too much in this life I know, but I know that. I'm going to bring you down some of my coconut cream pie if you'll just stick a pot of coffee on, maybe even squeeze in some girl talk. You just stick with Tianna on this one, honey. You won't be sorry.

(The lights fade.)

(Mrs. McGuigan speaks first from audience, then steps into a special as the scene is changed into the Ferrebys' living room, represented by a sofa, a coffee table and two chairs.)

MRS. McGUIGAN: The country's gone to hell, and it's the parents' fault. Plainly put, I don't know where the common sense is. You don't have to let the kids see those movies: bang, bang, bang, crash, crash, crash, sex, sex, sex. Hollywood doesn't have a gun to your head. You don't have to buy them cars at sixteen, you don't have to let them date at fourteen, you don't have to let them smoke and drink and come home at one A.M. And most of all you do not have to blame every darn thing but yourselves as if it's the teachers' fault or television's fault or the liberals' fault or the government's fault. You're like a bunch of second graders…it's Jimmy's fault, it's Letitia's fault, it's Wally's fault, it's anybody's fault but my fault! What in the world is going on here? You pull up your socks, mister! You raise those kids like you know is right. Don't take any baloney from them, be up when they get home at night, insist they treat other people with respect or get their butts whipped or their cars taken, and they won't have to say "no" to drugs. These parents are just too self-centered to do what they should. It's not a popularity contest or a part-time job or the babysitter's responsibility. Boy, they make me mad! This isn't exactly brain surgery, you know, just do it. And if the parents did the job we wouldn't need all these social services or Christian kooks getting into our business selling us their righty, lefty values and two-bit armageddons. Don't you go blaming anything else. Your kid is your damned fault, and that's flat!

(She moves into the Ferrebys' living room and sits on the sofa with the Bosuns. Robert and Catherine are in the chairs.)

ROBERT: You've been very quiet, Mrs. McGuigan.

MRS. McGUIGAN: When it's time to make noise, I'll make noise.

TIANNA: We just want you to speak up an' give us what-for if you want.

MRS. McGUIGAN: My opinion is I don't like the idea of the man, but I can't say I dislike him in person.

JIMMY RAY: There is a real clear law in this state says he has to register with the police within fourteen days of taking up residence, and the police have a further responsibility to notify those in proximity of his criminal record immediately and with dispatch. Now these officers have just been bumbledickin' around.

TIANNA: Pardon his French.

CATHERINE: What about his right to privacy?

JIMMY RAY: He doesn't have a right to privacy.

CATHERINE: Legally?

JIMMY RAY: Legally, he has no right to privacy. He wanted his privacy he should have kept his hands off those kids.

CATHERINE: What happened to those kids?

JIMMY RAY: Okay, we don't have that follow-up.

CATHERINE: And we don't know if he has registered with the police?

JIMMY RAY: That is one-hundred-percent correct. Now I've had considerable experience on this thing…real considerable, thirty, forty of these creeps cross this country an' I tell you, Missus, the point is not has he registered, the point is putting organized community pressure on the police department to inform the neighborhood of his presence because once that neighborhood gets goin' he will pack up and get gone so fast you'll see a yellow streak all the way to the Mexico border.

CATHERINE: For what?

ROBERT: Catherine…

JIMMY RAY: For what?

TIANNA: Now Jimmy Ray…

CATHERINE: I thought you paid for the crime when you served the time. I thought that was the social contract.

ROBERT: This particular crime…

JIMMY RAY: *(Riding over.)* See, there's a real high percent…

CATHERINE: Yes, exactly…

JIMMY RAY: *Real high.*

CATHERINE: During the first five years…

JIMMY RAY: Ma'am…

CATHERINE: No, it's my profession. High recidivism early…

JIMMY RAY: What it is...

CATHERINE: But after all these years...

JIMMY RAY: We don't know...

CATHERINE: Let me finish please...

JIMMY RAY: This boy has several years where we don't know...

CATHERINE: Let me finish!

TIANNA: Honey, you go right ahead now.

CATHERINE: This is thirteen years after his release with no repetition and the statistic is less than a two-percent chance of another sex crime. Way less than two percent. The man is over sixty years old and uses a cane. We can't afford to generalize here. You have to take it case by case. Mr. Bundy did what he did...

JIMMY RAY: Let's call it by its name...

CATHERINE:...in 1985.

JIMMY RAY: Sexually forced children...

CATHERINE: Thirteen years ago...

JIMMY RAY: To sexually service him...

CATHERINE: And it's time he was forgiven.

JIMMY RAY:...and that man was a teacher.

CATHERINE: Yes...

JIMMY RAY: A teacher. He didn't just meet those boys in an alley somewhere, he took advantage of his position in a classroom to turn them homosexual.

ROBERT:	CATHERINE:
Now wait a minute...	That is patently absurd.

JIMMY RAY: Because I investigated that...

ROBERT: Ridiculous.

JIMMY RAY:...up, down and sideways and those boys had no homosexual activity up to that point.

TIANNA: Jimmy Ray talked to everybody...

ROBERT: That much is mythology, Mr. Bosun...

JIMMY RAY: What's that, buddy?

CATHERINE: You just don't...

ROBERT: Wait, honey.

CATHERINE:...is so absurd that I can't...

ROBERT: Wait.

CATHERINE:...listen to this.

ROBERT: *(To Jimmy Ray.)* Homosexuality does not work that way. You don't turn somebody to it...

JIMMY RAY: Was a case on the Internet...

(Catherine has to leave her seat in frustration.)

ROBERT: Excuse me…

JIMMY RAY: Heck, you probably…

ROBERT: Just let me…

JIMMY RAY: This other teacher, see…

ROBERT: Can somebody else talk here? You say the boy was in drag…he gave them dresses? Well, the hemline didn't turn them homosexual. For God's sake, if we've learned anything, we've learned it isn't environmental.

JIMMY RAY: You keep the Lord's name…

TIANNA: *(Stopping Jimmy Ray and addressing Robert.)* Darlin', you're not blaming the boys, are you?

CATHERINE: Thirteen years ago…

ROBERT: I am certainly not blaming…

TIANNA: See, he's not blaming the boys, Jimmy Ray.

CATHERINE: Tianna, I'm not sure this whole thing…

TIANNA: These are good folks, they know who the victims are…

ROBERT: Yes, as a matter of fact…

TIANNA: No sir, he's not puttin' it on the victims!

ROBERT: Oh brother.

JIMMY RAY: I got some business to do here, Tianna.

CATHERINE: I'm not saying it's right, but he paid for that. I'm saying it's over. He did what he did…

TIANNA: What's over, darlin'?

ROBERT: I think we should…

JIMMY RAY: It is not over! I'm gonna tell you one time it's not over. You see my wife over there?

TIANNA: Now don't, Jimbo…

JIMMY RAY: Last night I wake up, she's out of the bed, down curled up on the kitchen floor cryin'…

TIANNA: Shoot, darn it…

JIMMY RAY: Had some half-done colorin' book she found of our little girl's, an' she's collapsed on the floor…

TIANNA: This man is a good husband…

JIMMY RAY: So don't sit here in your fancy house…

TIANNA: Now, Jimmy Ray…

JIMMY RAY: CATHERINE:

  With your import rugs…   That is not the point…

TIANNA: You got to…

JIMMY RAY: An' tell me what's over!

TIANNA: …shut up now.

JIMMY RAY: *(Moving away.)* Heck with you.

TIANNA: *(She gives a little laugh.)* Goodness me, did I say that? You're all gonna think I'm a witchy woman, which I'm not. Now I think we're havin' a real good discussion…real heartfelt…gettin' all points of view…'cept Helen here is held back. You got to put your ideas forth, darlin'. I bet you got some strong ideas.

ROBERT: It's getting a little late here.

TIANNA: Now you hold on, you bad boy. Come on, Helen, I got these bulls in a corner momentarily.

MRS. MCGUIGAN: I don't have too much to say.

TIANNA: See, that's a white lie.

MRS. MCGUIGAN: Mr. Bundy has been very nice to me. A good neighbor day-in, day-out. Helped me replace a very heavy garage door. I'm the boy's grandmother, you know, and a single person, his father and mother…well, we won't go into that. Mr. Bundy, well he's always ready to help out, fix things, always brings over his tomatoes, pies he makes. This other thing…my grandson Allen, I'm raising him, he's in his senior year…always lifting weights…plays all sports. Too many for his grades if you ask me. I don't believe anybody is going to turn him anywhere if that's the conversation here. On the other hand, I believe once you've done these things…well I'm not at all sure it's something a neighborhood can take in, it's just too…this may not be a Christian point of view…it's just too hard. It's such an emotional thing. Once everybody knows…well, it won't be too logical. I like the atmosphere so much the way it's been. Some people say it's not real life it's so nice here. I'd have to say I don't mind a bit doing without real life when I come home. I feel I've been through a lot. I need the quiet. Maybe Mr. Bundy should move on. I'm not sure.

TIANNA: See that's such a good point. You put that so well, you really did. Isn't that a good contribution, Jimmy Ray? Now this man Mr. Bundy, despite the fact he has this mark of Cain, he's been making a real effort from what you say…

JIMMY RAY: Tianna…

TIANNA: Well, all those years now like Cathy says. He could just make his own decision to move on, not go through this whole thing getting sour as Helen points out…

CATHERINE: It doesn't have to get sour…

TIANNA: That's right, he could be talked to private, honey. I would be glad to take that on as my part. They say a little sugar makes the medicine go down. I believe he might move right on as a neighborly thing, and nobody would have to be the wiser.

CATHERINE: I doubt he has a place to go. If he did…

TIANNA: Now, I believe…

CATHERINE: *(Riding over.)*…he would be there.

TIANNA: Well, honey…

CATHERINE: He's been living next door to us for two years. He has never bothered your grandson, has he?

MRS. McGUIGAN: Well, I don't believe he'd bother Allen.

CATHERINE: He has been with my daughter alone in his house many, many times, and no harm done.

ROBERT: We had two babysitters, but…

CATHERINE: *(Riding over.)* There have been no sex crimes in this area.

JIMMY RAY: Well…

CATHERINE: Within a wide area. He's been a good neighbor. There is not a shred of evidence that would lead us to conclude he had to be privately or publicly told to move on. Now I think this should be laid to rest with thanks to the Bosuns for their time and information. You can count on our being watchful, but other than watchfulness there is nothing to act on here.

JIMMY RAY: The man who raped and killed our Lucy, he had no record with little girls though he had previously harmed teenagers. He raped Lucy several times over six hours in a…an old gas station. Strangled her on a cement floor, threw her in the trunk of his car, took her back where he had a power saw, did the rest of what he did…*(Reaches in his coat.)* sometime during all that he must have stepped on her glasses…*(He puts the glasses on the coffee table.)* See it turned out…Charles DeYoung…Charles Gabriel DeYoung to quote his full name…well prior to Lucy he had confided to a couple people he had this rape record…served time but like this here the cops overlooked to notify…didn't have a taste for it, that department, it later came out…and the people he told, well they didn't tell no one. Had their reasons I don't doubt. So I have…Tianna and me…come to have a real firm belief in notification. Insiders, outsiders, whatever. *(A moment.)* Could be this Walker R. Bundy, to quote his full name…well, there is differences between him and Mr. DeYoung. *(To Catherine.)* Like you said about his age, all the different things. You can get him outta here private if you're willing to take that chance. I figure I'll give you three days to do that, but I want to make this clear…There is no place for these people next door anywhere. I find 'em, I'm gonna move 'em on for eternity. I will give them no rest and no roof. I will cast them out. Because any place I know they are I would be just too likely to come there and harm them and the Lord tells me I shall not kill, and I can't afford to be too tempted. I kid you not. You move him on or I'll move him on. It's going to happen one way or the other. *(A moment.)* Time to go, Tianna. *(She rises.)* We'd like to thank you for the fellowship. Thanks for the time in your home. *(He picks up the glasses.)* Only time I cried was when I saw these glasses. Ain't that somethin'? Go on, Tianna. *(Turns back.)* I'll be in touch.

(The lights go down but not out. As they come back up, Robert and Catherine are alone. It is minutes later.)

CATHERINE: I don't think this is right. Why didn't you say something?

ROBERT: I did say something.

CATHERINE: That gay isn't environmental?

ROBERT: He was using that to leverage Mrs. McGuigan.

CATHERINE: I'm talking about his using neighborhood pressure to get Mr. Bundy out of here.

ROBERT: I don't know where I am on that.

CATHERINE: You're kidding me?

ROBERT: No, I don't know.

CATHERINE: Robert…you had an affair, should they move you on? Out you? Run pickets in front of the house and pass out leaflets?

ROBERT: Come on, Catherine…

CATHERINE: No, turn it around. My dad had two drunken-driving arrests in the eighties. He still drives, isn't that a neighborhood issue?

ROBERT: Obviously not the same…

CATHERINE: Why not? He caused a very serious accident. The woman he hit had a child in the car. He still drinks, he still drives. Wouldn't everybody here be safer if we moved him on to Florida?

ROBERT: Okay, okay, we're both upset…

CATHERINE: Did it ever cross your mind that he could sue us?

ROBERT: He'd never get away with it.

CATHERINE: Are you kidding? He'd…

ROBERT: He'd have to be suicidal.

CATHERINE: In this day and age?

ROBERT: He'd lose.

CATHERINE: Robert, think about it…

ROBERT: But we have this child…

CATHERINE: Are you patronizing me?

ROBERT:…you love better than anything fifty feet from this guy.

CATHERINE: Yes, I do love her and he's not interested in little girls.

ROBERT: Interested enough to have her over there every spare minute.

CATHERINE: Older people like children, Robert.

ROBERT: They do, yes. Listen, you remember when those kids used to climb our wall to get up on the garage roof? Nobody ever fell, but you were the one who insisted we pay eight hundred dollars to take down the wall. So, the real question, you know, the heart of it is, why take any chance with this guy at all.

CATHERINE: Because…I don't know.

ROBERT: Then let's not, okay?

CATHERINE: Because I know him. Because he drinks coffee here. I don't know. Because it's not right to do harm to someone who drinks coffee in your kitchen.

ROBERT: Catherine…

CATHERINE: No, no I…there's no…because sometimes you have to take chances to stay human…or…because I know he's…maybe because I'm too fragile to do harm right now.

ROBERT: You're not fragile, you're rock.

CATHERINE: Is that what you see? Oh, Robert…never mind, look…Mr. Bundy isn't a wall we can tear down…hold on…it's easy to move to extremes here, really, it can be seductive…feels really…active to make assumptions that…Robert, he has lost those drives or controlled them.

ROBERT: Catherine, there is no way in this world to be sure of that.

CATHERINE: He's demonstrated it.

ROBERT: He may still do it and he hasn't been caught.

CATHERINE: Nobody condones what he did thirteen years ago, but you can't run a society with life sentences for every crime, Robert.

ROBERT: He takes little trips, where does he go?

CATHERINE: He has to live somewhere.

ROBERT: Maybe he drives fifty miles and hangs out in the malls.

CATHERINE: So the moral imperative is to move him on to somebody else's mall?

ROBERT: Don't give me that. That's not how you react. There is nobody… nobody fiercer than you are about protecting your family…nobody.

CATHERINE: Then why am I not concerned, Bobby? We may both work but you know I'm the basic safety net for Cassie. I screen the babysitters, I check out the camps, I'm the one who has coffee with Mr. Bundy. Why should your view prevail now?

ROBERT: Because of what I feel, okay? I don't agree, in this case, to take any risk whatsoever with Cassie. Bundy be damned. I don't agree, okay?

CATHERINE: Honey, not taking risks is one thing, riding him out of town on a rail is another.

ROBERT: And both those things make Cassie safer.

CATHERINE: It's overkill, Robert, until all these people are put on an island, we have to cope. We can't just ruin his life to get a statistical edge.

ROBERT: He already ruined his life.

CATHERINE: Where are you coming from? Who drags me to church every Sunday? Who tells me we don't need prayer in the schools but we do need Christian ethics taught in the classroom? Forgiveness is a central Christian precept. Bobby, I am back in this house on that principle. I am busy forgiving you as we speak. Do you want to be forgiven?

ROBERT: No fair.

CATHERINE: Do you?

ROBERT: Yes, I do. You know I do.

CATHERINE: Well, so does Mr. Bundy, Robert, so what do we do now?

ROBERT: Beyond what I may feel here, or you may feel here, the fact is that Jimmy Ray took this out of our hands.

CATHERINE: No he didn't.

ROBERT: He gave us three days to get Bundy out of here before he saw to it it became a community issue. He will go to the papers. You saw his eyes. He'll go door to door.

CATHERINE: And if he does that?

ROBERT: Yes? What is that supposed to mean?

CATHERINE: Then we would convince the neighborhood to leave him alone.

ROBERT: You...what?! Do you...people aren't going to listen on this issue. This isn't the International Debate Society...

CATHERINE: I never said...

ROBERT:...with points for style and research. Catherine, people fear and hate these guys, and with good reason.

CATHERINE: And sometimes that's wrong.

ROBERT: And sometimes...listen, what you suggest is the quickest way imaginable to become the biggest pariah in a hundred-mile radius.

CATHERINE: Robert, how can you...we're not talking about reputation here. We have several responsibilities.

ROBERT: Oh, my God. Can we get real here, okay? We bought a house we can't afford so we could have the neighborhood and the school district. I work in an advertising agency that is downsizing, and my job is to baby corporate clients whose personal politics are a little to the right of Vulcan the Barbarian. They should see me on local TV fronting for this issue? How would you like us to be moved on to another town?

CATHERINE: So it's not worry about Cassie, it's economic?

ROBERT: *(Slapping the table.)* Don't you dare say that to me!

CATHERINE: You said it.

ROBERT: You know exactly what I mean!

CATHERINE: Yes, unfortunately.

ROBERT: That guy is a sociopath… *(She throws up her hands.)*…no morals, no judgment, he proved it!

CATHERINE: Whatever.

ROBERT: And no, it's not economic, it's Cassie. The time she's spent over there makes my skin crawl, but all that…all that aside, you stood in this room and agreed with me that it was off-limits for her, and I saw her over there yesterday!

CATHERINE: Yes, I did agree, but that house has a slide and swings. She wasn't in the house. You won't even buy her a swing set. As a matter of fact, your chief argument was she could use the one over there. When I saw she'd gone over there I called her back. Why don't you come home on Saturdays and you can watch her!

ROBERT: *(Boiling.)* I don't want her over there, do you hear me? You see that she doesn't go over there, is that clear? I shouldn't even have to bring this up. Now you see it doesn't happen.

CATHERINE: I don't know who you think I am, but I don't take instructions.

ROBERT: Do not let Cassidy go anywhere near there.

(A pause.)

CATHERINE: Bobby, I am going to go over and talk to Mr. Bundy. I am going to tell him what we know about his past, and I am going to tell him there is likely to be trouble. I'm going to suggest he agree, in writing, to stay away from neighborhood children of any sex and age, and should he transgress that agreement we will have Jimmy Ray and Tianna make his life the living hell they suggest. I will then communicate this information to the Bosuns, and ask them not to proceed further. If they do I will organize support for Mr. Bundy, and what you do at that point is entirely up to you. I hope you will join me, but I have no "instructions" for you. I loved you once, and I came back here because I thought I could love you again. I think that's what we've been working on and hoping for. *(A moment.)* I understand what you feel, truly I do. It's just not what I feel. I wish it was. *(A pause.)* So, anyway, I think I should go over and see Mr. Bundy. *(Pause.)* It would really mean a lot to me if you would come with me. *(Pause.)* Robert?

ROBERT: I'll come with you.

(They look at each other.)

CATHERINE: Thank you.

(The lights fade and while they change to the furniture representing Mr. Bundy's living room, Tianna steps into a spotlight.)

TIANNA: Hey, I'm not getting fancy here, y'know, but, girlfriends, it probably comes down, don't you think, to whether there is such things as good an' evil? I mean, I'm no preacher now, shoot no, but I feel like we just got to come down on some side of that fence. Because evil, well if there was such a thing as that, well I don't think you can forgive evil, can you? Sure they got theologians, such as that, been working all this, but for simple folks…I don't mean dumb now…well, you know how I'd put it, darlin'? I'd say, honey, when you read the paper, some of these things people do, don't you just think "that there is evil"…like the word just attaches itself…you just can't explain it any other way. And the things you use that word on aren't any kind of a thing you can understand out of your human experience. These are acts you couldn't do, nor could anybody you know or ever met do those things, and yet they are done. They are done. So I believe that it does exist and, down where our instincts are, we know that. People who do evil, we can't recognize them as human, and this "evil" is beyond explanation, beyond forgiveness, an' beggin' your pardon here, they got to be stamped out or driven back to that darkness from which they come. Because once evil is the name of a thing, I say give it no quarter. 'Course as I say, I'm a simple person with simple ideas. *(She looks down at her hands.)* Got real nice finger polish though, don't I? Been likin' the red/brown tones, but I'm tryin' to get up the nerve to do 'em blue.

(The lights come up on Catherine, Robert, and Mr. Bundy in his living room. He is filling their kitchen glasses with lemonade.)

CATHERINE: So the thing is, Mr. Bundy, the thing is, we…we know now you have a…criminal record.

ROBERT: We didn't go looking for it.

CATHERINE: Nothing you did…someone outside brought it to our attention.

MR. BUNDY: Oh no.

CATHERINE: I'm sorry, I know it was a long time ago.

MR. BUNDY: I prayed to God against this.

CATHERINE: I know that you…

MR. BUNDY: I'm on my knees every day that I could live this down…for all these years.

ROBERT: *(Seeing the tipping pitcher.)* You're spilling the lemonade.

(He looks nonplussed as it continues to spill.)

CATHERINE: The lemonade, Mr. Bundy.

MR. BUNDY: Oh. I'm sorry.

CATHERINE: Are you all right?

MR. BUNDY: All right?

CATHERINE: Why don't you sit down, Mr. Bundy?

MR. BUNDY: You see, I wanted to have myself castrated. I looked into that.

CATHERINE: Mr. Bundy, don't.

MR. BUNDY: No, I suppose you are not interested in my regrets.

CATHERINE: Mr. Bundy…we have to talk about this, I'm sorry.

MR. BUNDY: I should clean up the lemonade.

CATHERINE: I'll do it.

MR. BUNDY: This carpet…

CATHERINE: It's all right.

MR. BUNDY: Stupid.

CATHERINE: Mr. Bundy, you've probably been wondering why Cassie hasn't been over.

MR. BUNDY: She is a beautiful child. I would never harm a child.

CATHERINE: This is hard. This is so hard.

ROBERT: Do you want me…

CATHERINE: No. No, it's all right. We told her she couldn't, Mr. Bundy. It's as much for your sake as it is for hers. It would be…I would still be pleased if you came over for coffee. *(Robert shifts position. Mr. Bundy notices.)* Mr. Bundy, there is some chance of this becoming public knowledge. *(Mr. Bundy sits with a hand over his face.)* Not from us. I do think there might be a way…to head that off.

MR. BUNDY: You can see some things are still in boxes. I've moved nine times in thirteen years. It's pretty hard. I uh…well, probably I deserve to be humiliated like they do but, my uh…nerves are…pretty bad now…pretty bad and uh…I don't know if you…know my age? *(They nod.)* So uh, I get…very nervous about things. I was hoping not to move again so soon. One time they filled up my car with feces. They spray paint…things…on my house. Killed a dog, my dog, one time. Cocker spaniel dog my sister gave me.

ROBERT: Could you go to your sister, Mr. Bundy?

MR. BUNDY: I don't believe she could afford to be…singled out…where she lives.

CATHERINE: I don't think you have to move, Mr. Bundy. I'm not in favor of that. *(She hands him a piece of paper from a file folder.)* I wondered perhaps if you would feel you could sign this? *(He reads it.)* You know if you…if you could, I think we could use it…um…to defuse anything, well, that came up. But if you…

MR. BUNDY: Damn children…these…damn children! I'm not…I don't harm them! *(Robert rises.)* I'm sorry. I'm sorry. God help me. *(A pause.)* I uh… yes, whatever you want…I could sign this. I'm surprised you offer…any kind of help. They would…they would drive me out though anyway. They need to do it. See? My hands shake now. Like the crying. I'm not in control of it. *(Puts his hands in his pockets.)* I would ask if you could give me till the eighteenth. All my sister's money is in this house. I don't know if you know I work weekends at the uh…the clothing outlet on Route 62… they pay every two weeks. I would need that money when I go.

CATHERINE: Where would you go, Mr. Bundy?

MR. BUNDY: Can't say. Somewhere else. Get some boxes. List the house. I don't know. I guess it doesn't matter where I go. I wouldn't be there too long.

CATHERINE: Mr. Bundy, I think you have paid. I don't think you need to pay anymore. You are welcome to live next door to me. My husband feels it is inappropriate for you to see Cassie. I don't know…perhaps I do too. He feels it strongly and I would have to honor that. Because she cares for you, I think we should address that with Cassie with you there. *(Seeing Robert's expression.)* I do, Robert.

MR. BUNDY: I don't believe I can go through this. To stay. I've been…having some irregular heartbeat. Nervous uh…nervous conditions. *(Wipes his eyes.)* I cry quite a bit over…over I don't know what. I don't…I can't listen to them shouting outside the house anymore.

ROBERT: Perhaps then, the best thing…

CATHERINE: If you had to go through it…if it came to that…I believe, after all these years there would be people here who…would feel this should stop now. Myself…people from our church…some of the people in the neighborhood…

ROBERT: Catherine, I believe I'll go back over to the house. I…

CATHERINE: *(Continuing to Mr. Bundy.)*…and after awhile they wouldn't shout anymore, and you could be done with it. I would encourage you to see if we couldn't put an end to it.

(Pause.)

ROBERT: I'll be there when you finish.

CATHERINE: Please stay.

ROBERT: Good-bye, Mr. Bundy.

MR. BUNDY: Oh. Yes.

CATHERINE: *(To Robert.)* Just stay one minute. Mr. Bundy, I know these are hard choices but…

ROBERT: *(By the door, has bent over and picked something up.)* What is this? What the hell is this?

CATHERINE: What is what?

ROBERT: This is the uh…the twirly thing, you know, that uh…that flying toy…the spinning fairy whatsit…from uh, from that thing I brought home to Cassie…you know the thing…come on, Catherine…the toy I brought Cassie two days ago.

CATHERINE: It could be from anything.

ROBERT: It's not from anything…it's the propeller part from that thing I bought Cassidy. She's been in here in the last two days.

CATHERINE: All right, calm down.

ROBERT: *(To Mr. Bundy.)* Has my daughter been in here? I made it clear a week ago…

CATHERINE: We'll talk at home.

ROBERT: No, we won't talk at home! Listen, Mr. Bundy, I don't want my daughter in here! I don't give a rat's ass about your nerves or your…palpitations, I don't want Cassidy anywhere near you, okay? I don't care what kind of pals you are with Catherine, I don't care how many years it's been, if my child knocks on your door you tell her, in no uncertain terms, she is not welcome. I can't believe this. I'm going to say this so everybody clearly, clearly understands it. If I ever find out you have spoken to my daughter, other than to send her home, I am going to hurt you, you understand, do you harm…*(To Catherine.)* Don't touch me…and break up your house, smash all these things I see, these things I see here, and drag every newspaper I can find right down here to your front door. Does that seem clear enough to you? *(To Catherine.)* Do you not listen to me? *(To Bundy.)* She was over here two days ago, and she better not ever, God help you, be over here again! *(He slams out.)*

CATHERINE: *(To Bundy.)* Are you all right?

MR. BUNDY: *(Shaking his head.)* I uh…I uh…

(They stand. Neither can speak. Robert, who has been moving since he left, walks by Jimmy Ray leaning against a building. Bundy's furniture is being cleared. The lights dim on Bundy and Catherine, who exit.)

JIMMY RAY: Hey, buddy. *(Robert stops and looks at him. He looks down and then back up.)*

ROBERT: What do you want?

JIMMY RAY: Been waitin' on you.

ROBERT: I work right over there.

JIMMY RAY: Yeah, I know, I didn't want to embarrass myself dressed like I am.

ROBERT: What is it?

JIMMY RAY: I said I'd be in touch. You want a cigarette? *(Robert shakes his head "no.")* You on the non-smokin' committee? *(A thin smile.)* Who runs your family, boy?

ROBERT: What are you talking about?

JIMMY RAY: There ain't squat goin' on is what I'm talkin' about. Bundy just sits there. What are you, pussywhipped?

ROBERT: Good-bye, Mr. Bosun. *(He starts off.)*

JIMMY RAY: Your kid said to give you this note from her teacher. Somethin' about parents' night, somethin' like that. *(Holds it out. Robert takes it and opens it.)*

ROBERT: Where did you get this?

JIMMY RAY: I went down to see your girl, ask her a few questions.

ROBERT: You went…no…you talked to Cassie at her school?

JIMMY RAY: Yeah, I dropped by.

ROBERT: Are you…you have got to be…I don't think that was any of your business.

JIMMY RAY: Me either, pal…

ROBERT: That's right…

JIMMY RAY: I think it was your business…

ROBERT: Hold it…

JIMMY RAY: …but you didn't take care of it so I had to make it…

ROBERT: Hold it.

JIMMY RAY: …my business.

ROBERT: *(Finger in his face.)* Don't you ever…

JIMMY RAY: *(Uninflected.)* Don't go there, man…*(An explosive moment.)* Don't go there, Bobby-Bobby. *(The potential passes.)* Now you want to know what I know, or you don't care?

ROBERT: What?

JIMMY RAY: *(Reaching out to his lapel.)* You got something stuck to your coat there. You remember how when Bundy abused those boys, he got 'em to put on women's clothes?

ROBERT: Yes.

JIMMY RAY: He dressed your girl up too.

ROBERT: No.

JIMMY RAY: Yeah, he did.

ROBERT: How do you know that?

JIMMY RAY: She told me.

ROBERT: In what way dressed her up?

JIMMY RAY: Had her undress, Bobby, had her put on some special little outfit he had an idea she should wear.

ROBERT: Why?

JIMMY RAY: Don't believe she said "why."

ROBERT: And then what?

JIMMY RAY: I figure that's your question to ask.

ROBERT: *(To himself.)* Goddamnit.

JIMMY RAY: Lord's name.

ROBERT: He had her undress?

JIMMY RAY: So she said.

ROBERT: *(Controlled.)* Is that all of what you have to say to me?

JIMMY RAY: You're a piece of work, man.

ROBERT: I think we're done now.

JIMMY RAY: Where are you, buddy?

ROBERT: Get out of my face.

JIMMY RAY: I think you're about three bricks shy of a load, pal. What kinda man are you foolin' with your daughter's life? You ought to be ashamed of yourself. You don't get him outta there, you're gonna be real, real sorry. I don't know where you're at, I don't know why you aren't takin' care of your family and, to tell the truth, I don't think you got any balls. When all this comes down it's gonna be straight up your fault. Oh yeah. Oh yeah. Batter up, man. Up to you, Bobby, big time. *(Starts off.)* Don't forget parents' night.

(He leaves. The lights come down. Cassidy steps into a spot. Behind her they reset the kitchen table and chairs.)

CASSIDY: Mr. Bundy told me that you should never go with a strange person and if they try to…the bad person…to pull you, you should yell and say, "You aren't my father. You aren't my mother!" Which is pretty stupid because nobody ever pays attention to kids anyway. Anne Marie said she tried it when she was with her daddy in the mall and everybody just laughed or smiled, or didn't even look when he carried her out. He was really mad, too. Why would anyone want to hurt a kid anyways? It's so stupid.

(The lights come up in the Ferreby kitchen. Cassidy and Catherine are seated at the table. Robert is on his feet talking to the child.)

ROBERT: It's not stupid. I want you to look at me, Cassidy. I said look at me!

CATHERINE: Don't scare her.

ROBERT: There are times to be scared. There are times when it is sensible and useful. Now you went over there when we told you very clearly you should not.

CASSIDY: No.

ROBERT: Don't lie to me, Cassidy.

CASSIDY: I didn't.

ROBERT: You went over there a day later.

CASSIDY: Just to play on the swings.

ROBERT: Was your mother watching you?

CATHERINE: Robert…

ROBERT: Did your mother know you went over there?

(Cassidy looks at her mother.)

CATHERINE: It's all right, honey.

CASSIDY: Just to play on the swings.

ROBERT: *(To Catherine.)* You knew.

CATHERINE: There is no reason she can't play outside there.

ROBERT: There is every reason but the simplest reason is we agreed she shouldn't.

CATHERINE: That isn't what we agreed.

ROBERT: How do you have the nerve to say that to my face?

CASSIDY: I don't like it when you fight.

ROBERT: We're not fighting, Cassidy.

CASSIDY: You are too.

ROBERT: I want you to be quiet, Cassidy.

CASSIDY: Oh fine. *(She turns away from him.)*

ROBERT: Were you watching her on the swings? After you sent her over there…

CATHERINE: I didn't send her over there.

ROBERT: Did you watch her, Catherine!

CATHERINE: What's the matter with you?

ROBERT: Because if I can't trust you to watch her, then maybe there should be someone else here.

CASSIDY: I don't want someone else.

ROBERT: I told you to be quiet!

CATHERINE: Now you're scaring both of us.

ROBERT: What is the matter with *you*? What is the matter with both of you? She didn't just play on the swings. Your mom and I told you that for grown-up reasons it was dangerous.

CASSIDY: Swings aren't dangerous.

CATHERINE: To be fair, Robert, what we said was…

ROBERT: There were a lot of things we didn't say because of you.

CATHERINE: *(Going to get Cassidy out of her chair.)* Come on, Cassie.

ROBERT: Not yet.

CATHERINE: Come to Mommy.

ROBERT: Are you deaf, I said "not yet."

CATHERINE: I think we should cool off now.

ROBERT: I want to know now, Cassidy, if you went in the house? And I want to know, clearly, if your mother knew you went in the house.

CASSIDY: Okay, yes.

ROBERT: "Okay, yes" what?

CASSIDY: For one minute.

ROBERT: Cassidy…Catherine, yes or no, did you know?

CATHERINE: Is this your…I don't know what…tough guy act?

ROBERT: Give me a straight answer!

CATHERINE: And are you more concerned about what she did in the house or whether you've been obeyed?

ROBERT: I'm not here to consider the fine points, Catherine, it seems to me I've made myself pretty clear. We agreed she wouldn't go in the house, and she was in the house.

CASSIDY: I wanted my train.

ROBERT: What train?

CATHERINE: The lawn decoration they'd been making together for weeks.

ROBERT: *(Punching the air in frustration.)* You let her go in there!

CATHERINE: No Robert. The furnace man showed up, so I said it would be all right to ring the bell and get the train.

ROBERT: Do you not take me seriously?

CATHERINE: That's an entirely different conversation. We can have that conversation later. Because of the furnace I might have been gone five minutes.

ROBERT: Five minutes?

CATHERINE: All right, seven minutes, eight minutes.

ROBERT: That is completely irresponsible!

CATHERINE: *(Explosive.)* And you are completely off the wall.

CASSIDY: No fighting! No fighting!

(Robert stops her with his hands on her shoulders.)

ROBERT: Honey…

CASSIDY: Let go of me! *(She struggles.)*

ROBERT: Stop it, Cassidy.

CASSIDY: You are mean. Let go!

ROBERT: Sit in the chair. *(Trying to break free, she accidentally hits him in the face and is momentarily free. In reaction, he lifts her roughly off her feet and over-firmly puts her back in the chair.)* Don't hit me!

CATHERINE: Leave her alone, Robert. *(She starts for the chair.)*

ROBERT: *(Warning her off.)* I'm talking to her.

CATHERINE: *(Trying to take his hands off Cassidy.)* Not like that.

ROBERT: I'm not hurting her.

CASSIDY: Mommy!

CATHERINE: You are hurting her! *(She tries to pull him away.)*

ROBERT: Get off me, Catherine.

CATHERINE: Just leave her alone.

ROBERT: *(As he pushes her away.)* I am talking to her.

(With the momentum of the push, Catherine missteps and falls to a sitting position on the floor.)

CASSIDY: Mommy!

(She runs to Catherine. Cassidy is intercepted by Robert who puts her back in the chair.)

ROBERT: Your mommy is all right.

CATHERINE: Stop it!!!

ROBERT: What did you do in the house?

CASSIDY: The lawn thing.

ROBERT: And what else?

CATHERINE: *(Rising.)* Get out of the room, Robert.

ROBERT: What else! Do you hear me!

CASSIDY: I asked him if I could play dress-up.

ROBERT: No!! Look at me!

(Catherine fiercely shoves him away from Cassidy. He stands there shaking,

trying to prevent himself from going after her. She takes a step toward him to comfort him.)

CATHERINE: Robert…
(He bolts out of the room, upsetting a chair. Cassidy is crying. Catherine goes to her and cradles her. During the following, the kitchen set is struck and an armchair representing Mr. Bundy's living room is brought on.)

CATHERINE: It's okay, sweetie, it's all right, Cassie.

CASSIDY: Daddy hurt you.

CATHERINE: He didn't hurt me, I tripped.

CASSIDY: I hate him.

CATHERINE: No you don't.

CASSIDY: It was scary.

CATHERINE: I know it was. *(Getting up.)* Let's go up, I'll read to you.

CASSIDY: Hold me.

CATHERINE: I want to hold you. *(She takes Cassidy up in her arms in a standing position.)*

CASSIDY: I hate him.

CATHERINE: *(Singing.)* "I'm looking over a four-leaf clover that I've overlooked before…"

(Catherine continues to sing, taking Cassidy off. Simultaneously, we are now in Mr. Bundy's living room. There is a single armchair, and he is sitting in it reading a woodworking magazine. There is an insistent knock on the door. He puts down the magazine and starts to get up. Another knock, he opens the door, and Robert is there. Robert grabs Mr. Bundy furiously by his shirt front and drives him back to the center of the room.)

MR. BUNDY: Wait…
(Robert hits Mr. Bundy full in the face. Mr. Bundy's hands go to his face. Robert grabs him by the hair and knees him in the groin. Bundy moans and bends over in pain.)

ROBERT: Never…never, never touch her, creep.
(Robert grabs him and straightens him up.)

MR. BUNDY: Please, no…
(Robert hits him twice more in the face, and Mr. Bundy collapses to the floor.)

ROBERT: Never! Do you hear?!
(He kicks him.)

MR. BUNDY: Please. Please.

(Robert pushes him down, gets astride him and bangs his head on the floor.)

MR. BUNDY: Animal!!

(Catherine enters.)

CATHERINE: Robert… *(Robert punches Mr. Bundy in the face again.)* Robert, in Christ's own name! *(Robert stops. He looks at her uncomprehendingly.)* Oh, my God, Robert. *(Robert gets up. His hands are covered with Bundy's blood. Bundy still moves slightly.)* Help him. *(Cassidy appears behind Catherine. Robert looks at Bundy, then looks at his hands. He wipes them off on his pants. Catherine sees Cassidy and pulls her in so her face is hidden and she can't look.)* Please help him.

(Robert stares at her. Lights down. A light up on Tianna elsewhere. During her speech, Bundy's chair is struck and we go to the Ferreby bedroom where we will see Catherine pack.)

TIANNA: All right then, Jesus Christ tells us to turn the other cheek and repay evil with good, but that's not about our kids. See, they are too tender and the evil too hard. This is where the humanists and such have got themselves confused, my friends. For our children we must be as a pride of lions and strike a blow, not turn away. For anyone who harms a child has broken covenant with the tribe and become anathema. And those who are anathema must be destroyed.

(She exits as the lights come up on Catherine packing. Her clothes are in piles on the bed. Three already-packed suitcases are on the floor. She packs into a fourth suitcase on the bed. Robert enters.)

ROBERT: Please don't go.

CATHERINE: *(Packing.)* My sister's work number and home number are on the sheet in the kitchen. She and Cassie left around lunchtime. I'll be getting there pretty late, and then Cassie and I will take off for a few days.

ROBERT: Please don't go.

CATHERINE: I went down to the hospital. He's off the critical list.

ROBERT: Forgive me.

CATHERINE: The movers will be here in a few days, there are people packing him up. Oh, packing. I packed all Cassie's Barbie stuff but the car is full. I addressed the box. It's in the garage. I'd appreciate it if you sent it on.

ROBERT: We don't know what he did.

CATHERINE: He did nothing.

ROBERT: We don't know.

CATHERINE: What are you, Robert? Are you sorry?

(A pause.)

ROBERT: What will happen to us if I answer that? Can you take my answering that? *(They look at each other.)* I guess I'm sorry for me. *(She looks down. He goes to her.)* Catherine.

CATHERINE: No.

ROBERT: *(Tries to lift her chin to look at him.)* Look at me.

CATHERINE: I said don't. *(Turns away.)*

ROBERT: *(Tries to turn her.)* Just look at me.

CATHERINE: I don't need to.

ROBERT: For one second.

CATHERINE: No!

ROBERT: *(Forcing her to turn.)* How much is that asking?

CATHERINE: *(Slaps him hard. A moment. They look at each other.)* Damn it.

ROBERT: Hey…

CATHERINE: I can't believe this!

ROBERT: It's okay.

CATHERINE: It's not okay. You…

ROBERT: I'm not hurt…

CATHERINE: All this time…Cassie, Mr. Bundy, Tianna, I wanted to stay…not this. Where did you think I was? You think I wasn't frightened for Cassie? You think it didn't cost me anything? Sometimes I wanted Bundy on the moon, in a cage, anywhere but next door to me. When you had the affair I fantasized coming back and setting fire to the house, but it seemed…important not to go there, not to be that. It was easy to hit him, Robert, easy…and it was easy for me to hit you, and we both did it, and now we are what we never wanted to be. All for nothing. Just part of this whole apocalyptic thing that seems to be rolling downhill. The one thing…*the one thing* I didn't want to be part of!

ROBERT: The guy destroyed children for pleasure. What part of the equation is that?

CATHERINE: *(Closing her suitcase.)* I have to go, Robert.

(They stand separated, in silence.)

ROBERT: What am I going to do without you and Cassie?

CATHERINE: *(Simply.)* Cassie doesn't want to see you, and I don't want to live with you.

ROBERT: I'll do whatever you want. What do you want?

CATHERINE: *(Putting the suitcase on the floor.)* I don't want her to learn what you have to teach her. That's what I want.

(She takes the suitcase out. The lights go down but not out. We hear bus announcements for various parts of the country. A waiting bench is brought on in one area and Mr. Bundy, bandaged and in a neck brace, sits on it. Tianna enters with microphone from another direction.)

TIANNA: I want to see Charles DeYoung fry, I do. More than that, I want eye contact with him, because I want to see the moment when the light goes out. It's my right to be the last thing he sees, so he knows I do not forgive him.

BUS ANNOUNCEMENT: Twelve-forty bus for Dayton boarding door nine. One o'clock Greyhound for Albuquerque with stops in Springfield, Tulsa and Amarillo door six. Also at one P.M., San Francisco Express, door change to fourteen. Door fourteen.

(Bundy takes out his ticket and looks at it.

He unzips the bag in front of him on the floor and takes out a "get well" card obviously made by a child and looks at it. He pulls out the dress that Cassie tried on in his workshop.

He puts the dress and the card back in the suitcase, zips it, and rises to go. He picks up his suitcase and walks down toward the audience. During the final bus announcement, the scene changers clear the stage of furniture.)

BUS ANNOUNCEMENT: Buses for Tampa, St. Petersburg, Orlando with intermediate stops, please proceed to door ten…door ten for all Florida destinations. Please do not leave luggage unattended in any part of the terminal.

(Mr. Bundy stands in a single light awkwardly holding the suitcase. Elsewhere on stage, Cassidy jumps rope.)

CASSIDY'S VOICE: Don't throw him pennies
　　or feed him sweets,
　　'cause you're just what
　　the oogey-boogey eats.

Don't open the cupboard
if you need a cup,
'cause the oogey-boogey's in there,
and he'll eat you up.

(The lights fade on Mr. Bundy and Cassidy.)

END OF PLAY

Anton in Show Business

A Comedy

ORIGINAL PRODUCTION

Anton in Show Business premiered at the Humana Festival of New American Plays in March 2000. It was directed by Jon Jory with the following cast:

T-Anne, Andwyneth, Don Blount, and Gate Manager	Saidah Arrika Ekulona
Lisabette	Monica Koskey
Casey	Gretchen Lee Krich
Kate, Ben, Jackey, Ralph, Wikéwitch, Joe Bob	Annette Helde Chick Reid
Holly	Caitlin Miller
Joby	Stacey Swift

and with the following production staff:

Scenic Designer	Paul Owen
Costume Designer	Marcia Dixcy Jory
Lighting Designer	Greg Sullivan
Sound Designer	Martin R. Desjardins
Properties Designer	Ben Hohman
Stage Manager	Deb Acquavella
Assistant Stage Manager	Amber Martin
Dramaturg	Michael Bigelow Dixon
Assistant Dramaturg	Ginna Hoben
Casting	Laura Richin Casting

CHARACTERS

T-ANNE: The Stage Manager—also playing: Airport Announcer; Andwyneth; Don Blount; Gate Manager

ACTRESS #1: Kate; Ben; Jackey

ACTRESS #2: Ralph, Wikéwitch; Joe Bob

CASEY: 36 years old; tall, lean, plain

LISABETTE: 24 years old; charming and energetic

HOLLY: 30 years old. A drop-dead gorgeous TV star

JOBY: 26 years old. A recent graduate with an M.F.A. in dramaturgy

The play is performed by women in roles of both sexes.

SETTING

Various locations in New York and San Antonio in the present.

There is one intermission.

DIRECTOR'S NOTE

It is possible to use a bare stage and minimal furniture. Many costumes must be rigged for quick change. You need six female scene changers/dressers, who handle the furniture moves and quick changes. Costume changes were full and were not done in sight. All changes were possible with the given text. I strongly suggest that you have the scene changers in several rehearsals prior to tech. Actors continued to play during scene changes. Have fun!

ANTON IN SHOW BUSINESS

A bare stage. In the darkness, rolling thunder, and then suddenly cutting across it, lightning. The flashes illuminate a mysterious cloaked figure. Thunder. A special. The figure speaks.

T-ANNE: The American theater's in a shitload of trouble. *(Flash, crash.)* That's why the stage is bare, and it's a cast of six, one non-union. *(Flash, crash.)* I'm T-Anne, the stage manager, but I'm also in the play. *(Flash.)* Like a lot of plays you've seen at the end of the 20th century, we all have to play a lot of parts to make the whole thing economically viable… *(Crash.)*…HOMAGE TO THORNTON WILDER. *(Flash, crash. She drops the cloak. She wears blue jeans, a T-shirt, many keys at her belt.)* The date is *(current date)*, 2000, just before noon. Well, I'll show you a little bit about how our profession is laid out. Up around here are the Broadway theaters, sort of between 42nd and 52nd Street, we like to think that's the heart of everything. City of New York, State of New York, United States of America, the world, the galaxy, the universe. Down over here is Greenwich Village, around there we do off-Broadway, that's good too. Now Tribeca, Soho, Lower East Side, we call that the "downtown scene," off-off stuff. An incredibly colorful group of people who despise realism and have all won the Obie Award…that's good too. Beyond that, radiating out in all directions for thousands of miles is something called "regional theater," which I understand once showed a lot of promise but has since degenerated into dying medieval fiefdoms and arrogant baronies producing small-cast comedies, cabaret musicals, mean-spirited new plays, and the occasional deconstructed classic, which everybody hates. After that, moving west, we reach the burning, uninhabitable desert and its militias who don't go to plays, and beyond that, singing a siren call, the twin evil kingdoms of Flick and Tube, the bourne from which no traveler returns. Now back to New York, thank God. Let's see, the Empire State Building, the Statue of Liberty and the Actors' Equity offices…that's our union. They make sure no more than 80 percent of our membership is out of work on any given day. And over there…yes, right over there is where we worship, yes sir, *The New York Times*. Well, that's about it. Now, with a short subway ride we get to one of the audition studios where producers and theaters come to find actors for their plays. Here's the front door, elevator up to the fifth floor, Studio C, where the San Antonio, Texas Actors Express has come to the big city to cast *The Three Sisters* by Anton Chekhov. He's Russian. At noon, you can always hear the actors doing their vocal warm-ups.

(Vocal warm-ups can be heard.)

Aya—there they are. Not much happens before noon. Theatre folks sleep late. So, another day's begun. There's Lisabette Cartwright walking into Studio C. She graduated from the S.M.U. (*Southern Methodist*) drama department and began teaching third grade. Then she was invited all the way to New York for an audition because the producer once had her appendix removed by one of her uncles. Lisabette's really excited, and her mom, who is at this moment canning okra, is too. Over there is Casey Mulgraw, the one dressed in the skirt/pants thing, a lot of people call her the Queen of off-off Broadway. She's a little hung over because she just celebrated the opening of her 200th play without ever having been paid a salary. She also has a yeast infection that is really pissing her off. In our town, we like to know the facts about everybody.

(NOTE: All scene and costume changes are done by six female "changers," dressed in a variety of contemporary styles, but all in black. T-Anne, the stage manager, moves to a small out-of-the-way table where she sits and follows the script. Three folding chairs are placed to create the waiting room of Studio C. Casey, a woman of thirty-six waits. Lisabette, twenty-four, enters. She has a rolling suitcase.)

LISABETTE: Hi. *(Casey nods.)* Is this the Studio C waiting room for Actors Express? *(Casey nods.)* *Three Sisters* audition? *(Casey nods.)* Oh, my heavens, it's so humid! I feel like I'm oiled up for the beach or something. I surely admire your fortitude in wearing both skirt and pants. Bet you're auditioning for Olga, huh?

CASEY: Why? Because Olga is older and homely and a spinster and has no life of her own and thus has assumed the role of caregiver to her brother and it's usually thought to be the least interesting acting role of the *The Three Sisters*. Would that be it?

LISABETTE: Well, no, I…

CASEY: It's what you meant.

LISABETTE: I think I'll just start over. *(She does.)* Hi.

CASEY: Hi.

LISABETTE: I'm Lisabette Cartwright, from La Vernia, Texas. Graduated S.M.U. but then I taught third grade for two years, bein' scared of an actor's life, and Maple Elementary loved me and wants me back anytime, but in a dream the Lord himself reaffirmed my calling so I made my comeback in *Fiddler on the Roof* but this is my first New York audition and I'm so jumpy my breasts bob even when I walk real slow. What's your name?

CASEY: Casey Mulgraw, one of my breasts had to be surgically removed because of a malignancy and I seem to be in remission but who knows how long that will last.

LISABETTE: Oh, my G-o-o-d-d-d!

CASEY: Want to do one more take?

LISABETTE: No, I would like you to forgive me for bein' such a dipshit, pardon the language, Jesus. I'm real sorry for your troubles and it looks to me like they did a real good match.

CASEY: *(Chuckles.)* And yes, I'm reading for Olga for the obvious reasons.

LISABETTE: Really, I think Olga is the most spiritual of all the sisters.

CASEY: Good try. You don't have a smoke by any chance?

LISABETTE: Ummmm, I don't.

CASEY: Cough drop?

LISABETTE: Beef jerky.

CASEY: No thanks.

LISABETTE: I'm auditioning for Masha.

CASEY: The dark, passionate, amoral poetess. I feel dark; men call me passionate; I'm definitely amoral, and I've actually had several poems published but they never, never, never let me read for that part.

LISABETTE: Because you're a little plain?

CASEY: Thank you for speaking the unspeakable.

LISABETTE: I did it again, huh? I'm, oh my, very nervous but that's just no excuse. I would like to say I'm in way over my head and could I have a hug?

CASEY: *(Not unkindly.)* If it's absolutely necessary.

(They hug. The stage manager enters to speak to the actors. A rolling door might divide the spaces. Behind her, a table with three chairs is set up as the audition room. Ralph Brightly, an English director, and Kate, the producer, are at the table. In a third chair, to the side, sits Holly Seabé, a TV goddess who is pre-cast as Irina and is helping audition.)

STAGE MANAGER: Ms. Todoravskia is ready to see you both.

CASEY: Both?

STAGE MANAGER: Both. Hustle it up, we're running behind.

LISABETTE: *(Still in the anteroom. To Casey.)* Do they usually see actors in groups?

CASEY: No. And we're not a group.

(Casey and Lisabette enter the audition room.)

KATE: *(Rising.)* Hi. I am Katrina Todoravskia, Producing Director of Actors Express. And you are?

LISABETTE: Me?

KATE: You.

LISABETTE: I'm sorry, I forgot the question.

CASEY: Your name.

LISABETTE: Oh, Lisabette Cartwright.

(Kate kisses Lisabette's hand extended for a shake.)

KATE: You are devastatingly beautiful. *(Turns to Casey.)* And I gather you're here to audition for Olga?

CASEY: How'd you guess?

KATE: You look like an Olga.

CASEY: Thanks.

KATE: This is the play's director, Ralph Brightly; he runs the Toads Hall Rep in London.

RALPH: *(Shaking hands.)* Well, a stone's throw outside, really. *(Shakes Lisabette's hand.)* Charmed. *(Shakes Casey's hand.)* Pleased.

KATE: *(Gesturing toward Holly.)* And this is…

LISABETTE: Oh my G-o-o-d-d, you're Holly Seabé. I can't believe it! Holly Seabé. I love your TV show! Your character is so kooky and glamorous. You have such great timing. I've learned practically everything I know about foreplay from that show. You are so liberated!

HOLLY: Thanks.

LISABETTE: Oh my God, pardon me Jesus, are you going to be in the play?

HOLLY: Irina.

LISABETTE: *(Clapping her hands.)* She's going to be in the play. This is way cool! *(To Casey.)* Isn't that cool?

CASEY: *(Smiling, but a bit reserved.)* Yes, cool.

HOLLY: Thanks.

LISABETTE: I am so stoked!

RALPH: Yes, well, off we go then. *Three Sister*s, as you know, by Anton Pavlovitch himself. I'll just drop some breadcrumbs along the path before we hear you…

KATE: Running forty minutes behind.

RALPH: Right. Straight along. Give you the gist in five words. Funny, funny, funny, funny, tragic.

CASEY: We're referring to *Three Sisters*?

RALPH: *The Three Sisters*, yes.

CASEY: Funny, funny, funny, funny, tragic?

RALPH: *Funny*, funny, funny, *funny*, tragic.

CASEY: Okay, I can do that.

LISABETTE: Do what?

CASEY: Show him that in our auditions.

LISABETTE: Gee, I didn't think it was funny.

RALPH: Precisely, that's to be our little revelation.

KATE: Forty minutes late.

RALPH: Right then, on we go.

(*A young woman in the audience rises and says:*)

JOBY: Excuse me.

RALPH: Let's get cracking.

JOBY: Excuse me.

(*The actors glance up, confused. The "director" tries to go on.*)

RALPH: It's Chekhov, don't you see, so we're certainly not ready to do text.

JOBY: (*From the audience.*) Excuse me.

(*The actors stop. They look to Kate.*)

KATE: Yes?

JOBY: Is the director...ummm...

RALPH: (*Supplying the character name.*) Ralph.

JOBY: Right, Ralph. Is it supposed to be a man played by a woman?

KATE: Yes. (*To Ralph.*) Go on.

JOBY: How come?

RALPH: You mean why am I playing a man?

JOBY: I mean what's the point?

RALPH: Could you possibly sit down and let us act?

KATE: Wait. (*To Joby.*) Hi.

JOBY: Hi.

KATE: What's your name?

JOBY: Joby. But I...

KATE: Joby, we want to thank you for coming to the theater; we need young audiences.

RALPH: But...

KATE: Shhhh. Now you'll understand this as a woman, Joby...

RALPH: Could she please...

(*Kate silences Ralph with a look.*)

KATE: Eighty percent of the roles in the American theater are played by men, and 90 percent of the directors are men. The point of having a male director played by a woman is to redress the former and satirize the latter. How's that?

JOBY: *(After a brief pause.)* Okay.

> *(She sits down. Kate nods at Ralph.)*

RALPH: Right. Onward and upward, eh? *(He looks at Casey.)* What I'd like you to do, sweetie, is use only the word "tiddlypee" as text... *(He looks at Lisabette.)* And you, dear, will say only "tiddlypoo." With these words, we will now play the scene where Masha tells Olga she's leaving her husband Kulygin and leaving town with the soldier Vershinin.

CASEY: But there is no such scene.

RALPH: Yes, precisely.

CASEY: So why?

RALPH: *(Sweetly.)* You don't wish to audition?

CASEY: That's the answer to "why"?

RALPH: Look, dear...

> *(Lisabette, trying to circumvent the oncoming conflict, goes into the improvisation.)*

LISABETTE: *(You wished to see me?)* Tiddlypoo, tiddlypoo?

CASEY: *(Is it true you and Vershinin are in love?)* Tiddlypee, tiddlypee, tiddlypee...tiddlypee?

LISABETTE: *(I am leaving Kulygin and going away with Vershinin.)* Tiddlypoo, tiddlypoo...tiddlypoo...tiddlypoo, tiddlypoo, tiddlypoo, tiddlypoo.

CASEY: *(If you go, what will happen to me?)* Tiddlypee...tiddlypee, tiddlypee, tiddlypee?

LISABETTE: *(You'll be fine.)* Tiddlypoo, tiddlypoo.

CASEY: *(To Ralph.)* How am I supposed to know what she's saying?

RALPH: Well, that would be the heart of the audition, wouldn't it?

> *(Casey tries once more.)*

CASEY: *(If you go, we'll be left with Natasha!)* Tiddlypee, tiddlypee...tiddlypee, tiddlypee. *(She stops.)* Look, this is ridiculous.

RALPH: *(Coolly.)* Really?

CASEY: Well, yes, really. Can't we just do a scene using the script? I mean that would be sensible, right?

RALPH: Perhaps to an American actress, dear.

CASEY: *(Not happy.)* Ummmmmmm...

LISABETTE: Oh, but this is fun. Don't you think it's fun? It's kind of interesting.

CASEY: *(Slow burn.)* American actress.

LISABETTE: *(Feeling the tension.)* Just really, really, really, really fun!

CASEY: *(Burning.)* You know, Ralph...dear...you Brits are arrogant, pompous, chauvinistic, smug, insufferable boors who take jobs from American actors and directors because of the toadying of the American press and the Anglophile American rich, and I've seen Chekhov done in London that really smelled up the place with its stiff-upper-lip, over practical, no-self-pity-or-despair-here-darling style that has nothing, nothing to do with Russian passion or spiritual darkness, so…

JOBY: Excuse me.

CASEY: *(Still on the emotional high.)* What?! What do you want?

KATE: Easy.

JOBY: Isn't this all just a little self-referential?

KATE: I'm sorry, Joby, but we are trying to perform a play and…

JOBY: I mean it's all just about the theater. Isn't that a little precious?

KATE: Why?

JOBY: Well, theater people talking about theater.

KATE: As opposed to theater people talking about the international monetary fund or the cloning of sheep?

JOBY: Well, is theater culturally important enough to be the subject of a play?

RALPH: Nice of you to buy a ticket.

JOBY: Actually, they're comps.

RALPH: Ah.

JOBY: I'd think your only hope is to work on a deeply personal and profoundly emotional level.

CASEY: Well, the thing about the Brits is very emotional.

RALPH: And plays aren't ordinarily deeply personal until after the exposition.

JOBY: Oh.

CASEY: Later on, the play takes hold, and there is devastating loss and a lot of really profound metaphors that will knock your socks off. I mean, knock your socks off!

JOBY: Oh.

CASEY: Okay?

JOBY: *(A brief pause.)* Fine.
(She sits down.)

CASEY: *(Going back,)* …with its stiff-upper-lip, over-practical, no-self-pity-or-despair-here-darling style that has nothing, nothing to do with Russian passion or spiritual darkness. So don't give me that American actress crap!
(A tense moment.)

RALPH: Right. Nicely done. I think I've seen more than enough. Thanks ever so for coming in.

LISABETTE: We're finished?

RALPH: Lovely work, sweetie. *(Turning to Casey, smiling.)* And I quite agree with you, dear, when Americans do Chekhov, it's just awash in self-pity.

(Casey gives him the finger and stalks out.)

LISABETTE: Well, anyway, this was my first professional audition, and it was really a lot of fun, and I want to thank you for calling me in and I really hope to work for you someday and... *(She begins to cry.)* ...and I'm sorry I'm crying. I didn't mean to cry, and I've never even been to London but...she's right, you're a real jerk.

(She runs out, leaving Ralph, Kate, and Holly alone.)

RALPH: *(Ironically.)* Well, that was a breath of fresh air.

KATE: Ralph, I want to apologize to you as an American...

RALPH: No, no...

KATE: I've seen hundreds, thousands of auditions, and I never...

RALPH: No need, sweetie...

KATE: I mean, who do they think they are?

RALPH: Made their beds, haven't they? Fat chance they'll be getting any work from this old British fairy.

(Kate laughs appreciatively.)

HOLLY: I liked them. *(They turn to look at her.)* I've been treated like dirt in situations like this, but now I'm rich and famous and you need me so you're sort of shit out of luck, huh? So here's the deal: I liked them and I'm bored with auditions so they're over and those two are in our play.

RALPH: Miss Seabé, they do not have the requisite talent.

HOLLY: Well, neither do I so maybe nobody will notice. *(She starts to exit.)* One thing, though. The little sweet one from Texas should play Irina, and I'll play Masha. Oh, and the Olga...well, she's Olga. Tiddlypee, tiddlypoo.

RALPH: So, Kate, love, I gather that's the horse that pulls our custard wagon, eh?

KATE: Well...

RALPH: Not to worry. In the kingdom of the barbarians, shit tastes like veal.

(Lights change. Furniture is removed as Casey and Lisabette move into two specials, where they talk to their mothers on the "phone.")

LISABETTE: Ma? It's me, Lisabette...

CASEY: Mother, okay, don't go ballistic...

LISABETTE: I got it! I got it! I got it! I got the part!

CASEY: Yes, I know I'm thirty-six years old, and I still have $40,000 in student loans...

LISABETTE: Ma, Ma, wait, no, there's more...

CASEY: Yes, I would have to leave my day job...

LISABETTE: I'm gonna act with a TV star!

CASEY: Okay, the real deal…

LISABETTE: Holly Seabé! Yes! Me and Holly Seabé; can you believe it?

CASEY: Yes, it's kind of a crappy part; it's some hick town in Texas; the salary is like pesos; I'll lose my job; you won't have anybody to abuse but, lest we forget here, I'm supposed to be an actress!

LISABETTE: Ma, it's Chekhov!

CASEY: Mother…

LISABETTE: He's a Russian.

CASEY: Mother…

LISABETTE: No, it's beautiful and wise and sad, and I get to be a real professional!

CASEY: Screw you! Mother!

LISABETTE: Love you, Ma!

CASEY: *(Hanging up.)* Damnit!

LISABETTE: *(Hanging up.)* Yes!

(Two connected plane seats are brought on. Lisabette and Casey move to sit in them. We hear an airport announcement.)

GATE ANNOUNCER: Flight number 270 to San Antonio, Texas, gate 27B, boarding is now complete. Flight number 270. All passengers…

CASEY: My dad's great. I worked weekends for a thousand years in his hardware store.

LISABETTE: You are kidding!

CASEY: What kidding?

LISABETTE: My dad has a hardware store.

CASEY: Yeah?

LISABETTE: You sorted screws?

CASEY: Oh yeah. *(They smile.)* Your dad want you to run it?

LISABETTE: Me? No. He sold it. He works in a community center.

CASEY: Well, my dad wants me. I dream I take it over and I wake up, stapled to three-quarter inch plywood, screaming. Okay, the hardware connection.

LISABETTE: You're not married, right?

CASEY: I'm not married, right. You?

LISABETTE: I can't abide sex.

CASEY: Oh.

LISABETTE: Well, temporarily. I've kinda had some bad luck.

CASEY: Doesn't hold me back.

LISABETTE: I was kinda doin' it with my high school boyfriend in the back of his car, an' we were hit from behind by a drunk in a pickup.

CASEY: Ouch.

LISABETTE: They said they'd never seen that kind of whiplash.

CASEY: Sorry.

LISABETTE: Meanwhile, back at school I was kind of bein' forced into an affair by my history teacher an' just after that I was sort of halfway raped by a plumber.

CASEY: *(Horrified.)* Jesus.

LISABETTE: No, it wasn't too bad really. I had to deal, y'know? The only bad part was for three years I couldn't touch a man, even like a handshake, without throwing up. Projectile vomiting, so there were some awkward moments at parties.

CASEY: You're kidding me, right?

LISABETTE: No, really, it wasn't so bad. I'm over it, except really, really occasionally when I first meet people. How about your relationships?

CASEY: A lot of casual sex.

LISABETTE: Really.

CASEY: A lot. Always with members of the cast. And I've done 200 plays off-off.

LISABETTE: Wow.

CASEY: Outside of rehearsal, I'm actually a virgin.

LISABETTE: Wow.

CASEY: Of course, I'm always in rehearsal.

LISABETTE: Oh, I really respect that. I'm a virgin too. Except for being harassed, whiplashed, and on New Year's Eve.

(Holly enters from first class.)

CASEY: Hi.

LISABETTE: Oh my God.

HOLLY: I saw you guys when you came through first class.

LISABETTE: We walked right by you!?

HOLLY: No problem. I was enjoying some brain surgeon hitting on me.

LISABETTE: Excuse me, but…shoot…I just want to say that when Kate, the producer person, made me the offer…well…she said you had put in a word for us…me and Casey…Casey and I…God, I am such a hick, pardon me Jesus, anyway…thank you, thank you, thank you!

CASEY: It was really nice.

HOLLY: Well, hey, yeah I did, thanks but, you know, I was like nobody once too. Really down on the food chain like you guys…ummm…I won't even tell you the stuff I went through. Well, okay, the easy stuff was being told I had no talent like that director piranha said about you, right? And my deal was that talent isn't the point here…I mean, we're going to whatever Texas or wherever. Like, nobody who is anybody will see us or care. Maybe excepting my manager who has time for one client, me, and who would not care diddly dick if you guys had talent or not. *(A brief awkwardness.)* But the point is…you didn't think I meant you had no talent, did you?

CASEY: No, no.

LISABETTE: No, no.

HOLLY: Because you can understand I have no way of knowing that. I mean… tiddlypee, tiddlypoo.

LISABETTE: Right.

CASEY: Right.

HOLLY: My point is you guys were disrespected and he had to pay.

CASEY: You mean…

HOLLY: I mean, once they said you had no talent, I had to see you were hired.

LISABETTE: Wow.

HOLLY: Because I had that pulled on me, and now that will not happen in my presence. Like I'm the respect police.

CASEY: Thanks.

HOLLY: No problem. So I just wanted to shed a little light.

LISABETTE: That is really so nice.

CASEY: Just think, all of us have been told we have no talent.

HOLLY: Exactly!

CASEY: Well, that's something to build on.

HOLLY: Yeah, that's the other thing. We have to stick together down there in…

CASEY: Texas.

LISABETTE: Oh absolutely.

HOLLY: Because I have this intuition it's going to be like combat, but we stick together, we make them pay.

LISABETTE: Like we were three sisters.

HOLLY: That is so sweet and so right. That like zaps my guts.

CASEY: There's an empty seat.

HOLLY: Nah, I got to go back, I don't eat pretzels.

LISABETTE: We're talking about guys.

HOLLY: Them I eat. See you later.

(Holly leaves. Three folding chairs are set, facing two other chairs for the next scene. Please remember the changes are cinematic. We never stop or take the lights out for a change.)

T-ANNE: Please place your seats and tray tables in an upright position; we are beginning our descent into San Antonio.

(We are now in the rehearsal room on the first day. Kate, Casey, Holly, Lis-

abette, and the new director, an African-American woman named Andwyneth Wyoré.)

KATE: *(Addressing them.)* Actors Express. Get it? Express? We are a serious theater. We are unique. What is our artistic policy? Well, I can state that policy clearly. We live these ideas. At Actors Express, we call them the Seven Virtues. Number one, we do plays that... *(She makes a complex gesture.)* Two: our style is surgically defined as... *(A series of sounds.)* And only that. Fourthly, multicultural new works from the classical repertoire that say to the audience... *(An even more complex gesture.)* So that, in summation, or seventh, we can say... *(She stares at the ceiling, thinking.)* and we say that with no fear of being misunderstood. Oh, I know, this policy makes us controversial. We offend, we pique, we challenge while at the same time bringing together, healing, and making our community one. In a nutshell. This unique mission has made us essential to San Antonio, not because...is there something out the window?

CASEY: Sorry.

KATE: Not because I have the best education money can buy...

LISABETTE: Wow.

KATE: Stanford, Harvard, Yale, but because... *(Holly is doctoring her lipstick.)* Holly, if you give this a chance, I think you'll find it's crucial to our work.

HOLLY: Stanford, Harvard, Yale...

KATE: Precisely.

HOLLY: *(Pointing at herself.)* Biddyup High, Biddyup, Nebraska.

KATE: But because...hear this...contemporary relevance.

CASEY: Contemporary relevance.

KATE: Contemporary relevance.

CASEY: Yes.

KATE: Our raison d'être! Does anyone find what I said moving? *(Lisabette raises her hand.)* Because I am moved, and it is central to our aesthetic. *(Lisabette applauds.)* Now I wanted to meet with you, our three sisters, before the rest of our cast arrived, to bond as sisters and to achieve a... It's now my pleasure to introduce our director, Andwyneth Wyoré, Artistic Director of San Antonio's Black Rage Ensemble. We're involved in an exciting cultural exchange with Black Rage.

HOLLY: Doesn't that happen between countries?

KATE: Excuse me?

HOLLY: Cultural exchange?

ANDWYNETH: *(Chuckling.)* You got that right, girl.

KATE: Interestingly enough, Andwyneth also went to Stanford, Harvard, and Yale.

ANDWYNETH: 'Course I went free.

CASEY: What happened to the Brit?

KATE: Well, there were...

KATE/ANDWYNETH/HOLLY: Artistic differences.

ANDWYNETH: Uh-huh.

KATE: And I came to feel a sister...

ANDWYNETH: Girl, I'm not your sister. My momma see you, she faint, girl. She smack my daddy with an iron skillet! Huh-uh, baby, we got a little mutual use goin'. How about that? Down here in San Antonio you get some black people, some white people in the same room, there's always some foundation goes orgasmic. *(Cries deep in the act of sex.)* Multicultural! Multicultural! Yes! Yes!! Multicultural!! *(Back to her own voice.)* Pay a little rent, right? Suck a little green. Hey, I never did no white play, dig? Y'all a mystery to me, but I tell you one thing on Brother Chekhov, he just talk, talk, talk, talk, talk! Lord have mercy!

KATE: Well yes, but...

ANDWYNETH: Whine, whine, whine. Man, he got the self-pity diarrhea! Gushin' it out all over! Cut all that shit, X it out! Get down on the race question, down on the poverty question, get down on abuse of power, baby! No more, "Whine and dine with Brother Chekhov." Huh-uh. We gonna heat this sucker up! No script, huh-uh. I don't do script. Hell with that! What I see is a little white sisters thing, an' a black peasants thing. Little dance drama thing, little street corner doo-wap. *(Holly raises hand.)* S'up, girl?

HOLLY: I'm doing the script.

ANDWYNETH: You didn't follow the conversation?

HOLLY: Yeah, I can follow it, but I'm not doing that.

ANDWYNETH: Who the hell are you, girl?

HOLLY: You watch TV?

ANDWYNETH: Hell no, colored people all live in a cave.

HOLLY: I'm a big TV star.

ANDWYNETH: Well girl, you just pat yourself right on the back.

HOLLY: They begged me to come down here to wherever Texas to do a classic style play. I don't give a shit about the race question or the poverty question. I don't have those problems. I got the film problem. I need to do film. No film, no respect. It's kind of like the race problem only in show business.

ANDWYNETH: You crazy, huh?

HOLLY: Yeah. So the rap is, you do TV you can't act. So my manager says to go backdoor. Get a little respect. Chekhov, Shakespeare, that stuff gives you shine. So like then you're a classical actress with fabulous breasts, and you can segue into sci-fi, action, cop-schlock, meet-cute, or any genre.

ANDWYNETH: Let's cut to the bottom line, sister.

HOLLY: I'm saying every syllable Chekhov wrote, slow and clear.

ANDWYNETH: See, you are so far from my trip I can't even find you on the map.

HOLLY: Ms. Wyoré, the real difference between the two of us isn't what you think.

ANDWYNETH: Well, little thing, you bring it on.

HOLLY: The real difference is, you're fired.

(Andwyneth looks at Kate.)

KATE: *(At a loss.)* Well…

HOLLY: Trust me.

ANDWYNETH: You are one straight-up, no kiddin' around, in-your-face, don't-misunderstand-me, bitch.

HOLLY: Sometimes, things just don't…work out.

ANDWYNETH: *(Focusing on Kate.)* What are you, invisible?

KATE: Ummmmm…

ANDWYNETH: She's the deal, or you're the deal?

(Holly also focuses on Kate.)

KATE: *(Finally, to Andwyneth.)* She's the deal.

ANDWYNETH: You get me down here, whip up a little money on my color, cast a buncha white girls an' then blow me off 'cause this prime-time toots shows up? *(To Kate.)* I'm gonna pin "racist" to your ass, Momma. They gonna burn you in the public square to get right with my people. There won't be nothin' left of you but little snowy white ashes, dig? You an' Chekhov is both toast!

(She exits.)

KATE: Ummm…if you'll excuse me.

(She exits to talk to Andwyneth. The sisters are silent for a moment.)

CASEY: Anyone want some Skittles?

LISABETTE: You just fired the director in front of the producer without asking.

HOLLY: I am saying the lines.

CASEY: She's saying the lines.

HOLLY: Directors are a very gray area for me. It has been my experience that they actually like to be fired because they suffer from severe performance anxiety. They have these pushy little egos but hardly any usable information, which makes them very sad and time-consuming. I wouldn't worry because after you fire them, they usually find successful careers on cruise ships where they are completely harmless.

LISABETTE: But to do that, is that ethical?

HOLLY: Lisabette, I like you. I do. You seem like a very nice person. I'm not a very nice person, but I can still appreciate one when I see her.

LISABETTE: Thanks.

HOLLY: In college plays, community stuff, arty nowheres-ville professional gigs like this, there is probably something called ethics, but up where the eagles fly and the wolves run, up where American presidents screw the actresses, there is only power. The ethics thing is a little foggy. Power, on the other hand, is clear, it's clear, it's understood. For a very short time, Lisabette, here in wherever-it-is Texas, you will fly with an eagle. Say whoosh.

LISABETTE: Whoosh.

HOLLY: Enjoy.

(At this moment, Ben Shipwright, a craggy actor, enters. He is playing Vershinin.)

BEN: Hello, ladies.

LISABETTE: Hi.

CASEY: Hi.

HOLLY: Hi.

BEN: Ben Shipwright. Gonna play Vershinin.

CASEY: Olga, the boring sister.

LISABETTE: Masha. But I can't shake your hand right now. I'll explain later.

HOLLY: Masha.

LISABETTE: You're playing Masha?

HOLLY: We'll talk. Where are you from, Ben?

BEN: Right around here. I do some acting but I actually make my living singing country.

LISABETTE: Oh my God, you're Ben Shipwright?

BEN: Yeah.

LISABETTE: Oh my God, I love your records!

HOLLY: You record?

BEN: Little bit.

LISABETTE: Little bit? This week he has two singles in Top 50 Country!

HOLLY: Really?

CASEY: Mazeltov.

BEN: *(To Holly and Casey.)* You girls from New York?

CASEY: Yeah.

HOLLY: L.A.

BEN: *(To Lisabette.)* Now I know you're a home girl.

LISABETTE: How do you know?

BEN: Well, you talk San Antonio and you listen to a bunch of no-good pickers like me.

HOLLY: Ben?

BEN: Yes ma'am.

HOLLY: This relationship thing that goes down between Masha and Vershinin? We probably should get together and talk that out.

BEN: Be my pleasure. I'll let y'all get settled.
(He starts to exit.)

HOLLY: Dinner?

BEN: I'm sorry, you speakin' to me?

HOLLY: I was speaking to you.

BEN: Well…ummm…I don't believe I caught your name.

HOLLY: Holly Seabé.

BEN: Well, Miss Seabé, I got me a couple of kids want me to barbecue some ribs tonight.
(Starts to exit.)

HOLLY: Drink later?

BEN: Well, ummm, no ma'am. No ma'am, I can't. No offense intended.

HOLLY: *(Smiling, but not pleased.)* Really?

BEN: No ma'am, I better not. My wife…

HOLLY: How old are your kids?

BEN: Four and seven. Seven and a half.

HOLLY: Won't they be asleep?

BEN: *(They regard each other.)* Just no-can-do, ma'am. *(Shakes her hand.)* Real pleased to meet you. Lookin' forward to rehearsal. Catch y'all later.
(He exits.)

LISABETTE: I don't think he knew who you were! Can you believe that? I mean, you are on the cover of *TV Guide!*

HOLLY: I'll have to buy him a copy.

LISABETTE: But, am I right or am I wrong, he is really cute!

CASEY: My take is if you… *(She indicates Holly.)* …come on to a guy, looking the way you do, and he stiffs you while talking about his kids, he is *really* unavailable.

HOLLY: If I come on to a guy…and I'm not saying I did…that guy can kiss his previous life good-bye for as long as I find said guy entertaining. And on this I would be willing to wager some fairly serious money.

CASEY: I think serious money to me and serious money to you could be seriously different.

LISABETTE: But what about his wife and kids?

HOLLY and CASEY: Shhh.

HOLLY: Okay, forget the money thing. We'll bet hair. Loser shaves her head.

LISABETTE: Wow.

CASEY: You can't afford to shave your head.

HOLLY: I won't have to.

CASEY: The guy's straight from Norman Rockwell.

HOLLY: I could screw anybody Norman Rockwell ever drew.

LISABETTE: This is so yeasty!

CASEY: Let's get it on.

(She holds out her hand. Holly shakes it.)

HOLLY: He's going down.

LISABETTE: You aren't Baptist, huh?

HOLLY: Hey, Lisabette?

LISABETTE: Uh-huh?

HOLLY: I'm going to play Masha because it's the best part, and the most powerful person plays the best part. That's one of Hollywood's ten commandments. You'll play Irina, because I say so, but also because she's the youngest and you're the youngest and you would be really good doing her because you have yet to become a completely calcified diva.

LISABETTE: (Not at all upset.) Okay.

HOLLY: Everything's copasetic. Hey, let's go to the apartment hotel and get settled in fleabag hell and then find some cowboy dive with pine paneling and get unbelievably plotzed before tomorrow's first rehearsal, because I need to be hungover to face whatever director she digs up next.

(A scene change starts. Eventually, there will be two single beds, two chairs, and a rolling door in place. This scene is played during the change.)

JOBY: (From the audience.) Excuse me. (Scene change continues.) Excuse me.

T-ANNE: What?

JOBY: Well, I…didn't you…

T-ANNE: Hey, spit it out; I'm busy.

JOBY: Well, didn't you consider that role offensive?

T-ANNE: Did you notice we're doing a scene change?

JOBY: Golly, as a person of color…

T-ANNE: You're a person of color?

JOBY: No, you are.

T-ANNE: Ooooo, I hate it when I forget.

JOBY: But, wasn't that... *(Whispers.)* ...stereotyped behavior?

T-ANNE: *(Again stopping her work.)* Listen, I have to...all right, okay...listen, Babyface, I would like to do something, almost anything, where nice white people like you didn't feel like they had to defend me. Particularly... *(Whispers back.)* ...in the middle of a scene change. *(Goes back to work.)*

JOBY: But it satirizes your political...

T-ANNE: Got to go.

JOBY: But, aren't you...

T-ANNE: No, I'm not. Want to know why?

JOBY: Oh, I do.

T-ANNE: 'Cause if I didn't do the plays that offended my color or politics or sex or religion or taste, I'd be shit out of work. Lights!

(She exits. The scene light snaps on. Joby is still standing.)

CASEY: *(To Joby, not unkindly.)* Sit down, Joby. *(Starting the scene.)* I am leveled by that last drink. I am, as my beloved father would say, schnockered. *(Sings.)* Tell me I can't sing Karaoke?

HOLLY: You can't sing Karaoke.

LISABETTE: This is so amazing, it's like a pajama party.

HOLLY: *(Patting her knee.)* It is a pajama party.

LISABETTE: I mean, here I am, just out of drama school, and I am completely drunk, talking with real actors in a real way, including a great actress of the stage and a great actress from TV, and it just makes me want to cry.

HOLLY: Don't cry. Where did the vodka go?

LISABETTE: Holly, can I ask you a question?

HOLLY: Here it is. *(Pours herself another drink.)*

LISABETTE: It's something about acting.

HOLLY: I don't know anything about acting.

LISABETTE: Okay then, have you had breast implants?

HOLLY: Yes.

LISABETTE: Yes?!

HOLLY: Yes.

CASEY: That actually makes me feel better.

HOLLY: I have had seventeen separate surgical procedures to make me the completely natural beauty you see before you. They have even reshaped my toes because I do a lot of swimsuit.

LISABETTE: Those are artificial toes?

HOLLY: They are not artificial, they have been slimmed.

CASEY: How much?

HOLLY: Altogether?

CASEY: For the toes?

HOLLY: Seventeen thousand dollars.

LISABETTE: Wow.

CASEY: How much would it take to make me beautiful?

HOLLY: You're serious?

CASEY: Yeah.

HOLLY: Take off the sweatshirt.

(She does.)

LISABETTE: But beauty is subjective.

HOLLY: Not in Hollywood. Stand up and turn around. Over here. Over here, over here. *(Casey does.)* Look at the ceiling. *(She does.)* Hold your arms out like wings. Look left. Look right. Okay. I could be off 10, even 15 percent here depending on bone and muscle structure, but my estimate would be $600,000.

CASEY: Go ahead, flatter me.

HOLLY: Oh, there are divas who have paid more, and the kicker is even then there's no guarantee the camera loves you.

LISABETTE: Oh my God.

HOLLY and CASEY: Pardon me Jesus.

CASEY: I'm giving it one more year.

(Refreshes her drink.)

LISABETTE: Give what?

CASEY: This. I don't have to put up with this hellish life. I have other skills.

HOLLY: Let me guess…

CASEY: For six years I worked in a slaughterhouse.

LISABETTE: No.

CASEY: Yeah.

LISABETTE: No way. You worked in your dad's hardware store.

CASEY: That was earlier. Where's the chocolates?

HOLLY: *(Handing her the box.)* There's only creams left.

CASEY: I took the slaughterhouse job because it paid more than waitressing, and I could cut the pigs' throats at night, which left my days free to audition.

HOLLY: Was there a lot of blood?

CASEY: Gouts.

HOLLY: I hate blood.

LISABETTE: I faint. I fainted the first time I had my period.

CASEY: I mean, look at us. Holly's the Frankenstein monster. You teach third grade. I support myself as a murderess from midnight to dawn so I can do godawful plays for free in black box theaters built into linen closets in welfare hotels. This is a career in the arts in America.

LISABETTE: But now we get to do Chekhov! It's like lacework. It's beautiful and delicate and demands everything. Everything! It's unbearably sweet and sad and painful, just like our lives.

HOLLY: Don't you love her.

CASEY: Plus I get a paycheck so my mother will think acting is actually a job.

LISABETTE: No, but it's Chekhov!

CASEY: As long as it pays the bills.

LISABETTE: That's so cynical.

CASEY: Lisabette, sweetie, I'm not cynical. Look at me. I'm like a beating heart you can hold in your hand. I just happen to live in a country where they give people who do what I do endless shit.

LISABETTE: But why can't it be beautiful? I want it to be beautiful.

CASEY: Lisabette, you're drunk.

LISABETTE: I am, I'm really drunk. But the three of us are so sad, right? I mean, I'm sad because I'm hopelessly naïve and have absolutely no idea what will become of me, like I'm running down the railway tracks and the train is coming. *(To Casey.)* And you're sad because you're hoping against hope when you really probably know there is no hope. *(To Holly.)* And you're sad because…why are you sad, I forget?

HOLLY: I am sad because that beautiful country singer dissed me, and now I'm going to have to make him pay, and that'll make me feel bad about myself, and that'll put me back in therapy which means I have to switch therapists because my last one is too busy writing screenplays.

LISABETTE: See, Chekhov knows us.

CASEY: *(Nodding.)* 'Fraid so.

LISABETTE: To Chekhov.

(There is a knock on the door.)

LISABETTE: Who is it?

KATE: *(Outside.)* Lisabette? It's Kate. Kate Todoravskia. I wondered if you would like to drink red wine with me and make love?

LISABETTE: *(Sotto voice to the sisters.)* Oh my God.

KATE: I find you unbearably beautiful. I can't think, I can't eat. I want to produce *Romeo and Juliet* for you.

LISABETTE: *(To the sisters.)* What do I do?

(Holly beckons her over and whispers.)

KATE: I just want to hold you. You could move into my apartment. I have a satellite dish.

LISABETTE: Kate?

KATE: *(Still outside.)* Yes?

LISABETTE: It's a little awkward because I'm in here having sex with Holly.

(She mouths "Pardon me Jesus" to the ceiling.)

KATE: With Holly?

HOLLY: With Holly.

KATE: Oh…never mind…good-bye.

(They wait as Kate's footsteps recede.)

CASEY: Now that's Chekhov.

LISABETTE: Thank you, thank you, thank you!

HOLLY: No problem.

LISABETTE: *(Turning to Casey, meaning Kate's crush.)* Did you know that?

(Casey indicates "yes.")

HOLLY: Hey, Lisabette.

LISABETTE: What?

HOLLY: In my world, you'd be right there looking at her satellite dish.

(A change now moves from the apartment to a circle of folding chairs. It takes place during the opening half of Kate's speech.)

KATE: Dearest friends. Dearest, dearest actors. You may wonder why at this our first rehearsal I have spoken of my childhood for three hours. Why, I have told you of my mother, the only American killed by prairie dogs, of my father whose love of literature inspired him to inscribe three chapters of Tolstoy's *War and Peace* on the convex side of a single contact lens, which was then tragically lost at Daytona Beach. These then are the threads with which I wove my love of the Russian Classics, and then carried in my heart here to San Antonio…San Antonio is to Houston as rural Russia is to Moscow. The sisters of San Antonio, their hearts beat with this play. We know what it is to be isolated, vulgarized, we know what it is to work! This play runs in our veins. Its pain is our pain. The pain of the women of San Antonio. So I say to you, on the brink of rehearsal, the final lines of Chekhov's Texas play, *The Three Sisters*, "In a little while we shall know why we live and why we suffer!"

(Applause from those gathered.)

CASEY: But that's not the final line, right?

KATE: I was speaking metaphorically.

CASEY: Because the final line is, "If only we knew."

KATE: Yes, Casey, that is the final line. Thank you.

CASEY: Said twice.

KATE: I'd like to move on if that's all right?

CASEY: Hey, it's your theater.

KATE: Thank you. Thank you. And now it is my extraordinary pleasure to introduce our fabulous director, Wikéwitch Konalkvis, a fellow Pole and recent émigré who has directed seventy-one Chekhov productions and…

WIKÉWITCH: Seventy-two.

KATE: …Seventy-two productions and…

WIKÉWITCH: No, you are right, seventy-one.

KATE: …Seventy-one productions and…

WIKÉWITCH: Every one jewel. Make beating heart of Chekhov.

KATE: …and I just want to say…

WIKÉWITCH: Make beautiful from the pain of love this life which is like some…

KATE: …he is so…

WIKÉWITCH: You, I know, will play Olga. You have pain. Have loss. Radiating of loss. Good. Good Olga.

KATE: I just want to say, and I'm likely to get a little emotional…

HOLLY: Could we go around the room and meet the other actors?

KATE: Oh.

HOLLY: So we like know who we are. Like we were beginning a process.

KATE: Absolutely.

HOLLY: Holly Seabé, which probably goes without saying, Masha.

CASEY: Casey Mulgraw, radiating of loss, Olga.

LISABETTE: Lisabette Cartwright, Irina.

(Now T-Anne moves from chair to chair, being all the other actors.)

GUNTER: Gunter Sinsel, Solyony.

ALLEN: Allen Greif, thrilled to be Andrey.

JAMES: James George, the hapless Tusenbach.

WIKÉWITCH: *(Ferocious.)* Not hapless!

JAMES: The definitely-not-hapless Tusenbach.

(T-Anne indicates it would take too much time to do every introduction.)

T-ANNE: *(On book.)* Talk, talk, talk, talk, talk, talk, talk, talk, talk. Introductions over.

WIKÉWITCH: Okay, now I talk…

KATE: Could I…

WIKÉWITCH: You are going to speak of deep love you feel for Chekhov…

KATE: Yes, because when I was fifteen…

WIKÉWITCH: Stop! This love for Chekhov is like American fantasy. You make God from Chekhov. You say Chekhov, bullshit, Chekhov, bullshit, Chekhov, bullshit, bullshit, bullshit. From God we can't make play. From

God we make worship. Worship makes boring play. You want to know in this room who is God? Who is God here?

LISABETTE: *(A guess.)* You are?

WIKÉWITCH: This is very intelligent young actress. God in theater is interpretation of play. I, Wikéwitch, make interpretation…. In this room, in this time, I, Wikéwitch, will be God.

JOBY: Excuse me.

WIKÉWITCH: This is audience. Audience is talking!

JOBY: I mean, this is driving me crazy! This is the whole problem with 20th century theater. This is part of the reason nobody wants to buy a ticket. We used to get stories; now we get "interpretations." The director is not God!

WIKÉWITCH: I am God.

JOBY: You are not God!

CASEY: Joby…

JOBY: What?!

CASEY: A character is talking.

JOBY: I know a character is talking, so?

CASEY: Who says it's the author's view?

WIKÉWITCH: *(Triumphantly.)* You are making interpretation!

JOBY: I don't care whose view it is, it's pernicious.

WIKÉWITCH: You are being God. Who gave you this position?

JOBY: I have a ticket!

WIKÉWITCH: If I do not make interpretation, you cannot make interpretation of my interpretation. You are secondary! I am artist! I fuck you with my art and you cry out.

JOBY: What the hell are you talking about?

WIKÉWITCH: Sit down, little audience, I give you *Three Sisters*. From big soul.

CASEY: *(Trying to calm her.)* Joby…

JOBY: I have never heard such unadulterated…

CASEY: Joby…

JOBY: Sit here and listen to…

CASEY: Joby! *(Joby stops talking.)* Not now.

JOBY: Then "now" what?

CASEY: You are the audience, Joby. If you talk to us all the time, you become an actor, and then you would have to come down here. Do you want to come down here?

(Joby, still upset, stands in silence for a moment, then, making a decision, sits back down. Don Blount enters.)

KATE: Don!

DON: Running a little late.

KATE: Don Blount, everybody, Vice President for Grants and Contributions at Albert & Sons Tobacco, our wonderful corporate sponsor.

DON: Don't mean to interrupt. Please go on with the Art.

KATE: Thanks Don. Now, we have the opportunity to make Chekhov with… *(Indicating Wikéwitch.)* this fine artist…

WIKÉWITCH: Great artist.

KATE: Great artist, and I feel deeply, even profoundly, that…

DON: *(Back in the scene.)* Could I just say a couple of things… *(Taps watch.)*

WIKÉWITCH: Okay. I pee now.

DON: …because, uh…well, I'm not part of your world…I'm a businessman. I actually have things to do.

KATE: Oh, Don, absolutely. Don Blount, everybody. Our underwriter.

DON: This is really a…revelation…for me to get to see what art's really all about. It's just that, uh… *(Taps watch.)* So I wanted to say that Albert & Sons Tobacco is really pleased to make this gift to the community of …*Four Sisters*… *(Casey holds up three fingers.) Three Sisters.* Sorry. Because Albert & Sons Tobacco International…we're in 130 countries, but we feel our role in this community is to…

CASEY: Kill people.

DON: Excuse me.

CASEY: Your role is to kill people, to target children and African Americans and to seek profit independent of any ethics or morality.

KATE: Oh dear.

CASEY: And by involving yourself in the arts who have no money and have no alternative to taking your minuscule handout, you hope to give the impression that you are on the side of life, when actually you are merchants of death.

DON: *(Pause.)* Thank you so much for the feedback. Albert & Sons respects others and their disparate and useful points of view. But in closing, I will say to you personally that if you take money from us it is disingenuous to make a pretense of morality and that historically, insofar as I understand it, actors were traditionally pickpockets, whores, and parasites on the body politic. Of course, given that your very profession is pretense, I still have the pleasure of enjoying your morality as entertainment. *(Taps watch.)* Got to go. Good luck with however many sisters you've got. *(He leaves. There is a stunned moment. Lights down.)*

END OF ACT ONE

ACT TWO

The act opens with a bare stage, one folding chair, and an inch-high, two-foot square box that Holly stands on while being fitted for her dress as Masha.

JACKEY: *(The costume designer.)* Baby-darlin'-honey-dear, your luscious body is a costume designer's dream! You have proportions goin' on like Greek statuary on a good day! Oh, my goodness! Your "out arm center back to wrist bent" is a world-class pisser. Your "shoulder point to mid-bust to center waist" is to die for, and your "depth of crotch and nipple to nipple" would turn Cleopatra mauve with envy. Golly-goodness-gracious, darlin', you are Masha the bomb!

HOLLY: But this is like, "Why have a body?"

JACKEY: Well, a little draggy, but 1901, if you see what I mean?

HOLLY: I am not going out there dressed up like a funeral cake. This would be, in fact, a good dress for somebody ugly. I mean, Olga might look like this, sure.

JACKEY: Au contraire, my goddess, au contraire. Every man in that audience is gonna hafta keep his program over his lap.

HOLLY: Ugly does not enhance luscious. People who wear ugly become ugly. Are we trying to make me ugly? I am not here to suffer the revenge of the ugly Texans. And I am not beautiful in this dress!
(Wikéwitch enters.)

WIKÉWITCH: Okay, okay. So. Masha is great beauty, yes? But is hiding. Hide-and-go-seek Masha.

HOLLY: The West Coast, we don't hide it. All right, a slit—waist to floor—let a little leg out.

JACKEY: 1901, honeydoll, no tits, no slits.

WIKÉWITCH: Repress. Very constrict. Very dark. This is sex for brain peoples.

HOLLY: Brain peoples. Reality check, all right?

JACKEY: *(Working.)* Ooooo, reality, I don't live there.

HOLLY: I spent $114,000 on my legs. I was in rehab for three months with animal, killer, monster rehab nurses in the Dominican Republic. An Internet survey shows that my legs alone, without the rest of me, have nineteen million fans. I either have legs or I walk. *(Jackey has his head in his hands.)* Jackey, will you stop crying. Every time we have a fitting, you weep.

JACKEY: You think I want to make women ugly because I'm a gay man.

HOLLY: Oh, please.

JACKEY: You think I'm hostile because you make millions, and I do consignment store windows.

HOLLY: Okay, all right, I'm going to try something completely new for me. I'm going to try compromise.

WIKÉWITCH: No compromise.

JACKEY: I love compromise.

HOLLY: Everybody listening? Floor length/see-thru.

WIKÉWITCH: I am in madhouse.

JACKEY: Well, lil' darlin', you would look delicious, but I keep rememberin' what you said the day you got here as to how the play was about like a tidal wave of vulgarity sweepin' everything good and beautiful away, which just made me bawl like a baby, and how the vulgarity of the rich was not to see the desperate need of the poor, and how the vulgarity of the poor was to be blind to beauty, and the vulgarity of the intellectual was to separate thought from action. So that everyone in the play was as different as they could be but in this funny way they all shared the same despair.

HOLLY: When did I say that?

JACKEY: Well, it was such a pretty thought, you are such a talk-diva, baby love. But it made me think maybe Masha could be this little simplicity in the sea of vulgarity and get all the attention, an' reviews, an' applause, applause, applause.

HOLLY: Well, if I said that, that's what we should do.

WIKÉWITCH: *(To Jackey.)* You are God in other form.

JACKEY: *(Sweetly.)* Well, she said.

HOLLY: No more talking!!! The dress rocks. I gotta book to make rehearsal.
(The scene now transitions into rehearsal. At first we see only the director because Holly has a costume change.)

WIKÉWITCH: Okay. Okay. Please stopping. Good. Okay. Leave brain. Brain no more. Brain outside, art inside. What you are doing in this time? Hah? Okay, good. Is very clear, is very smart, is very beautiful, is very professional. But is not art. No more professional. No good to Chekhov, this professional. No, no, no, no, no, no, no! Peel off skin. Rip open body. Lungs, liver, spleen. Okay. Begin.

HOLLY/MASHA: "I don't know. I don't know. Of course, being used to something means a lot. For example…"

WIKÉWITCH: *(Interrupting.)* You say line.

HOLLY/MASHA: *(Confused.)* I did.

WIKÉWITCH: Yes, you say "you don't know."

HOLLY/MASHA: I know the line.

WIKÉWITCH: You don't know!

HOLLY/MASHA: I just said it!

WIKÉWITCH: Saying is not being.

HOLLY: What are you talking about?

WIKÉWITCH: Look, little television actress, Masha say, "I don't know," but you don't know what this is not to know, so you just say line. So this little thing, this "I don't know" is dead, and more you say, you go from corpse to corpse over this dead Chekhov. You make graveyard of scene by just say lines. No good. Okay. Her father, military man, is dead. Real corpse, not acting corpse. Since that moment, this Masha lives, imbeciles all around, peasant idiots, animals, mud, stupidity. Peasant thirsty for drink, they spit in hand, like spit for drink. Only soldiers, like father, have brain. She is thirsty for brain. She says soldiers honorable, educated, worthwhile. Vershinin is soldier. His soul is dead. He knows soldier is animal too. He says this. How can she bear this? This is break her heart. He says this before scene. It is like stone. Like stone. You understand? She says, "I don't know." Yes! This is heart bleeding. Yes! Now you say.

HOLLY: I don't know.

WIKÉWITCH: No.

HOLLY: I don't know.

WIKÉWITCH: No!

HOLLY: What the hell do you want?

WIKÉWITCH: I want you to *be* line, not *say* line!

HOLLY: I don't know!

WIKÉWITCH: No.

HOLLY: I don't know.

WIKÉWITCH: No!

HOLLY: You think I know what the hell you mean but I'm telling you *I don't know!*

WIKÉWITCH: Yes! *Now* you know!

HOLLY: What?!

WIKÉWITCH: What you don't know! Chekhov is back from dead!

(*A pause.*)

HOLLY: Okay, I get it.

WIKÉWITCH: You get it.

HOLLY: Yes.

WIKÉWITCH: One line. Twenty minutes. You get one scene, I'm dead from old age.

HOLLY: I really get it.

WIKÉWITCH: Enough. Rehearse. Say "I don't know."

HOLLY: *I don't know.*

WIKÉWITCH: Okay. Next line.

> *(There are now a series of short Ben/Holly scenes with minimal furniture being brought in and out during a continuous flow.)*

BEN: Hey.

HOLLY: Hi.

BEN: Ummmm.

HOLLY: Ummmmm?

BEN: Coffee?

HOLLY: Sure.

> *(Chairs are placed under them and a table between them.)*

BEN: I held that kiss too long.

HOLLY: I noticed.

BEN: That was unprofessional.

HOLLY: Nice tongue, though.

BEN: Ma'am, I never meant…

HOLLY: You did.

BEN: I have to go.

> *(He moves away from the table.)*

HOLLY: Ben?

BEN: Yeah?

HOLLY: You kiss your wife like that?

> *(They meet outside rehearsal.)*

HOLLY: What the hell's going on in rehearsal?

BEN: Please don't call me at home.

HOLLY: When we're doing the scene, don't avoid the kiss and then say, "Kiss. Kiss over." I feel like I'm in middle school.

BEN: That scene is driving me crazy.

HOLLY: Why is that?

BEN: You know perfectly well why.

HOLLY: Yeah. I do.

BEN: I am married. I have two kids.

HOLLY: I have a live-in lover.

BEN: My wife is ill.

HOLLY: My lover's an ex-convict.

BEN: The kids are waiting for me to come.

HOLLY: Me too. All right, Ben. Come over in the morning.

*(A rolling door moves on. Ben knocks. Holly opens it. He steps in and imme-
diately kisses her. They start ripping off clothes. Dialogue along this vein ensues.)*

HOLLY: My neck. Yes. Yes! My mouth.

BEN: Oh God.

HOLLY: *(While being kissed, she is trying to undo his belt.)* Belt.

BEN: Belt.

(She keeps trying.)

HOLLY: Can't. Ouch. Hate that belt.

*(She steps back and takes her blouse off over her head. He is working on the
belt.)*

BEN: Beautiful. Goddamnit, you're beautiful!

HOLLY: I know. *(Trying to undo his buttons.)* Hate these buttons.

BEN: Boots.

HOLLY: *(Pulling his pants down.)* Screw the boots!

JOBY: Excuse me.

BEN: *(Freezes. Pants around his ankles.)* Yes, Joby, we've missed you.

JOBY: I don't think this love story is necessary.

HOLLY: Does anybody have any Tylenol?

(T-Anne brings her some.)

BEN: The Ben/Holly relationship is a crucial parallel to Masha and Vershinin
in *The Three Sisters*.

JOBY: I never read *The Three Sisters*.

HOLLY: Shut up. I'm a character, and you're a character, and I'm cutting your
character's lines!

*(He kisses her more roughly. They freeze. The lights change. It's now post-coital.
Ben pulls up his pants.)*

BEN: You were incredible.

HOLLY: Lots of practice.

BEN: What in the hell did you say that for?

HOLLY: Because it's true. It doesn't mean I didn't like it.

BEN: I'm not kidding around here, Holly.

HOLLY: Okay. It was my first time.

*(The scene breaks up. Two period chairs and a standing lamp become the set
for rehearsal.)*

HOLLY/MASHA: What a noise the stove's making. The wind was…line?

T-ANNE: *(Prompting.)* Moaning in the chimney.

HOLLY/MASHA: …moaning in the chimney just before Father died.

T-ANNE: The same sound exactly.

HOLLY/MASHA: The same sound exactly.

BEN/VERSHININ: Are you superstitious?

HOLLY/MASHA: Yes.

BEN/VERSHININ: Strange. *(Kisses her hand.)* You magnificent, magical woman. Magnificent, magical! It's dark in here but I can see the shining of your eyes.

HOLLY/MASHA: There's more light over here…

BEN/VERSHININ: I'm in love, I'm in love, I'm in love…

> *(He stops.)*

T-ANNE: *(Prompting.)* In love with your eyes, with the way you move.

BEN: *(Out of scene.)* I don't want to do this.

HOLLY: *(Out of scene.)* Are you?

BEN: Am I what?

HOLLY: In love?

T-ANNE: *(Prompting.)* In love with your eyes, with…

HOLLY: Can it, okay? You are or you aren't.

BEN: I have a real life. I can hurt real people here.

HOLLY: And what am I, animation? You think I'm not susceptible? Hey, man, three years ago, I'm involved with a guy commits suicide jumping off the Golden Gate Bridge in a wedding dress. Two years ago, the guy I'm living with whacks me, breaks my jaw so I couldn't work for three weeks and they almost pulled the show. Right now, as we speak, my significant other is an actor who has an immobilizing drinking problem mainly because in high school he murdered his prom date and served eleven years. You see why I might be susceptible to some ordinary, straight-up guy? Okay, it's mutual.

> *(Light comes up on Joby. Holly sees it.)*

JOBY: Excuse me.

HOLLY: Don't even think about it!

> *(Holly leaves. Furniture is struck. An exercycle and some mats become the gym.)*

CASEY: So, the casting agent says to me, "You're not right for it; you're a character woman." I die. My blood congeals. Fissures appear. It's the actresses' death knell. I go through menopause in five seconds. All fluids dry. I become the Mojave Desert. Character woman! I, who have screwed every leading man on the East Coast, become their mother. Vertigo. I scream out in a silent, unattending universe: "I'm too young to be a character woman!" and the echo replies, rolling out of infinite space: "They want to see you for the funny aunt at the wedding!"

> *(She ritually disembowels herself. Holly enters in exercise clothes. All three begin to work out; Holly particularly exercises fiercely.)*

CASEY: Bad day?

HOLLY: Bad day.

LISABETTE: Bad day.

CASEY: Bad day.

(They exercise.)

CASEY: Why does every actor in America go to the gym?

HOLLY: Because it's a beauty contest, not a profession.

(They exercise.)

LISABETTE: Damn it to hell! (She drops the weights.) Wikéwitch called me dense
    as a turkey, an' I'm a lot smarter than a turkey. An' then he picked on me
    for three hours an' I cried an' he patted me on my shoulder an' I threw
    up all over him. Then I ran out an' tripped over the doorjamb an' cracked
    a tooth an' I could just spit fire an' eat broke glass.

CASEY: (Exercising.) He called you a turkey?

LISABETTE: He didn't call me a turkey. He said I had the brain of a turkey.

HOLLY: Wikéwitch is a tyrannical, woman-hating buttwipe, but he seems to
    know what he's doing.

(They exercise.)

HOLLY: Meanwhile, my boyfriend has just been arrested for sexually soliciting
    a seven-foot transsexual on Hollywood Blvd. who turned out to be a
    policewoman on stilts, so People magazine called me for a quote.

(They exercise.)

CASEY: What'd you say?

HOLLY: I said it just showed he missed me.

(They exercise.)

CASEY: Play's going pretty well. (They exercise.) Whattayathink? (They exercise.)
    Play's going pretty well.

HOLLY: I wouldn't know, I've never done a play.

(Casey and Lisabette stop exercising.)

CASEY: You are kidding? Are you kidding?

HOLLY: From high school to TV…well, I was in one play, but I had to leave
    to get an abortion. One play and one porn flick.

LISABETTE: You didn't do a porn flick!?

HOLLY: (Still exercising.) Yeah.

CASEY: Tell.

HOLLY: Actually I got fired.

LISABETTE: How do you get fired from a porn flick?

HOLLY: I came. Joking. I got fired because I started crying uncontrollably on
    camera. It depressed the porn divas so they dumped me.

LISABETTE: Why were you crying?

HOLLY: Because I came. First time. Consider those implications.

(They all exercise.)

LISABETTE: What if it were good?

CASEY: What?

LISABETTE: You know.

CASEY: Our little Russian skit? The Sisters Three?

LISABETTE: I mean, what if it were *really* good? Really. Really, really good. Could we? You're good. You're both good. We could do something good. Could we do something good? It could be good. It could be really, really good. Could it? Be good?

CASEY: I once believed I could be very good. I wanted to be so concentrated, so compressed, so vivid and present and skillful and heartfelt that anyone watching me would literally burst into flame. Combust.

LISABETTE: That kills me. I want that. Did you ever do it? Did it ever happen?

CASEY: No.

LISABETTE: But maybe we could do that? What would happen if we did that?

HOLLY: Nobody would care.

LISABETTE: That's so cold. How can you say that? It could change people's lives.

CASEY: God love you, Lisabette, two months later the audience can't remember the name of the play.

LISABETTE: *I don't believe that. I don't believe that.*

CASEY: Has anybody you know to be a sentient being ever walked up to you and said the play changed their life? No, fine, okay. You know who is changed by Chekhov? Me. I finish a play, it's like, "Get me an exorcist!" He eats my life. He chews me up. He spits me out. I'm like bleeding from Chekhov. The audience? Who knows what their deal is? They come from the mists; they return to the mist. They cough, they sneeze, they sleep, they unwrap little hard candies, and then they head for their cars during the curtain call. And once, once I would like to step out and say to the ones who are up the aisles while we take the bows, "Hey! Excuse me! Could you show a little mercy because I just left it all out here on the stage and even if you don't have the foggiest notion what it was or what it meant, could you have the common courtesy to leave your goddamn cars in the garage for another forty seconds and give me a little hand for twenty years of work!"

JOBY: That is unmitigated hogwash!

HOLLY: Oh, please...

JOBY: I don't cough or sleep or unwrap little candies, I come to feel. *(She taps*

her head and chest.) Here and here. Because if I'm ever going to understand my own life, it will have to be through feeling, and my own life
and experience isn't big enough so I come for enlargement. Plus I want
the highest quality moments for my life I can get, and you're supposed
to provide them, though you usually don't, so when I write my review…

CASEY: Hold it.

JOBY: …I need to point out whether there is any enlargement…

HOLLY: Your review?

JOBY: …to be had by the audience…

CASEY: You're a critic.

JOBY: …in this particular experience!

CASEY: You have been interrupting us all night…

JOBY: I am part of the process.

CASEY: After the play, not during the play.

JOBY: After the play I'm not part of the process. After the play you revile and
dismiss me. Some of you claim you don't even read reviews, which is a
complete joke!

CASEY: I don't read reviews.

JOBY: You do.

CASEY: Don't.

JOBY: Do.

CASEY: Don't.

JOBY: Do.

CASEY: Okay, sometimes.

JOBY: Hah!

CASEY: Look, we only put up with you because half our audience is three
months from the nursing home.

HOLLY: I can't believe it—a critic!?

JOBY: Well…

HOLLY: How are we doing so far?

JOBY: Well, it's definitely interesting, sometimes amusing, well-paced, but a
very uneasy mix of…

LISABETTE: Stop! Not while we're doing it! Critics are gods to me. I completely
measure my self-worth by my reviews.

HOLLY: Who do you write for?

JOBY: *(A pause.)* I don't want to talk about it.
(She sits down.)

CASEY: That is completely unfair. We have to go on here. Do we have to be
afraid of you or not?

JOBY: It doesn't matter who I write for; it matters what I perceive.

CASEY: Joby, even you don't believe that. Don't tell me there isn't a critical hierarchy when you would poison your colleagues for the six best jobs.

JOBY: Not my job.

CASEY: Who do you write for, Joby?

JOBY: *Bargain Mart Suburban Shoppers Guide.*

CASEY: *(Turning back to the stage.)* She's nobody, let's act.

JOBY: I am not nobody!

CASEY: *(Referring back.)* I didn't mean you personally, Joby.

    (Joby sits down. The actresses exercise.)

LISABETTE: What was wrong with your day, Casey?

CASEY: Forget it.

LISABETTE: We told you.

CASEY: Forget it.

LISABETTE: We're not important enough to tell?

    (They exercise a moment in silence.)

CASEY: I felt a lump in the shower. I saw a doctor. She wants to do a biopsy.

HOLLY: When?

CASEY: On the day off.

LISABETTE: Oh my God.

    (Casey exercises. Lisabette is frozen. Holly stops exercising, stands, and walks over to Casey, who keeps working out.)

HOLLY: *(Standing above her.)* Stop. *(Casey does. Holly puts out her hand.)* Get off. *(Casey does.)* Hug me. *(Casey does.)*

BEN: Excuse me?

LISABETTE: Yes?

BEN: It's Ben.

HOLLY: Come in.

    (He does.)

BEN: I left my wife.

    (A moment.)

CASEY: Well, either way I lose my hair.

    (Holly and Casey exit. The gym is struck and a desk and two chairs are brought on for Don Blount's office.)

DON: Don Blount of Albert & Sons Tobacco calling for Martha Graham. Then why is it called the Martha Graham Dance Company? Oh. No, I knew that. Little joke. Listen, the grant's in the mail. Yes. Well, it's our pleasure to support a dance company of your caliber, and if you might find an opportunity to mention to the chairman of your board that we'd be thrilled if she'd tell her brother the congressman to stop sodomizing the tobacco industry just because he's personally in the pocket of the HMOs, I think you'd find your grant is definitely renewable. My pleasure.

(Don hangs up the phone, picks it back up and dials.)

Mom, it's Don. Your son Don. I need the favor, Mom. I know we did it yesterday, but I'm feeling a little alienated…a little remote. Wonderful. Good. I knew I could count on you, Momma. Ready? All right, light it up, Mom. Inhale, Mom. Would I encourage you to smoke if there was any danger? That's right, I wouldn't. I would never harm my mom. I must be a good person if I would never harm my mom. If I'm a good person, it must be all right to do what I do. Thanks, I feel a lot better. Put it out now, Momma. Everything's all right. I feel damn good. Go back on the oxygen, Ma. See you Sunday.

(Kate enters Albert & Sons. Don rises, smiling and affable.)

DON: Ms. Todoravskia, it's really nice of you to come over on short notice.

KATE: No, I've been wanting to…

DON: Can I get you something?

KATE: Well…

DON: At this level in the executive suite, we could fly in crabs' legs from Iceland. Just kidding. But in Iceland the crabs have pneumonia. Wouldn't affect their legs though. Just kidding. Tea, coffee, soft drink, bottled water, mixed drinks of all kinds, munchies, brownies my mother sends in… *(Does his Dracula imitation.)* Cigarette?!

KATE: No, I…

DON: You know, Kate…may I call you Kate? Nice dress, by the way. I deal with a lot of artists, and usually they look like they bought their clothes from the llama shop in Costa Rica.

KATE: Well, I…

DON: I can't tell you how impressed I was by that rehearsal of whatsit you let me see.

KATE: *Three Sisters.*

DON: Well, it just seemed like a metaphor for the lives we all lead, don't you think?

KATE: Well I…

DON: Plus it confirmed my every doubt about corporate investment in Russia. In that way it was very personal for me.

KATE: I'm glad that you…

DON: So it's a real downer to have to pull the funding. Oh, I think we also have fruit juices.

KATE: The funding.

DON: The funding. In a way here, Ms. Todoravskia, I have to tell you I personally blew it. I've only been in Grants and Contributions with Albert & Sons for a couple of months—before that, they let me do real work—just kidding, and I didn't realize when I gave you the okay that there had been a policy change up top.

KATE: Do you mean…

DON: Let me just wrap this up and then we'll relate. We had sort of turned our contribution policy on a dime based on the fact that all this tobacco legislation, politically motivated lawsuits, advertising restrictions have made it clear to us that our market focus in the future will be overseas where they just plain old like a good smoke. Plus their life expectancy is so low that we don't really constitute a health hazard. Hah! Just kidding. Just kidding. And it's in those communities in our target market we'll be looking to leverage our contributions. So the bad news is that I didn't have the authority to give you the money. I hope this won't inconvenience you?

KATE: But you did authorize it.

DON: *(Smiling.)* Poof.

KATE: But we're in the middle of the work.

DON: Poof.

KATE: We will have to default on the salaries and the Board will fire me.

DON: You know, I'm very interested in artists and how they function, and a little research shows an overwhelming percentage of the best work didn't have grants. As far as I can see, good art is almost invariably a product of good old-fashioned adversity and rage. Anger is the engine of art, so in an odd way this is a good situation for you. You don't want to be the lap dog of big tobacco. We're the bad guys. Great art is a personal passion, not a grant. Ms. Todoravskia, Albert & Sons Tobacco is sorry to defund you, but that doesn't mean we aren't proud to fuel your anger.

KATE: I cannot believe…

DON: I'm afraid that's all the time I have for you. I do however want to make a $75 personal contribution to your theater. If you wonder about the cost basis, it's the same amount I give to public radio, which I actually use. *(She takes the envelope. He heads back for his desk.)* Oh, listen, I wonder if you have Holly Seabé's phone number?

(Office is struck. The girls are talking—one seated. Kate enters with her suitcase.)

KATE: Hi.

(She puts down her suitcase.)

LISABETTE: Hi.

CASEY: Hi.

HOLLY: Hi.

KATE: I, uh…are my eyes red? *(Furious.)* I hate it when my eyes are red!! Sorry, I'm sorry. Look, I want to…uh…tell you how proud…proud I am of you… *(She pauses on the brink of something. It explodes.)* To hell with everybody!! Okay, that feels better…umm, it was very emotional to see this great play being so well done in our little theater that has…struggled and…held on by its fingernails…believe me…for all these years. When I settled here, having attended Stanford, Harvard, and Yale, I hoped…I hoped!!…well, those rehearsals were what I hoped for as an artist. They surpassed my hopes. It's one hell of a time to be fired, I'll tell you that.

LISABETTE: Oh my God…

KATE: Albert & Sons removed the funding.

CASEY: Oh God.

KATE: And when I told Joe Bob Mattingly, the Chairman of our Board of Directors, he said…

JOE BOB: *(From somewhere out in the house.)* Damn woman! You got no more sense than a hog on ice! I been pourin' my money an' the money of my friends down your double-talk rathole since Jesus was a pup, so my wife could drag me down here to see plays nobody can understand with a buncha people I would never invite to dinner, on the basis it creates some quality of life I'm supposed to have since I figgered out how to make some money. Half the time, that stuff doesn't have a story, and it's been five years since you done one takes place in a kitchen, which is the kind all of us like. The rest of the time it's about how rich people is bad and Democrats is good and white people is stupid and homosexuals have more fun an' we should get rid of the corporations an' eat grass an' then, by God, you wonder why you don't have a big audience! Now you just blew 15 percent of your budget 'cause you riled up the tobacco interests, plus you got the colored rattlin' on my cage, an' as of this precise minute, you are out of luck, out of work, an' outta San Antonio, Texas. See, I am closin' us down, lockin' the door, an' then, by God, we can go back to hittin' each other up to give to the United Way where it will, by God, do some poor handicap some actual, measurable good, an' I won't have to hear anybody say "aesthetic" from one year to the goddamned next! Now, vaya con Dios, darlin'.

JOE BOB and KATE: You got three minutes to clean out your desk.

(He disappears. Kate speaks to Casey.)

KATE: So that's it. They said if I was out of the city before five o'clock I'd get six months' severance and my plane ticket. What, do you suppose, I thought I was doing here? Making theater because… See I just can't remember. Well, I guess nobody told us everything has a purpose.

CASEY: Man cannot live by bread alone.

KATE: No, he needs salsa. *(Shakes Casey's hand.)* Actually, I think I hate theater. It makes you think it was about something when it was actually only about yourself. It fascinates you. It seduces you. It leaves you penniless by the side of the road. Screw Thespis! *(She looks at the women.)* Run for your lives.

(She exits. The women look at each other.)

LISABETTE: Goodness gracious. *(Wipes tear.)*

CASEY: You okay?

LISABETTE: I guess.

JOBY: *(From audience.)* Don't let it get too sentimental.

CASEY: *(Without looking up.)* Thanks for the tip. *(Turns to Holly.)* So that this doesn't get too sentimental, why don't you pay for the production? You have the money.

HOLLY: Why would I do that?

CASEY: Self-interest?

HOLLY: Ah.

CASEY: You want the credit. You don't like to be pushed around. You're secretly thrilled you're good in the part. Based on proving you can act, you might get a film where you kept your clothes on. And I could use the distraction from the fact the biopsy was positive.

HOLLY: That's not too sentimental. Anything else?

CASEY: No, that's about it.

HOLLY: *(Seeing Ben enter.)* Hi.

BEN: Stay.

HOLLY: *(Turns to Lisabette.)* And you, little one?

LISABETTE: It might make you happy.

(Holly chuckles.)

HOLLY: Well, that aside, why not?

CASEY: You'll pay to get us open?

HOLLY: I'll get us open.

LISABETTE: No way?

HOLLY: They screwed with us, now they lose.

LISABETTE: You really mean it?

HOLLY: I don't want to talk about it, I want to do it.

(At this point, Wikéwitch walks in with his suitcase.)

WIKÉWITCH: So. Is not to be. Okay. I put life in small suitcase. You. You. You. On we go, yes? Is hard to tell what is good, what is bad. Everything is doorway to something else. *(Shaking hands.)* Little Irina, okay, good-bye. Olga. Olga, she goes on. Vershinin. He finds another girl next town. *(To Holly.)* Like cat you land on feet, yes?

CASEY: It's not over.

WIKÉWITCH: No?

CASEY: We have the money. We can open.

WIKÉWITCH: Where is money?

HOLLY: Here is money.

WIKÉWITCH: Ah. Is for what?

LISABETTE: So we can do your beautiful play.

WIKÉWITCH: Ah. Okay, okay. Honorable sisters and Lieutenant Colonel. Okay. I wake, wake, wake. No sleeping. Okay. I get up, pack suitcase, close suitcase. Knock, knock, knock. Theatre producer says no more money. Dead Chekhov. Okay. Bye-bye. Money, money, money. But, dear American actors, before knock-knock, I am pack. So why is this? Because work is finish. When do Chekhov, now, now, now, young, middle, old. So much you can do, only what you know. No more. Then wait for life to teach. You are sweet young people, but what I know… *(Points to head.)* …you cannot do. What for I do this? No sleep, no sleep. We must be a little realistic in this time. For you, Chekhov is fantasy. For me, life. You have nice, small talent. We can do together baby-Chekhov. Okay, but I have…short time…short time now…no sleep…no time for baby-Chekhov…I must take small suitcase, find big souls to do play, so I don't die with this Chekhov in my head. This you understand or not understand?

HOLLY: We're not good enough.

WIKÉWITCH: You do not understand. OK. Bye-bye. *(Goes to exit and turns back.)* You are good enough to do the Chekhov you are good enough to do. But is not good enough. *(He tips his hat and is gone.)*

LISABETTE: See, I've always been terrified that some guy dressed in black would show up and tell me I'm not good enough.

HOLLY: Yeah, but what he said was:

CASEY and HOLLY: You just have to do the Chekhov you're good enough to do.

LISABETTE: He did say that.

HOLLY: Okay. We'll do the Chekhov we can do.

LISABETTE: Really?

HOLLY: Really.

LISABETTE: Yes! Oh yes! *(To Casey.)* Can you believe this? Can we please work on the last scene? *(She picks up the script.)* I want to work on the last scene.

HOLLY: Where from?

LISABETTE: The band. Ta ra ra boom de ay.

CASEY: We're over here.

HOLLY/MASHA: "Oh, but listen to the band! They're leaving us."

T-ANNE: *(Entering.)* Sorry. Sorry to interrupt. Phone for you, Holly.

HOLLY: Take the message.

(She turns back to the scene.)

T-ANNE: Dreamworks.

(A moment.)

HOLLY: *(To the others.)* I'll be right back.

(She goes.)

LISABETTE: What's Dreamworks?

CASEY: Who are you? What planet do you live on? Spielberg.

LISABETTE: Oh, you mean…

T-ANNE: *(As a stage manager, cutting to another place in the text.)* Talk, talk, talk, talk, talk, talk, talk. Holly comes back.

(She does.)

HOLLY: I got a film.

CASEY: You are kidding?

(Holly shakes her head. No, she's not kidding.)

LISABETTE: That is great! That is so exciting! What is it! I never heard anybody say that, "I got a film." I was right here when you said it!

CASEY: When?

LISABETTE: What when?

CASEY: *(Directly to Holly.)* When film?

HOLLY: Now. Yesterday. I'm replacing somebody who walked.

LISABETTE: Now?

HOLLY: They want me on a flight in ninety minutes. Jesus, I gotta pack. Rental car? How will I get rid of the rental car. Damn it, my dogs? How the hell am I going to do that? I'm supposed to film tonight.

CASEY: How long?

HOLLY: One month, L.A.; one month, Thailand. I mean, the part is dogmeat. Girlfriend stuff. Two scenes naked, three scenes I listen to the guy talk, one scene I get crushed by pythons. Two months I say a dozen sentences. Listen, I am…I am sorry, I am really sorry, but I am really happy…bad for you, good for me…me, me, me…and I can't even pretend I'm anything but euphoric! Kill me, I'm horrible! Gotta go, gotta go.

(She starts to race out.)

BEN: I'll come with.

HOLLY: Damn.

BEN: I don't have anything here. I got rid of everything here. You're it.

HOLLY: You just don't have a clue who you got mixed up with, do you?

BEN: I love you.

HOLLY: I got the call. We've just been fooling around while I waited for the call.

BEN: I'll just come out and hang.

HOLLY: Oh Ben. You just don't get it. This is the shot. You are a very sweet cowboy, but it makes you, don't you see, completely disposable, babe. Trust me, you don't want to hang around Malibu while I give head for billing. This is it. I will take no prisoners. You have to blow me off. You know what? *(She kisses his cheek.)* Go back to your wife. Sorry to be the meat grinder. It's just the way it plays out. *(Looks at him.)* I got a couple minutes, tell me to go screw myself. *(He shakes his head.)* Okay. *(She kisses him.)* Bye L. *(Hugs Lisabette. Appraises Casey.)* More I see of you, you could probably get it done for a hundred thousand. *(Casey chuckles; they hug.)* Anything I can do, you call me. We almost made it, huh?

CASEY: Almost.

HOLLY: I'm no surprise to you guys, I know that. Gotta go. Want to know the really worst part? I-am-so-happy!

(She leaves.)

CASEY: You okay, Ben?

(He nods yes.)

LISABETTE: *(Concerned.)* What will you do?

(He shakes his head "I don't know.")

CASEY: She was really beautiful, huh? *(He nods yes.)* Kind of like really sexy Russian roulette, right? Only you're alive.

BEN: *(A pained smile.)* Thanks.

(He exits.)

LISABETTE: What will we do?

CASEY: When the play's over, you pack.

LISABETTE: I live here.

CASEY: Then I will allow you to skip the packing.

LISABETTE: What will you do?

CASEY: What will I do? Oh, probably get my other breast lopped off, and then

I think I will try to accept that you don't necessarily get to do what you want to do. I will try to be a grown-up about that. And after I'm a grown-up, I will try to like doing the things grown-ups like to do. Right now, I'm thinking hardware store. I am worried, however, that I will make a lousy grown-up and that I will cry a lot and be depressed.

LISABETTE: Oh God.

CASEY: Can I tell you something about theater?

LISABETTE: Sure.

CASEY: Never ask an out-of-work actress what's next.

LISABETTE: Okay.

CASEY: *(Giving her a hug.)* Pardon you Jesus.

(Chair is struck. An airplane gate table is rolled in, as well as three waiting room chairs that move as a unit. Holly enters with luggage.)

AIRPORT ANNOUNCER: Because of weather, the following flights have been canceled or rescheduled: Flight #1726 to Los Angeles, Flight #343 to Dallas/Ft. Worth, Flight #2121 to Seattle, Flight #1643 to San Francisco…

(Holly begins talking to a gate check-in person, overlapping the flight cancellations.)

HOLLY: No, you don't understand, I have to be in L.A. by 6 PM.

GATE MANAGER: Ma'am, we have weather cancellations or long delays on everything going west.

HOLLY: You said that. I am a famous television star who is shooting a movie at 7 PM. tonight.

GATE MANAGER: Wow, what movie?

HOLLY: Get me on a plane!

GATE MANAGER: Ma'am. Weather is weather, ma'am. There is nothing flying.

HOLLY: *(Overlapping his speech.)* And if I'm not there for the shoot, I will lose the most important job of my career!

GATE MANAGER: I can get you on Flight #1077 arriving L.A. 7:30 A.M. tomorrow.

HOLLY: Too late.

GATE MANAGER: All I've got.

HOLLY: Look, is there a VIP lounge?

GATE MANAGER: Sure.

HOLLY: Is there a sofa in it?

GATE MANAGER: Absolutely.

HOLLY: I'll fuck you for a flight.

GATE MANAGER: You are one sad chick, and I don't have a plane.

HOLLY: *(Apoplectic.)* I'll have your job, do you understand me?!

GATE MANAGER: *(Gently.)* No, you won't, ma'am.

(He exits.)

HOLLY: *(Utter frustration.)* Arrghrrrahhhhh! *(Smashes the bag down, kicks it, throws an enraged fit. She then sits with her head in her hands in a row of gate seating. Casey enters with her bag. Lisabette tags along.)*

CASEY: Holly? *(Holly rocks, keening.)* What's the deal?

LISABETTE: Are you okay?

HOLLY: Do I look like I'm okay?

LISABETTE: Oh no, what is it?

CASEY: Holly? *(Holly, crying, doesn't look up.)* What's the deal?

LISABETTE: What, what is it?

HOLLY: My flight's canceled, nobody's flying. I called my agent, he says they'll replace me.

LISABETTE: Oh no.

CASEY: You can't connect through another city?

HOLLY: You can't land on the West Coast. I'm cursed. It's my karma.

(She leans on Casey who now sits beside her.)

LISABETTE: I drove Casey out for her New York flight. We thought we'd check to see if you left.

HOLLY: No, I haven't left! You can't see I haven't left? I can't take this, I can't, I'll kill myself. *(A band is heard in the distance.)* No planes! It's like some incredibly murderous cosmic joke. *(The band's sound intrudes.)* What the hell is that?

CASEY: There's some high school band playing in the terminal.

HOLLY: Does anybody have a goddamn Kleenex? That was my last Kleenex. My life is like a nightmare. I'm a nightmare. *(She blows her nose.)* What happened to Ben?

CASEY: He threw his stuff in his car and drove to Nashville. Said Texas was over, acting was over, his marriage was over, and you were over, the end.

HOLLY: Eat me!

(She puts her head back in her hands. Silence, except for the band. Lisabette makes the connection with the last scene in The Three Sisters *and sings softly.)*

LISABETTE: Ta-ra-ra boom-de-ay, ta-ra-ra boom-de-ay.

HOLLY: Oh please.

(Casey wipes at her eyes with another Kleenex.)

LISABETTE: (Quoting.) "Let them have their little cry. Doesn't matter, does it?"

(They are in the familiar tableau. Holly and Lisabette sitting, Casey behind them. She looks at Holly.) Your line.

HOLLY: So?

CASEY: *(A pause.)* It is, it's your line.

HOLLY: Do I give a damn?

CASEY: Yeah, you do.

HOLLY: "Listen. Hear how the band plays. They are leaving us. One has already gone, gone forever, and we are alone, left behind to start life again. We have to live; we must live."

LISABETTE: "A time will come when everyone knows what it was all for and why we suffer. There will be no secrets, but meantime we must live; we must work, only work! Tomorrow I set out alone. I'll teach in a school and give the whole of my own life to those who can make some use of it. Now it's autumn, but winter will come, covering everything with snow, and I will work; I will work."

CASEY: "The music plays so gaily, vigorously, as if it wants itself to live. Oh, my God. Time will pass, and then we shall be gone forever. They will forget us, our faces, voices, even how many of us there were. But our sufferings will become joy for those who live after us. A season of happiness and peace, and we who lived now will be blessed and thought of kindly. Oh, dear sisters, our life is still not finished. We will live. The music plays so bravely, so joyfully, as if in another moment we shall know why we live and why we suffer. If we could only know, if we could only know!" *(A moment held in the traditional pose, and then Casey and Holly leave the stage. Everyone has gone except Lisabette. She looks up in the audience and speaks to Joby.)*

LISABETTE: So how did we do?

JOBY: Oh fine. Not bad. Is it over?

LISABETTE: Sort of. I mean I'm the only one left. Their planes left.

JOBY: But not really.

LISABETTE: No, not really. I mean, in the play they left.

JOBY: They don't give me much space in the paper. I'm kind of between the car ads and the pet ads.

LISABETTE: I didn't have a lot of lines either. Not like a lead character or anything.

JOBY: You were good though, with what you had.

LISABETTE: Thanks. And?

JOBY: Oh. Well I…okay umm. So I would say…it played ___*(the time)*, you know ___ *(the date)*, at ___*(the place)*, and umm…a seriocomic, ummm, look at the creative drive and how the culture and, like, human frailty warp that, make it less pure…almost ludicrous, maybe breaks it…umm, calls into question whether it's kind of over for the theater…you know. Pretty good acting and everything…minimal set. I guess my question would be if plays, doing plays, doesn't speak to the culture, then examining why, or satirizing why, is kind of beating a dead horse…from the inside. So, uh, anyway, I only have about a hundred words to say that. You were good.

LISABETTE: Wow.

JOBY: Yeah. I could send you a copy.

LISABETTE: Thanks.

JOBY: I mean, I'm not a real critic…yet.

LISABETTE: Oh, you will be.

JOBY: Yeah. I don't know.

LISABETTE: Really.

JOBY: Yeah. Anyway. Bye.

LISABETTE: Bye.

JOBY: Bye.

(*Joby leaves. Airport is struck. T-Anne enters and sets a ghost light.*)

T-ANNE: 'Night, baby.

LISABETTE: 'Night. (*Lisabette remains in a single light. She looks around her.*) Wow. Crazy. It's so stupid, but I love to act. It always feels like anything could happen. That something wonderful could happen. It's just people, you know, just people doing it and watching it, but I think everybody hopes that it might turn out to be something more than that. Like people buy a ticket to the lottery, only this has more…heart to it. And most times, it doesn't turn out any better than the lottery, but sometimes…my dad runs a community center, and back in the day they did this play called *Raisin in the Sun*, just about a black family or something, and it was just people doing it. He said there was a grocery guy and a car mechanic, a waitress, but the whole thing had like…I don't know…aura, and people wanted to be there…so much that when they would practice at night, 'cause everybody had jobs, they had to open the doors at the center and hundreds of black people would just show up, show up for the play practice. They brought kids, they brought dinner, old people in wheelchairs, and they would hang around the whole time, kids running up and down, until the actors went home, night after night at practice, and when they finished, these people would stick around and they would line up outside like a…reception line…like a wedding…and the actors would walk down that line… "How you doin'? How you doin'?" shaking hands, pattin' on the kids, and the people would give them pies and yard flowers, and then the audience and the actors would all walk out, in the pitch dark, to the parking lot together. Nobody knew exactly what it was or why it happened.

Some day I'd like to be in a play like that. I would. So I guess I'll go on...keep trying...what do you think? Could happen. Maybe. Maybe not. *(She looks at the audience.)* Well, you came tonight anyway. *(Blackout.)*

END OF PLAY

Flaming Guns of the Purple Sage

A "B" Western Horror Flick

ORIGINAL PRODUCTION:

Flaming Guns of the Purple Sage was first produced at the 25th Humana Festival of New American Plays, at the Actors Theatre of Louisville on March 8, 2001. It was directed by Jon Jory. The cast was as follows:

Big 8 . . . . .Phyllis Somerville*
Rob Bob . . . . .Leo Kittay*
Shedevil . . . . .Monica Koskey*
Shirl . . . . .Peggity Price*
Black Dog . . . . .Mark Mineart*
Baxter Blue . . . . .William McNulty*
Memphis Donnie Pride . . . . .Atticus Rowe**

and with the following production staff:

Scenic Designer . . . . .Paul Owen
Costume Designer . . . . .Lindsay W. Davis
Lighting Designer . . . . .Amy Appleyard
Sound Designer . . . . .Kurt Kellenberger
Properties Designer . . . . .Mark R. Walston
Fight Supervisor . . . . .Drew Fracher
Production Stage Manager . . . . .Paul Mills Holmes
Assistant Stage Manager . . . . .Amber D. Martin
Dramaturg . . . . .Michael Bigelow Dixon
Casting . . . . .Laura Richin Casting

* Members of Actors' Equity Association

** Member of Actors Theatre's Apprentice Company

SETTING

A house on a small ranch near Casper, Wyoming. The present.

CHARACTERS

Big 8
Rob Bob
Shedevil
Shirl
Black Dog
Baxter Blue
Memphis Donny Pride

FLAMING GUNS
OF THE PURPLE SAGE

ACT ONE
SCENE 1

> *A kitchen in a small $40,000 house built in the Fifties in Casper, Wyoming.*
> *There are two posters of early cowboy movies on the wall, and a stitched "Home*
> *Sweet Home." The only unusual feature is a butcherblock island in the mid-*
> *dle of an otherwise working-class, run-down space. There are beer cans scat-*
> *tered about and a new six-pack (with two missing) on the island. It's 2:00*
> *A.M., and Rob sits at the island chugging a beer and perusing the magazine*
> *Western Screen. He is a good-looking twenty-six, and the youngest rodeo rider*
> *to have won the "World's Top Cowboy" silver buckle. He is recovering from*
> *back and leg injuries inflicted by a rodeo fall. Big 8, a substantial woman of*
> *forty-eight, an ex-rodeo star and expansive personality, carries a beer and is*
> *cooking up bacon and eggs in a frying pan on the stove. She is, as usual, in*
> *the midst of a rodeo reminiscence. A storm, lightning and all, rages outside.*

BIG 8: Yeah, cowboy, the rodeo it's gone to hell in a handbasket.
(She chugs the rest of her beer, as does Rob. She has a spatula in her other hand. Thunder!)
All sold out to the corporations. Guy in a banker suit finally called me in, said, "Lurlene…" "Hold it," I said. "Who's this Lurlene? 'Round here they call me Big 8."

ROB: Yeah, boy.

BIG 8: "Well, Big 8," says he, "my name's Wallace." "Well, that's a real surprise to me," I said, " 'cause everybody here just calls you dumbass." My, he laughed real big, slapped his big ol' desk an' then he said I wasn't suitable for the rodeo no more. Said they was lookin' for another type, somethin' a little more in the showgirl line.

ROB: *(Digging into his breakfast.)* Yummy, yummy.

BIG 8: Ol' Wallace said ridin' an' ropin' wasn't the thing no more. Talked on about floats, costumes, chor-eog-raphy.

ROB: Oh, yeah!

BIG 8:…*Astro-dirt!* Dust free. Artificial damn dirt, honey, Lord have mercy!

If I was a man, I woulda pissed on his shoe. Said he'd give me a lifetime pass, though. Said I could come to his rodeo anytime I wanted. Pissed me off. From that day to this, I just stay pissed off all the time.

(He nods. He's heard it before. He picks up the Western Screen.*)*

You hear what I'm sayin'?

(She looks at him immersed in the magazine. She takes a slug of beer and then knocks the magazine out of his hands and across the room.)

ROB: Hey!

BIG 8: Hey what?

ROB: I'm just checkin' facts, okay?

BIG 8: An' what facts would those be?

ROB: Facts on Gabby Hayes.

BIG 8: Good Lord, Rob Bob, we got that settled afore dinner.

ROB: I'm just sayin'…

BIG 8: You got your sidekicks ass-betwixt an' backwards.

ROB: *(Frustrated. Louder.)* Dude, Gabby Hayes didn't come on as Hoppy's side-kick till *Moon Over the Mojave.*

BIG 8: Big wrong.

ROB: Gollee, it was still Burt Smoot.

BIG 8: Burt Smoot? Burt Smoot?! Gabby was on three pictures before that.

ROB: Darn-a-doodle, Big 8, Smoot's finale was *Guns of Thunder.*

BIG 8: Smoot's last sidekick was *Hoppy Serves a Writ!* An' that picture wasn't worth heifer piss.

(Big thunder. He goes to the windows. A silence. She picks up.)

BIG 8: Whatcha lookin' at?

ROB: Just lookin'.

(He turns and stares out the window again.)

BIG 8: Gittin' antsy, huh?

ROB: Boy my age jest wants to be up and doin'.

BIG 8: Hey.

ROB: Hey what?

BIG 8: You wouldn't jes' walk off on me, would you?

(He doesn't answer.)

'Cause, cowboy, I'd take that right unkindly.

(He looks back out the window.)

BIG 8: You hear me?

ROB: Yes, ma'am.

BIG 8: An' don't never, ever, or forever call me ma'am.

(He nods.)

ROB: You my healin' angel, ladybird.

BIG 8: Walk on it full for me.

(He walks.)

'Zat yer *full* weight?

ROB: *(Walking.)* I ain't comin' off 'er at all.

BIG 8: Got a little hip hitch in there still.

ROB: Shoot.

BIG 8: Six more weeks.

ROB: Six more weeks!? I got to get busy in my life. You show me where Randolph Scott spent six weeks sittin' himself around.

BIG 8: Hey, who's the number one rodeo healer on the circuit, Rob Bob?

ROB: You are.

BIG 8: *(Unbuttoning his shirt.)* Don't need no X-ray machine when you got me.

(Kisses his chest.)

ROB: Hey, that there tickles.

BIG 8: Now, it's s'posed to tickle, ain't it?

(She reaches for his belt buckle, undoes it.)

ROB: Come on, girlfrien', that ain't right in the kitchen.

(He steps back and turns to the window, buttoning himself up.)

BIG 8: 'Zat so?

ROB: Well, every room's got a purpose, don't it? Come on now. Rainin' frogs out there, man.

BIG 8: When it's sunny, I miss the rodeo.

ROB: *(Finishing buttoning.)* You in the hall of fame, babe.

BIG 8: Hall of damn fame ain't the rodeo.

ROB: Dude, you cain't ride rodeo all yer life.

(Turns her to him.)

You rode till you was forty years old!

BIG 8: Don't never say that number. I mean it now, Rob Bob, don't never.

ROB: Sorry, ma'am.

BIG 8: An' do not, damnit, call me ma'am!

(He moves away from her.)

Hey?

(He doesn't turn.)

BIG 8: Rob Bob Silverado, Top Cowboy, '98. Hand me over yer belt, boy.

(He does.)

Ain't no buckle has that heft, is there?

(Holds the belt up, looking at the buckle.)

Oooooo, baby, ain't you pretty. There's still ten thousand cowboys, but there's but one buckle looks like this. You jes' that little bit different that makes all the difference, ain't you?

(There is a knock at the door.)

BIG 8: Hell, it's 3:00 A.M.

ROB: Three-thirty.

(Knock repeats.)

BIG 8: You git the door an' I'll get the shotgun.

(Takes one off the wall. Gets cartridges from a drawer.)

ROB: Say when, 8.

(She chambers the cartridges.)

BIG 8: If that's State Land Agents come to foreclose my property, they'll by God have to clean 'em up with a tweezers.

(Closes the shotgun. Shoulders it.)

Okay, Rob Bob, let's git us a big look.

(Rob pulls the door open. A young girl, completely drenched, wearing Army fatigue pants and an odd leopard print blouse, wrapped in a sodden blanket, stands there. She has many piercings, a couple of tattoos, electric pink short hair, one long glove and carries a duffel bag. She has a southern accent.)

SHEDEVIL: *(She speaks a strange tongue.)* Ca-ching, eeeyow, kaboom!

BIG 8: *(A moment.)* You an American citizen, darlin'?

SHEDEVIL: I'm…kaboom, schwang…looking for Lucifer Lee. Thwang, splat?

ROB: Holy mackerel.

SHEDEVIL: Doing!

BIG 8: She got a little problem.

ROB: *(Admiringly.)* She does.

SHEDEVIL: Just, rat-tat-tat-tat-tat, happens when I'm nervous.

ROB: Oh, I get nervous, too.

BIG 8: Oh.

SHEDEVIL: Is this number 125 West Hacienda?

BIG 8: Child, do you wear a watch or carry a timepiece of any kind?

SHEDEVIL: I'm wet through.

ROB: She's wet through, Big 8.

BIG 8: *(Who has lowered the shotgun.)* All right, step in an' say your piece.

SHEDEVIL: You Lucifer Lee's mama? Big 8?

BIG 8: Could be.

SHEDEVIL: I met him…bam!…when he was singin' at the La Cienega Best Western Motel Sparkle Lounge. He let me…ka-lonk…crash in the suite they put him up in. He had a driftwood lamp by his bed carved to look just like Lucille Ball.

ROB: You know, you got a bunch of metal stuck in yer face.

SHEDEVIL: Yeah.

BIG 8: Looks like a junkyard. *(Her piercings.)*

SHEDEVIL: Thanks.

ROB: You take off your blanket an' I'll git you a towel.

(He exits.)

SHEDEVIL: Waka-waka-waka-waka.

BIG 8: Jes' take 'er easy now.

SHEDEVIL: Waka-waka.

BIG 8: Jes' take 'er easy now.

SHEDEVIL: We stayed in the Best Western fourteen weeks, then I told Lucifer I was knocked up, so we drove up to Vegas an' had a real nice ceremony at the Wee Chapel of Jesus Resurgent.

BIG 8: You kiddin', huh?

SHEDEVIL: *(Shaking her head.)* My daddy runs it.

BIG 8: Yeah, well, Lucifer always liked to git married.

SHEDEVIL: Three days later, I woke up. He'd packed up his Mel Tormé records and split.

BIG 8: Lucifer Lee has a dog's taste in music.

SHEDEVIL: You ever hear of Mel Tormé?

(Rob re-enters.)

ROB: Gotcha a towel.

SHEDEVIL: Ga-boing.

(He hands it to her, taking the wet blanket an' hanging it on the stairs.)

ROB: I'm Rob Bob by the way.

(He holds out his hand; she takes it gingerly.)

SHEDEVIL: Go a little easy, I got a plastic hand.

ROB: *(Going really easy.)* Oh, sure.

BIG 8: How'd you get a plastic hand?

SHEDEVIL: Look, Lucifer's not the first guy split on me.

(Puts her hand to her forehead.)

ROB: You okay?

SHEDEVIL: *(Waves him off.)* So, one night while he was doing his lounge act, I got this address from his address book.

BIG 8: I haven't heard nothin' from Lucifer in three years, darlin'.

SHEDEVIL: You mean he's not here?

ROB: Not here.

SHEDEVIL: He has to be here, goddamnit!

BIG 8: Well, darlin'…

SHEDEVIL: I hitchhiked 1500 miles.

BIG 8: Long gone.

> *(Shedevil stands staring at them and then, suddenly, collapses in a faint.)*

ROB: Damn.

BIG 8: Well, this is real nice.

ROB: *(Goes to her.)* Littlebit? You okay girl?

BIG 8: Really needed this.

ROB: Lemme get her up, over to a chair, Big 8.

BIG 8: Well, don't get no lice on you.

ROB: Stick her right by the kitchen table. I'll get her a wake-up call. *(Pours her a drink from a pint bottle of whiskey.)*

BIG 8: What's all them noises she makes?

ROB: *(Shrugs.)* Maybe she's Catholic.

BIG 8: *(Not sold.)* Okay.

ROB: *(Regarding her.)* Now, what color would you call that hair?

BIG 8: Throwed-up strawberry milkshake.

ROB: Listen, you believe she's with child?

BIG 8: Question is, who put the roast in the oven?

ROB: Golly! Ol' Lucifer.

BIG 8: See, we don't know that.

ROB: Them two is married!

BIG 8: Baby, jes' cause you an angel on earth don't mean the devil ain't workin'.

> *(Shedevil opens her eyes.)*

ROB: Looky there! Hello, li'l darlin'.

SHEDEVIL: Kerthunk. Boom.

ROB: Get you a glass water.

BIG 8: You okay?

SHEDEVIL: How the hell would I know?

> *(Starts to rise. Big 8 puts a hand on her shoulder.)*

BIG 8: Stay sit.

SHEDEVIL: Walked the last few miles.

> *(Rob re-enters with water.)*

BIG 8: How far's that?

> *(Takes glass from Rob, puts it in the girl's hand.)*

SHEDEVIL: Bison's Hole.

ROB: Bison's Hole!

BIG 8: Girl, that's twenty-seven mile.

> *(Gives her a drink.)*

SHEDEVIL: *(Suddenly irate, aggressive, and loud.)* Well, what the hell am I supposed to do?! I'm hitchhiking, okay!

(On her feet.)

Yo, *twenty-two* rides from L.A. to wherever the hell I was when I started
walking. And hey, yo, excuse me, I'm pregnant!

ROB: Whoa.

SHEDEVIL: Your baby boy owes me 17,000 bucks, okay! Plus, excuse me, he
took my…gaboom…comic book collection, Disc Man, my charm
bracelet, my ecstasy stash, an' hey, yo, I'm *wet*, goddamnit!

(She starts crying and sits.)

ROB: Well, gollee, darlin'.

BIG 8: *(To Rob, pointing to the stairs.)* Git.

ROB: Well, darn-a-doodle, Big 8…

BIG 8: You get up those stairs!

ROB: Okay, I'm goin'.

BIG 8: Move it or lose it!

ROB: *(Disappearing.)* Geez Louise.

BIG 8: *(To Shedevil.)* Y'see that whiskey on the table.

(Shedevil looks.)

Slug on it.

SHEDEVIL: You got any Kahlua?

BIG 8: I said drink it down!

(Shedevil does.)

Lord, I got me a headache. Strip off your T-shirt.

SHEDEVIL: Doogie, doogie, kapow.

BIG 8: An' don't go makin' them noises.

SHEDEVIL: Eeeeeyow!

BIG 8: Looky here, I ain't your mama. I ain't into no "alternative lifestyles." I
got problems of m'own, okay? I got mortgages, I got arthritis, got my
cowboy lookin' at yer little pointy tits, it's three A.M., an' why the hell
should I believe you're carryin' Lucifer Lee's baby anyhow?!

SHEDEVIL: *(Holding out her glass.)* Can I have some more?

BIG 8: No, you can't! Now I got questions girl, and you prevaricate on me I'll
drop-kick you out on the highway, let you get hit by lightnin'. There was
a hitchhiker up here got hit by lightnin' they didn't find nothin' but his
contact lenses an' his foreskin.

(Shedevil starts to blubber.)

Hell, here…

(Pours another hit in Shedevil's glass.)

Now. Numero son-of-a-bitching uno: What shape is the mole on the inside of Lucifer Lee's thigh?

SHEDEVIL: Looks like a purple rose.

BIG 8: Middle initial?

SHEDEVIL: X for Xavier.

BIG 8: What's the signature tune in his lounge act?

SHEDEVIL: "I Did it My Way!"

BIG 8: Je-*sus*, I hate that song!

SHEDEVIL: *(On the attack.)* First thing he eats?

BIG 8: Snickers bar.

SHEDEVIL: Has he ever, *ever, ever* done it in anything but the missionary position?

BIG 8: How the hell would I know?

SHEDEVIL: Well, I lived it! An' the answer's no!!

(The two women stare at each other.)

BIG 8: I ain't takin' you in.

SHEDEVIL: You think I care?

BIG 8: Where's your wedding ring?

SHEDEVIL: Didn't buy me one.

BIG 8: What the hell'd you give him $17,000 for?

SHEDEVIL: 'Cause I'm a damned fool!

(She knocks back the whiskey.)

BIG 8: How'd you get $17,000?

SHEDEVIL: I screwed R.V. salesmen for an escort service.

BIG 8: *(Shocked.)* That ain't no all-American way.

SHEDEVIL: You asked me, Mama hick.

BIG 8: Don't be callin' me "hick," child. Rode me barrel races front of the Queen of England. You want a place to lay your head, you damn well respect me.

SHEDEVIL: Thwack!

(A standoff.)

BIG 8: You got a good size cut up in your hairline.

SHEDEVIL: Yeah.

BIG 8: Nasty lookin'; how'd you git it?

SHEDEVIL: Fell down walkin'.

BIG 8: Sit.

(Shedevil stares.)

When I say sit, you sit.

(She does.)

Rob Bob!

ROB: *(Offstage.)* Yeah?

BIG 8: Run me down a needle an' thread.

ROB: *(Offstage.)* Okay.

SHEDEVIL: "Rob Bob"?

BIG 8: Yeah. An' while we're on that subject, just who the hell are you?

SHEDEVIL: Shedevil.

BIG 8: Nah, I mean, what's your name?

SHEDEVIL: Shedevil.

BIG 8: What's yer daddy's name?

SHEDEVIL: Front Load.

BIG 8: What's yer mama's name?

SHEDEVIL: Meretorius.

BIG 8: We're just gonna move on past this, hon.

> *(Rob shows up with the needle and thread.)*

ROB: Here you go.

BIG 8: Sit back, I'm just gonna sew up your head.

SHEDEVIL: Sew up my head?

BIG 8: Yeah.

SHEDEVIL: Nuh-uh.

BIG 8: Rob Bob, give her the chewin' stick.

SHEDEVIL: Look, it's just a little cut and…

BIG 8: Nine, ten stitches, we don't take care of it, yer like to get an infected brain.

SHEDEVIL: I don't want anybody stickin' needles…

> *(Big 8 sticks the "chewing stick" in her mouth, silencing her. Shedevil rises.)*

BIG 8: Hold her still, Rob Bob.

> *(Rob Bob sits her down and holds her.)*

> When I'm cuttin' or sewin', there ain't nothin' like a chewin' stick.

> *(Shedevil makes sounds. Big 8 goes to work.)*

ROB: She's *real* good, Littlebit. Gonna fix you right up.

BIG 8: *(Big 8 sews. Shedevil makes muffled pain sounds.)* Now, you ain't should've got mixed up with Lucifer Lee. Hold still. Twenty-seven years old, an' been married four times I know of.

> *(Shedevil spits out the stick. Big 8 picks it up.)*

> Now girl, we gonna put you out with a wooden mallet you don't suck it up.

> *(Sticks the chewing stick back in.)*

> Wipe that blood off, Rob Bob, so I can see where I'm at.

> *(He does.)*

As to him stealin' your money, it wouldn't be the first time…steady now…
not knockin' you up neither…hell, that's his damn hobby. Now, this might
hurt some.

(She sews. Shedevil makes muffled sounds.)

Don't go messin' me up.

(Feeling pain, Shedevil wrenches to the right.)

Dang! Okay, smarty, now I got the needle stuck in your eyelid. Git aholt,
will you Rob Bob?

SHEDEVIL: *(Big 8 removes it.)* Ow.

ROB: Had me aholt.

SHEDEVIL: Off me!

BIG 8: Well, git you a bigger holt! Damn, I hate sloppy work.

SHEDEVIL: Let go of me.

BIG 8: Girl, I'm a healer. Lay my hands on a fracture or break…

SHEDEVIL: Ow!

BIG 8: Sit still an' sit quiet!…that break'll knit up maybe twice as fast as a doctor could do. Stop twitchin'. Healin' just come on me, I didn't no way
go lookin' for it.

ROB: You gone be all right.

BIG 8: Now, Rob Bob here is defendin' his World's Top Cowboy title…look
up now…an' he's broke up off a fall in nine pieces I can feel. Top a'
that, I'm a full-time cheese grater for Beatrice Foods down the road…last
stitch…what I'm sayin' here…got it.

(She leans in and cuts the thread with her teeth and then steps back.)

How's that feel?

ROB: Feels good, huh?

SHEDEVIL: *(Amazed.)* It feels good.

ROB: Don't hurt, huh?

SHEDEVIL: Feels real good.

ROB: See?

BIG 8: What I'm sayin' here is I can't provide no surcease for your storm, girl.

ROB: Gol-lee……

BIG 8: Now the Rainbow Trail Motel down three mile got perpetual vacan-
cies, an' ol' Rob can run you down there, end of story, amen.

ROB: That's pretty cold, Big 8.

BIG 8: You worry about your own self.

SHEDEVIL: Hey! I got $24, that's what I got.

BIG 8: Uh-huh.

(Turns back to Rob.)

SHEDEVIL: Twenty-four dollars! Stitched up head, walking *to* nowhere *through* nowhere, an' Black Dog's coming.

BIG 8: Girl...

SHEDEVIL: *BLACK DOG!*

ROB: Whazat?

SHEDEVIL: He's a Ukrainian, one-eyed Hells Angel's biker.

ROB: What's a Ukrainian?

SHEDEVIL: See, when Lucifer split, I met Black Dog in a Pep Boys. I don't know... fifteen minutes later, we were screwin' in a dumpster. Stayed with him awhile, an' he's got this dumb idea I took $9,000 of his stupid cocaine money.

ROB: But...

SHEDEVIL: He's the one chopped off my hand!

BIG 8: Doubly glad to have you for a houseguest.

ROB: So, he's bad?

SHEDEVIL: Bad what?

ROB: Okay, there's good guys an' bad guys, okay?

SHEDEVIL: I saw him bite the head off a cat.

ROB: Well, that's rough.

SHEDEVIL: Stabbed some cop who spit on his hog. Killed two bikers from the Idaho Skulls with a pool cue and a No. 6 power stapler.

ROB: Okay, that's a bad guy, see.

SHEDEVIL: Yeah, well, he'll be by here soon.

BIG 8: She's goin' to the Rainbow Trail.

ROB: You think Roy or Gene or Randolph or the Duke would leave her unaccompanied with this Black Dog comin' on? That ain't the Cowboy Code.

BIG 8: An' she ain't my deal.

ROB: Gollee, jes' look at her, with child, shiverin', wet, cut up, degraded by life an' too much time in California. We got hearts as big as the West, Big 8.

BIG 8: Listen here, Shedevil.

SHEDEVIL: Yes, ma'am.

ROB: You got the majesty of the mountains lookin' at you.

BIG 8: Will you bite your tongue?! *(A moment.)* Okay, you can sleep out front in the hammock.

ROB: Yeah boy!

SHEDEVIL: Outside?

BIG 8: Don't keep no hammock in the house.

SHEDEVIL: It's pouring rain.

BIG 8: Got a nice view, though.

SHE DEVIL: I left my address book…Black Dog…

BIG 8: Ain't my problem, darlin'.

SHEDEVIL: An' if he rides in?

BIG 8: I was you, I'd run for the trees. *(To Rob.)* Go pull her off a blanket.

ROB: *(Fascinated.)* Why'd he cut off your hand?

SHEDEVIL: I was jerkin' off some rock star, and Black Dog cut it off with a hatchet.

ROB: Holy moley!

BIG 8: Well, I sure needed to hear that.

SHEDEVIL: Thwack!

(Lights fade.)

SCENE 2

The next morning around 7:30 A.M. Big 8 making coffee and cleaning. Shirl, Big 8's sister, an attractively blowsy woman of forty, has just entered. She carries a somewhat bloody package of spareribs.

SHIRL: An the Viagra just made his thumbs swell up.

BIG 8: Poor ol' Baxter.

SHIRL: Poor ol' Baxter? What about your poor ol' sister?

BIG 8: He's a good ol' boy.

SHIRL: He's a limp ol' boy, is what he is. *(Searches in her bag.)*

BIG 8: Shirl, don't go drippin' blood on my linoleum.

SHIRL: *(Pulls out a couple of letters and hands them to Big 8.)* Sis, you didn't pick up your mail. Honeybunch, pour me a cupper, wil'ya? *(Runs a hand along the kitchen island.)* This turned out nice, didn't it? How much that old man charge?

BIG 8: Died before he could send a bill.

SHIRL: Well, there's bad luck an' good luck. Sis, I was thinkin', you get foreclosed on…'nother sugar…you just come on over, I can set you up with Daddy's ol' iron bed in the living room

BIG 8: I ain't wakin' up with Baxter.

SHIRL: Don't you worry about Baxter.

BIG 8: Why you keep on with him's a mystery to me.

SHIRL: I don't like rattlin' around a house on my own. Oh-oh.

BIG 8: Oh-oh what?

SHIRL: I did drip a little blood.

BIG 8: Sponge's over by the toaster oven.

SHIRL: Bad ol' me. Say, you know, there's a young girl with stupid hair layin' in your hammock?

BIG 8: Uh-huh. *(Scans a letter brought by Shirl.)* I am not openin' another letter from that bank.

SHIRL: "Uh-huh?" What do you mean "uh-huh?" Who is she?

BIG 8: She woken up?

SHIRL: Said something like "ca-ching" when I walked by.

BIG 8: I don't want to hear about it.

SHIRL: Okey-dokey. *(The presentation.)* So, I brought you some spareribs!

BIG 8: Shirl, you always bringin' me spareribs. I got more spareribs than a herd.

SHIRL: What's the use workin' down to the slaughterhouse I can't bring my sweet little sister spareribs. Say, listen, you think I should go fer a breast reduction?

BIG 8: Break Baxter's heart.

SHIRL: Oh-oh, I'm still drippin'. Drip, drip, drip.

BIG 8: Will you stick them ribs in the freezer?

(Shirl goes to do it. Big 8 takes the sponge and cleans up.)

SHIRL: How's your little cowboy?

BIG 8: He ain't little an' I ain't little, will you stop callin' everbody little?

SHIRL: Well, I wish you'd send him over to me for about one night. Say, you know how ol' Mr. Dawson cut his finger off with the lawnmower?

BIG 8: *(Knowing what's coming.)* Shirl…

SHIRL: Well, I found it. *(Getting it out of her purse.)* Well, actually, my dog Rusty found it. *(Unwrapping a Kleenex.)* You think it's too late for it to get reattached?

BIG 8: Damn Shirl, that happened last month.

SHIRL: Yeah, it's lookin' a little ragged.

BIG 8: Get that thing away from me.

(Shirl moves to the freezer.)

Don't you go puttin' that in my freezer.

SHIRL: Should I take it over to him?

BIG 8: Put that thing down the disposal!

SHIRL: You think so?

BIG 8: Yes, I think so, do it!!

(Shirl pops it in her mouth.)

My God, Shirl, you gone crazy!

SHIRL: April Fool.

BIG 8: What??

SHIRL: It was just a Vienna sausage I bloodied up a little so we could have some fun!

BIG 8: Jesus, you made my cross too big.

SHIRL: April Fool. Now tell your little sister what that little girl's doin' out there?
(Big 8 explodes with laughter.)
What? What?

BIG 8: That was pretty damn funny, Shirl.

SHIRL: Well, all your troubles, I thought you needed a laugh.

BIG 8: Well, I did. Lord girl, you are stranger than dirt.

SHIRL: Well, you are so nice to say so. *(She jerks her thumb to the door.)* Now, for heaven's sake, tell!

BIG 8: If I'm believin' what I'm hearin', that chile seems to be the pregnant fourth wife of Lucifer Lee.

SHIRL: No!

BIG 8: Yeah. It was, maybe, three A.M. and…
(Shedevil walks in. She's not in a good mood.)

SHEDEVIL: Okay I use your goddamned john to change my goddamned clothes?
(Shedevil exits to bathroom.) See how you like bein' rained on all night!

SHIRL: *(Looking after her.)* Well, she's personable.

BIG 8: Sign on her forehead says, "I'm a world of trouble."

SHIRL: *(Pouring herself another cup.)* Oh, I read the sign.

BIG 8: She's bein' pursued across America by some Russian biker with an ax.

SHIRL: Well, you know young people.

BIG 8: All I needed. *(Picks some torn-off signs off the counter.)* Went around rippin' these off m'land. They gonna auction off my property, all but the house.

SHIRL: Well, little girl, you'll still have the house then.

BIG 8: I got horses, Shirl, I got stock.

SHIRL: How much you need?

BIG 8: Six damn thousand.

SHIRL: Lord, I don't have six thousand.

BIG 8: I know you don't have six thousand.

SHEDEVIL: *(Offstage.)* I can't see a damn thing in this mirror!

BIG 8: She can't see a damn thing in the mirror.

SHIRL: That child doesn't look pregnant.

BIG 8: Shirl, I know when a woman's pregnant.

SHEDEVIL: *(Still off.)* An' the toilet don't flush!

BIG 8: You put her brains in a bluebird, it'd fly backwards. Push in on the button!

SHIRL: Now, it's not your job takin' the child in, Sis.

BIG 8: I suppose not.

SHIRL: Time you look out for yourself. I mean it now.

BIG 8: I know you mean it.

SHIRL: Had you two husbands worthless as cat litter. Got you the head injury couldn't rodeo no more. Raised Lucifer Lee so stupid he couldn't roll rocks down a steep hill.

BIG 8: Shirl…

SHIRL: Workin' night shifts and half shifts try to keep this place together…

BIG 8: Okay, Shirl…

SHIRL: Got you a nice boy around the house now, don't go temptin' him with twenty-year-old flesh!

BIG 8: Shirl! Thank you, darlin', I *got* the *point.*

SHIRL: *(Going through cabinets.)* You got you any Goo-Goo Clusters?

BIG 8: Fried pie, maybe.

SHIRL: Lord girl, I can't be eatin' fried pie before I slaughter pigs. Now, you do or you don't know where Lucifer's at?

BIG 8: Playin' cocktail piano at some raggedy-ass Holiday Inn, I'd guess.

SHIRL: Little girl, that child should clean up his own damn mess. Where's Lucifer's daddy at?

BIG 8: Well, wherever he is, he's drunk.

SHIRL: *(Jerking her thumb toward the bathroom.)* This is *not* your deal.

BIG 8: What's she gonna do though?

SHIRL: You choose the pleasure, you pay the measure, babe.

BIG 8: Yeah, but…

SHIRL: No "yeah, buts," girl's rough as hog gristle, she'll keep on tickin'. Hey, you know what I wanna know.

BIG 8: What's that?

SHIRL: *(Pointing upstairs.)* Does that boy go as good as he looks?

BIG 8: *(Grinning.)* Well, he rides hard but fair.

SHIRL: There's many ride hard, but few ride long.

BIG 8: Sister, he can do a night's work.

SHIRL: Ooooo. You givin' me the shivers. *(Checks her watch.)* Whoa! We got to get goin'! *(Shows Big 8 the time.)*

BIG 8: Oh my.

SHIRL: You give her some marchin' orders, you hear me? Go on now!

BIG 8: *(Calling.)* Shedevil?

SHEDEVIL: *(Offstage.)* Yeah?

BIG 8: We got to vamanos, me and Shirl. There's biscuits and spoon gravy, you hungry…

SHIRL: An' then out.

BIG 8: Then get you to goin'.

SHEDEVIL: *(Off.)* Can't hear you.

BIG 8: I'm leavin' twenty bucks on the butcher block…

SHIRL: *(Warningly.)* Sister?!

BIG 8: I got no line on Lucifer, sad to say.

SHIRL: Now don't you be 'round here when she gets back!

BIG 8: Shirl, I can do my own dirty work in my own dirty house. *(To the offstage Shedevil.)* Good luck travelin', an' don't be wakin' up Rob Bob, he's healin'.

SHIRL: An' don't be 'round here when she gets back!

BIG 8: *(Irritated, to Shirl.)* Will you fridge those ribs?

SHIRL: I fridged 'em. Don't be cleanin' up. Lord, my supervisor's goin' to fry eggs on his forehead.

BIG 8: Well, come on then.

(They are gone. A moment, and Shedevil enters from the bathroom in a little white dress she picked up in a consignment store. She looks, well, virginal. She looks around; then tries a half-hearted, experimental hail.)

SHEDEVIL: Yo? *(No answer. She walks over to the butcher block and picks up the twenty dollar bill. She looks at it; then holds it up to the overhead light. She sticks it in her blouse. A little louder.)* Yo?
(Still no answer. She stands still, listening, then explodes into action. She opens the kitchen drawers, rummages, shuts them. She opens cabinets, throwing out food items. Nothing she can use. She pulls out a box of cereal, rips it open and pours it out on the butcher block. Nope. She stands thinking and looking at the stairs. She experimentally eats a handful of the cereal dry. She takes off her shoes and moves upstairs. All is quiet and still. She comes back down with a cheap jewelry box in one hand and a shoebox in the other. She opens the jewelry box and pours the contents on the butcher block in among the Cheerios. She picks up a silver ring, holds it up to the light and puts it on. She picks around in the rest of the jewelry, discontent. She picks up one more ring, starts to toss it down, stops, listens. She stands frozen for a moment; then puts the second ring on. She brushes the cereal and jewelry over to the corner of the butcher block to make a clear space. She dumps the shoebox out. It's all silver rodeo buckles, close to two dozen.)

Bingo! *(She picks several up and reads the backs.)* Sterling, sterling, sterling, sterling. Oh, yes.

(She leaves the buckles and goes over to the sink, opening the cabinet below it. She pulls out a box of Hefty tall garbage bags. She takes the bag over to the butcher block and in two or three swipes she gets all the buckles in the bag. She puts the garbage bag on the counter and goes back to the bathroom, emerging with the duffel bag and the clothes she changed out of. Hurriedly, she jams the dirty clothes in her duffel, grabs the garbage bag and heads for the door. Rob appears on the stairs with a silver-plated traditional cowboy sixshooter in his hand. He wears only a jockstrap.)

ROB: Turn around real slow. I got you covered.

(She turns. She laughs.)

Excuse me, I was sleepin'.

(She continues to laugh.)

It's the way God made us, okay?

SHEDEVIL: Okay, nutcase, now what?

ROB: Damn, you look pretty. Whew. Lookin' like ice water on a hot day. Darn. I get this. I get what this is. Sure, I recognize it. Oh, man. I seen this in *Bells of Rosarita, Plainsman and the Lady.* By golly, straight out of *Cimarron Petticoats.*

SHEDEVIL: What the hell are you talking about?

ROB: Love at first sight.

SHEDEVIL: Kaboom, whack.

ROB: It happens between the hero and the schoolmarm, or sometimes it's the deceased kindly rancher's daughter an' the travelin' sheriff, has amnesia from the avalanche. *(He's still holding the gun on her.)* Put the bags down, okay?

(She does.)

Never thought it would come on me 'cause I ain't the hero. I'm sort of more the young man the hero befriends. See? 'Cept they usually got their clothes on.

SHEDEVIL: Hey, doofus, I got to find Lucifer Lee and, yo, I can't do it on twenty dollars.

ROB: Love at first sight. Boy, it's painful.

SHEDEVIL: What good's a bunch of silver buckles in a shoebox?

ROB: At's all the cowboys Big 8 has healed.

SHEDEVIL: Yeah?

ROB: What's love at first sight feel like to you?

SHEDEVIL: You're retarded, huh?

ROB: Beg your pardon?

(Sound of a motorcycle.)

SHEDEVIL: *(Holds out her hand for silence.)* Motorcycle.

(Rob Bob opens front door.)

No!

(They listen; it approaches; it roars by.)

Wasn't him.

ROB: How'd ya know!

SHEDEVIL: It's some two-bit Japanese bike. Okay, here's the deal. I'll go upstairs with you. Then I leave with the buckles.

ROB: Lord, I 'preciate that, but I'm savin' myself for marriage.

SHEDEVIL: What about Big whatsername?

ROB: Well, that don't count. That's customary.

SHEDEVIL: She screwed every one of these buckles?

ROB: Just a mark a' respect. Like when Gene or Roy tip their hat to the fan dancer when they ride off.

SHEDEVIL: Shazaam!

ROB: Beggin' your pardon, but what's them noises?

SHEDEVIL: Nuthin'.

ROB: Hey, they're somethin'.

SHEDEVIL: Just started when my daddy'd lock me in the basement.

ROB: My daddy locked me in the basement too!

SHEDEVIL: No way.

ROB: Yeah! Well, we didn't have a basement, kinda chained me under the house.

SHEDEVIL: Yeah? How come you sleep in a jock strap?

ROB: I don't like woolly pajamas. Say, I got mucho respect you're huntin' for your husband.

SHEDEVIL: Whatever.

ROB: Sounds like he's bad though.

SHEDEVIL: Like in those movies?

ROB: Yeah. See, there's good people an' bad people, an' funny sidekicks an' the love interests, an' the bystanders, which it don't matter what they are.

SHEDEVIL: *(Sort of charmed.)* Yeah?

ROB: Yeah. Now, the good people, no matter what happens, what they have to do…whatever…they are good people, an' the bad people, they're bad.

SHEDEVIL: So what am I in the movie?

ROB: Schoolmarm.

SHEDEVIL: I look like a schoolmarm?

ROB: You look real nice in that white dress.

SHEDEVIL: What about me takin' the buckles?

ROB: It's real sweet 'cause you're doin' it fer your unborn child. Now, if you were one of the bad people, it would be bad to do it.

SHEDEVIL: You're goofy as hell, huh?

ROB: I guess.

SHEDEVIL: Listen, can I ask you a question?

ROB: Yes, ma'am.

SHEDEVIL: Does it bother you talkin' to me bareass?

ROB: Guess I mainly forgot about it. *(Looks down at himself.)* Didn't mean no harm.

SHEDEVIL: It's okay. *(A pause; they look at each other.)* Cowboy, what the hell are we going to do now?

ROB: Well, in a love-at-first-sight deal, we could do a little kiss. Nothin' real involved.

SHEDEVIL: I don't have the love-at-first-sight deal.

ROB: Shore you do. 'Member back now. I came round the corner. Our eyes met like. It was real still.

SHEDEVIL: You scared me pissless.

ROB: It feels like that.

SHEDEVIL: You were pointing the gun!

ROB: That jes' gives the love scene a little pep. Little originality. It's still a damn love scene. Looky here…you go to the movie an' there's a boy an' a girl… you followin' me?

SHEDEVIL: You know, you're talking when we could be screwing.

ROB: Ummm, no, I didn't know that.

SHEDEVIL: You nervous or what?

ROB: Well, sort of am, yeah.

SHEDEVIL: Okay, kiss me then.

ROB: You don't mind I'm in the buff?

SHEDEVIL: I can deal with it.

ROB: I'm jus' gonna kiss the outside of yer lips now.

SHEDEVIL: Okay.

ROB: Real easy like.

SHEDEVIL: Okay.

ROB: Tilt your head up.

SHEDEVIL: Shut up, okay?

ROB: Okay.

(He moves toward her, putting the six-shooter on the butcher block as he comes. He stops a step from her.)
Close your eyes.

SHEDEVIL: I don't close my eyes.

ROB: You sure?

SHEDEVIL: I'm sure.

ROB: Well, people got to get used to each other.

SHEDEVIL: Smack!

(She puts her arms around his neck.)

ROB: Smack right back atcha.

(They kiss gently. The lights fade.)

SCENE 3

Rob is now wearing a pair of jeans but is still naked to the waist. Shedevil wears his western shirt, but her legs are bare. The two sit, legs crossed under them, on the butcher-block island in the center of the kitchen. They are passing a quart of orange juice back and forth and eating from a bag of Reeses Pieces. A motorcycle is heard coming closer.

SHEDEVIL: So, after he hit me, I waited till he was asleep an' then I tied him to the bed an' left my initials in his chest with pushpins. That's when they started calling me Shedevil.

(They stop. The motorcycle roars by.)

Naw, that wasn't his Harley. *(Looks at the walls.)* How come she got the guns?

ROB: Some's family. Use 'em huntin', puttin' down sick stock. Burglars, need 'em if the Chinese come, Democrats try to take over. Citizen got to be armed.

SHEDEVIL: *(Watches him carefully.)* Uh-huh.

ROB: What's your true life name?

SHEDEVIL: I don't tell my name.

ROB: Okay. Shoot, I like a good nickname. All the riders got nicknames. Only me, I don't got one.

SHEDEVIL: When your name's Rob Bob, you don't need one.

ROB: So you're a preacher's daughter, huh?

SHEDEVIL: *(Raises a warning finger.)* Don't go there, mister.

ROB: Okay. *(A brief pause.)* Hey, one thing I like about you is how real your plastic hand looks.

SHEDEVIL: One thing I like about you is you got a lazy eye.

ROB: I do. Left one.

SHEDEVIL: You'll be goin' bald, too.

ROB: Naw.

SHEDEVIL: Yeah. I can tell from the way a guy's hair comes together in front.

ROB: *(A moment.)* It's nice to notice things about each other.

SHEDEVIL: It's okay.

ROB: How come you took up with a biker?

SHEDEVIL: Well, sometimes guys is kind of contiguous. See, one leaves while you're in the 7-Eleven, so you just take another one that's in there.

ROB: Like a relay race.

SHEDEVIL: Yeah. The first night with Black Dog he took me to a Chinese restaurant that had this grande fish tank, you know, an' he says, "I can catch those fish barehanded, an' swallow them raw."

ROB: Did he do it?

SHEDEVIL: Yeah. It started a hell of a fight. He finally broke the fish tank with a waiter.

(Shedevil giggles.)

ROB: I once fought nine guys in a Best Western parking lot.

SHEDEVIL: *Nine?!*

ROB: Yeah. They beat the holy Toledo out of me. *(She laughs.)* You ain't gonna leave with the buckles, are ya?

SHEDEVIL: I can't spend my life sittin' on this butcher block.

ROB: All right then, I got to say my piece. *(He hops down.)* Listen, I don't feel comfortable callin' you Shedevil.

SHEDEVIL: Too bad.

ROB: Well, shoot, okay. Shedevil…I already tol' you I got love at first sight. I'm a aces high bronc rider, bulldogger, and Brahma buster. Big 8 heals me up, be maybe the all-time best. See, Shedevil…you're the one, girl. A hero, he mates for life like a swan. He can't be contiguous. Now, I ain't a hero yet, but I'm a good guy…no holds barred on that, so I just got to take it to the next level. And to do that, Shedevil, I need the love of a good woman. I got to have it. Now, hells bells, we both got a ways to go. Listen here, I got to tell the truth an' shame the devil. You got to get rid of that pink pus-colored hair…an' we probably got to tone down your lovemakin' some, but we kin git this right, girl. *(She gets off the butcher block and starts retrieving her clothes, which are scattered about.)* Now don't git nervous, I ain't callin' in the preacher, what I'm sayin' here is let's get in practice. See, my hip's healin' real good an' I'm thinkin' I could ask Big 8 could I have a few days off, follow my drift? Shedevil, I got my daddy's huntin' cabin up in the cottonwoods in the Greaser Mountains.

Sits real pretty on a bluff. What I'm sayin' is, we could take off from here, ride up there. Big 8, she's got a mare handles soft as butter…hell, it's like ridin' in a Buick…I'm not kiddin'. We could go up there an' git used to each other, see? Go on up there an' practice! *(He is finished. A pause.)*

SHEDEVIL: I hate love.

ROB: No you don't.

SHEDEVIL: Yes I do.

ROB: I'm sayin' you don't!

SHEDEVIL: An' I'm sayin' I do!! Hey, I always end up getting treated bad. An' I don't ask for it, okay? Yo, have I asked you to treat me bad?

ROB: No, ma'am. Did I treat you bad?

SHEDEVIL: You will.

ROB: Swear on the Bible I won't.

SHEDEVIL: Hey, as soon as the sex wears off, a man's got no idea what to do with you. "What's this?" they say. "How did this get in the house? What's it for?" Only thing they can think of is to have you watch 'em do stuff. Black Dog wanted me to watch 'em sleep. Like his old grunts and moans was entertainment. An' when you won't watch 'em, hey, they start treatin' you bad.

ROB: I ain't like that.

SHEDEVIL: The hell you're not.

ROB: I ain't. What I would want is to have you explain things to me. 'Cause most of what goes on, I don't get it. Shoot, that would be paradise to me.

SHEDEVIL: Are you for real?

ROB: Far as I know.

SHEDEVIL: How in hell did you get this way?

ROB: Well, I'm just naturally kind of out of it.

(She considers this phenomenon.)

SHEDEVIL: Lemme show you somethin'.

ROB: You bet.

(She opens her mouth wide. He moves in close to look.)

Holy mackerel, you got a nail through your tongue! Holy mackerel, you want me to take you to the hospital?

SHEDEVIL: Look again.

ROB: It's real shiny and pretty.

SHEDEVIL: You sure it doesn't gross you out?

ROB: *(Working hard.)* You gimme a couple of minutes, I'll like it. *(Revelation.)* Hey, it's sorta like jewelry, huh?

SHEDEVIL: Yeah.

ROB: That's good.

SHEDEVIL: *(That was pretty good. She observes him.)* You notice I'm pregnant?

ROB: Hardly.

SHEDEVIL: I mean, yo, do you mind?

ROB: Why would I mind?

SHEDEVIL: It's nice at your cabin, huh?

ROB: There's antelope.

SHEDEVIL: Kiss me.

ROB: Did once.

SHEDEVIL: Again.

> *(He moves to her and kisses her gently, chastely, the way one might in an old western. Shedevil pulls back and roars at him.)*

I said kiss me!

> *(She pulls him into a wild kiss. Just at that moment, Big 8 and Shirl enter, home from work. They carry grocery bags. Big 8 is dumfounded. She watches. She looks at Shirl. She exits. Shirl looks after her, dumfounded. The kiss continues. Big 8 re-enters, raging.)*

BIG 8: Sonufagunufabitch, curl my hair an' suck my toes! Let go of me, Shirl. Hey, far as I know, Hopalong Cassidy kept it in his pants.

ROB: Now, girl…

BIG 8: *(Riding over him.)* What in hell do you think would be the hardest thing on a hip, huh? How about screwin' in a rotary fashion, Rob Bob? You think maybe that's it?

> *(She throws her bag of groceries at him, and they fly all over the kitchen.)*

ROB: Hey…

BIG 8: What the hell am I haulin' my ass on your behalf, huh? Get off me, Shirl. You just followin' yer li'l baby dick around in a circle!

> *(Grabs Shirl's groceries and throws them at Rob.)*

SHIRL: Hey, I got mayonnaise in there!

BIG 8: *(To Shedevil.)* Did I tell you to git off my place? Well, I'm tellin' you, bitch!

SHIRL: *(Intervening. To Big 8.)* Now you think what Jesus would do in this situation?

BIG 8: Goddamnit, Shirl, there's a commandment on this. *(To Rob.)* What the hell do you have to say for yourself?

ROB: Love at first sight.

BIG 8: Dick at first chance is more like it.

ROB: One swan sees another swan an' that's it.

BIG 8: Don't start in on the swans.

ROB: Love is good!

BIG 8: She ain't no All-American way.

ROB: *(Truly riled.)* Don't start, Big 8!

SHEDEVIL: Hey!!!

BIG 8: What!!!?

SHEDEVIL: Yo!! Am I alive or am I dead!!?

SHIRL: *(Soothing the multitudes.)* How 'bout we all go out get us some ribs?

SHEDEVIL: *(Flashing a switchblade.)* I...am...with child...okay? Do I have to slice myself open to prove it? I dropped by Loony Tunes here, lookin' for my husband an' my $17,000. I'm lookin' for some place to rest! All this dilly-dally, shill-shally...yo, you are in a world of trouble you can't even imagine, because Black Dog, the psychopath from Kiev, is out there on the road, headin' this way! I can smell him. Now, let's get down an' get some modus operandi worked out before we're roadkill!

BIG 8: What happened to your southern accent, girl?

SHEDEVIL: None of your damn business!

ROB: Now, I am the man of the house...

SHIRL: *(Head in hands.)* Oh, my God.

ROB: *(To Big 8.)* Ma'am. Rodeo been my life. Shoot, you *are* the rodeo, Big 8, but a good man's got to have a good...

SHIRL: Will you just hush up!

SHEDEVIL: Hold it!

BIG 8: What?

(Shedevil puts a warming finger to her lips. There is a far-off hum.)

BIG 8: What is it?

SHEDEVIL: Too late.

ROB: Too late for what?

SHEDEVIL: He's comin'.

ROB: Don't hear nuthin'.

SHEDEVIL: I know that bike.

ROB: Black Dog?

SHEDEVIL: You just wouldn't listen, would you?

ROB: You just come on over here.

SHEDEVIL: The bunch of us are toast.

ROB: *(Seating Shedevil.)* Sit yourself down.

SHEDEVIL: *(Head in hands.)* I can't believe this! Don't you get it? He's a walking time bomb! He's the Frankenstein freakin' monster. I've seen him suck the brains of a pet monkey out its nose!

SHIRL: Ohhhhhh my.

SHEDEVIL: I am dead meat.

ROB: *(Still to Shedevil, who has begun to cry.)* You kin blow on my neckerchief.

SHEDEVIL: Thwang, ka-boom!

SHIRL: I think I got to go to the bathroom. *(Goes to bathroom door. Closes herself in.)*

BIG 8: Ain't nobody, no-body, settin' foot in here with hostile intent. This is *private property,* buddy.

(Rob is strapping on his belt and holster.)

ROB: Yes, ma'am; yes, ma'am.

BIG 8: Rob Bob, what the hell are you doin'?

ROB: *High Noon,* my damn favorite.

BIG 8: *(Goes for the wall.)* I'm gettin' my shotgun.

ROB: I believe everybody is born for one special moment. And this is, by God, mine!

BIG 8: Simmer down, Rob Bob.

ROB: Back off, Mama, give me room to roll.

SHEDEVIL: *(Rising.)* I'll just go with him.

ROB: Hell you will. Clear the floor now. By God, a man's got to do what a man's got to do.

(Rob takes the familiar ready-to-draw position. Gravel crunches. Footfalls approach the door. Big 8 appears on the stairs.)

BIG 8: You let me take care of this.

ROB: This is my town, and my time. Stay off me, Big 8, this is a man's fair fight.

(Suddenly, with a murderous kick, the door explodes inward, completely off its hinges. Into the room steps a monstrous, Harley-clad, mustachioed, eye-patched, tattooed, fierce, forty-five-year-old Ukrainian biker, the dreaded Black Dog. He takes in the room and roars.)

BLACK DOG: I'm here to crush some goddamned skulls!!!

ROB: Go fer yer gun, Black Dog!

(Black Dog laughs a sharp croaking laugh.)

BLACK DOG: Fuck you, little American idiot!

ROB: Bet 'em or fold 'em, cowboy!

BLACK DOG: *(Laughs, slaps his side with his bare hand in an imitation of a draw and points his finger-gun at Rob.)* Bing, bang!

(Rob draws right on top of this and fires three times. The bullets slam Black Dog back against the wall.)

What the hell is this?

(Rob fires three more times, and Black Dog slides down the wall, leaving a

trail of blood. Shedevil screams. Big 8 runs downstairs with the shotgun. Black Dog lurches to his feet.)

You kill me!

(Blood pours out of his mouth. He pitches over stone dead. Shedevil runs to the body. Big 8 kneels down and tries his pulse. Shirl comes out of the bathroom. All three women turn and look at Rob. He blows on the end of the pistol, twirls it expertly, and slides it coolly into the holster.)

ROB: Man got what he came for.

(Blackout.)

END OF ACT ONE

ACT TWO
SCENE 1

The whole group is gathered silently around the body of Black Dog. They stare down at him.

SHEDEVIL: What kind of beer is this?

ROB: Local.

BIG 8: *(Nodding.)* Local beer.
(They look at the body.)
Shit.
(They all drink beer.)

SHIRL: He's dead, huh?

BIG 8: Oh, yeah.

SHIRL: Broke your door.

BIG 8: Tore that sumbitch right off.
(Shedevil explodes in tears and throws herself in an embrace with Rob.)

ROB: It's okay, girl. Gonna be okay, little lady.
(She grabs him by the back of the hair and kisses him; then she pulls back and hits him square in the face.)

SHEDEVIL: Kaboom! *(She kicks him.)* Crunch! *(Hits him again.)* Skreek! *(Then she grabs him and kisses him again.)*

SHIRL: Makes me feel old.

BIG 8: *(Still looking at the body.)* He just inhaled.

SHIRL: Huh-uh.

BIG 8: Seemed like it.

SHIRL: *(Peers at him.)* I kill things all day long an' this here is dead.
(Rob and Shedevil have let their passion drive them up on top of the butcher block, where they are making love.)
We got some modified shock goin' on here.

BIG 8: Rob Bob, get offa that girl! Git offa her right now!
(He does.)
You don't think I have any feelings here? You can jes' rape an' pillage an' shoot an' it's all jes' part of the wallpaper?

ROB: Sorry, Big 8.

BIG 8: You should be sorry. Gollee! Did you never care for me or what?

ROB: Did, an' I do.

BIG 8: Well, you got one hell of a strange way of showin' it!

(A strange, low growl emanates from the body of Black Dog. Everybody shrinks back. It stops.)

SHIRL: I believe corpses let off gas.

SHEDEVIL: Was that gas?

ROB: You sure that was him?

BIG 8: Well, it sure as hell wasn't me.

SHEDEVIL: He used to growl; he used to growl in bars.

BIG 8: Used to growl?

SHEDEVIL: Yeah. It was a sign, you know, that you should back off. Yo, I would always tell whoever was on his case that they might, you know, want to drive to another state or whatever.

SHIRL: See, I'm pretty sure that was gas. Happens all the time with deceased pigs. *(Sees their concerned, incredulous faces.)* Cross my heart. It was nasty gas, too. Sometimes, one person would press on the belly and another one would hold a match, and the gas would catch fire an' shoot out.

BIG 8: No kiddin'.

SHIRL: Not with steers though. Wouldn't catch fire with steers.

BIG 8: Well, I'm glad to hear that.

(There is another ominous growl from Black Dog.)

SHEDEVIL: I don't think that's gas.

(Another growl and Black Dog rolls over on his side.)

SHIRL: Jesus.

SHEDEVIL: Look out.

(Black Dog, his bad eye a bloody hole, several bullet holes in his chest oozing, blood running down his arms, begins a monstrous, agonizing struggle to rise to his feet. He grabs hold of a stool by the butcher block and uses it to drag himself up.)

SHIRL: Oh my God, oh my God, oh my God, oh my God, oh my God, oh my God, oh my God.

(Simultaneously with that.)

SHEDEVIL: We ought to run. Everybody should really ought to. We shouldn't just stand here. It's a mistake just to stand here. Everybody run. Everybody run.

(Black Dog's growling becomes a kind of roaring. It's like a horror movie. He forces himself upright, using the butcher block for leverage. Rob goes for his gun, drops it on the floor. Picks it back up. Fires repeatedly. It is, of course, empty. Black Dog is now erect; across the butcher block from him is Shedevil.)

SHEDEVIL: Hi there, baby.

BLACK DOG: *(He swivels, looking at them around the room, speaks in tortured English.)* Give…me…beer!

SHIRL: *(To Big 8.)* He wants a beer, Sissy.

BIG 8: Uh-huh.

SHIRL: I'll get you a beer, darlin'.

(She goes to fridge. Black Dog moves around butcher block. Shedevil moves too, staying away from him.)

You bet I will. Nice cold beer.

(Pops top. Black Dog turns toward the sound.)

Here you are, Honeybunch, and I know you'll enjoy it.

(She hands it to him gingerly. He upends it and chugs it down. They watch, hypnotized. As he drinks, liquid stains his shirt. He feels it. He looks down. Shirl speaks, hysterically cheerful.)

SHIRL: It's leakin' out his chest, see there, it's leakin' out his chest.

BLACK DOG: What is this I am seeing with my eyes?

SHIRL: It's comin' out the bullet holes.

BLACK DOG: *(In English.)* Can't even drink beer, you son-of-bitch! *(Throws the beer can through the window, shattering glass. A guttural roar.)* I eat you, kill you, crack your bones! *(He spins around and falls to the floor once more like a concrete block.)*

BIG 8: I'm switchin' to bourbon.

(She goes to a kitchen cabinet and pulls out a bottle. At the same time, Shedevil, sickened, runs into the bathroom and slams the door.)

Shirl?

SHIRL: What?

BIG 8: How you feelin' over there?

SHIRL: Oh, well, I guess I'm good to go.

BIG 8: You think you could lean over, check around fer a pulse.

SHIRL: Well, it's sweet of you to think of me.

BIG 8: Shirl!

SHIRL: Yeah, I…I can do that.

ROB: What should I do?

BIG 8: You should stand there.

ROB: Okay.

BIG 8: *(Drinks.)* What's the verdict down there, Shirl?

SHIRL: He got but nothin' going on.

BIG 8: You sure now?

SHIRL: If he got a pulse, I got a hard-on.

BIG 8: We was doin' rodeo in Wisconsin, so they took us down fer some ice fishin' an' this bronc rider fell through the ice. Two hours later, he smashed up outta there like a damn Jack inna box.

SHIRL: I'm tellin' you, this dude is dead.

BIG 8: Rob Bob.

ROB: Yeah?

BIG 8: Walk yourself over there, kick that body real hard.

ROB: Do I have to?

BIG 8: Rob Bob, you have betrayed my trust. An' I'm not gonna lie to ya, I'm hurtin'. Hurtin' in the rain.

ROB: It stopped rainin'.

BIG 8: Damnation! I just want me an ordinary life. Is that too damn much to ask!?

(Shedevil comes wanly out of the bathroom.)

What is it?

SHEDEVIL: I'm shakin'. I'm shakin' bad.

BIG 8: Well, hell, Rob Bob, git over there an' hold her! You know, I blame every goddamned bit of this on Lucifer Lee. *(Sees Rob hugging Shedevil.)* An' that's enough of that. *(To Shirl.)* Shirl, walk over there an' kick that corpse.

SHIRL: My sneakers are bran' new.

BIG 8: Shirl.

SHIRL: All right.

(She does.)

BIG 8: I mean *kick* him!

(Shirl gives him a good one. Nothing.)

SHIRL: *(Looking down on Black Dog.)* Since he's layin' on his face, I'd haveta notice he ain't packin'.

ROB: He went for his gun.

SHIRL: In your dreams, Rob Bob.

ROB: Hey, this was a fair fight, okay? We was eyeball to eyeball, I tol' him to draw, an' y'all saw him reach.

BIG 8: Got him a sheathed huntin' knife.

ROB: See there, betcha he's an expert knife thrower.

SHIRL: *(Irritated.)* He can't throw it when it's sheathed.

ROB: Code a' the West is no shooting a unarmed man, okay... *(He unsheathes the knife.)*...but he had him a razor sharp 10-inch bear gutter. He went for his an' I went for mine. This ain't shabby. This here passes muster.

SHIRL: What are we doin' here?

ROB: What are we doin'?

SHIRL: Have we lost our damn minds?

ROB: We are discussin' whether I'm the good guy or the bad guy.

SHIRL: This is the first of the month, right?

ROB: Yeah, but...

SHIRL: Does my boyfriend Baxter, without fail, propose to me ona first of the month?

ROB: Yeah, but...

SHIRL: What time does my honey pick me up at my sister's?

ROB: Around six o'clock, but...

SHIRL: An' is it six-fifteen?

ROB: Shirl, we got important issues, girl...

SHIRL: What does my honey do for a livin'?

ROB: He's a deputy sheriff, Shirl.

> *(They look at Black Dog. Rob looks heavenward in frustrated recognition.)*
> Oh-oh.
>
> *(The room explodes into action. Rob grabs hold of Black Dog's arms and tries to drag him around the island so he can get him out the back door. Moving Black Dog however is no simple task. Shirl is rushing around picking up the beer cans. Big 8 opens the mop closet, grabs a mop, and heads for the sink to wet it. Shedevil closes her eyes and sings "Rock of Ages" in a small, clear soprano. Shirl now moves to the door, trying to set it back in the frame. Big 8 is mopping up the blood trail left as Rob drags the riddled Black Dog.)*

BIG 8: Rob Bob. Rob Bob! Where the hell you takin' him?

ROB: *(Dragging.)* Out.

BIG 8: *(Mopping.)* Where? Out where?

ROB: Backyard.

BIG 8: You can't take him in the backyard. Backyard's flat. Backyard's empty. It's completely damn empty clear to the horizon. Rob Bob, goddamnit, hold it!

ROB: *(Finally in a fit.)* How the hell am I supposed to git anything done you yak-yak-yakking upside down an' backwards while I'm workin' here? *("Rock of Ages" finally irritates him.)* Shedevil, honey, will you jes' shut the hell up, sweetie? Will you, little darlin', for God's sake, stick a sock in it?

BIG 8: Rob Bob.

ROB: What?!

BIG 8: Out in the backyard he will be the only object of size in five miles.

ROB: There's cows out there, fer God's sake.

BIG 8: He don't look nothin' in the known universe like a cow.

ROB: I'm not jes' gonna leave him there! I ain't a complete moron, am I; I'm gonna bury him.

BIG 8: On'y a complete moron would think we got time to bury him!

SHIRL: Put him in the icebox! *(She rushes to the fridge and starts throwing stuff out.)*

BIG 8: *(Rushing to help Shirl.)* See, put 'im in the icebox.

ROB: *(Leaving Black Dog.)* He's bigger nor a damn steer, you cain't git him in the icebox!

BIG 8: *(Furious.)* See, that the deal, see. You always lookin' on the dark side. You got to accentuate the positive, goddamn it.

(Shedevil is down with dishtowels, mopping blood and singing again.)

ROB AND BIG 8: *(To Shedevil.)* Stop singing!

SHEDEVIL: *(Simply.)* Yo, you can't get him in the icebox!!

(There is the sound of a car driving in onto the gravel. Shirl whirls and runs to the empty door.)

BIG 8: Oh-oh.

SHIRL: It's Baxter in the cruiser. Baxter's comin' up the drive. Stick him in the broom closet!

ROB: In the broom closet.

SHIRL: *(Yelling and waving out the door hole.)* Hi, there, Baxter puddin'! How you doin', sweet thing?

(They reverse direction. Shirl pulls brooms, mops, and buckets out of the broom closet and hurls them out the back door. Shedevil rushes about, mopping up blood fiendishly. The two older women and Rob exert superhuman strength and get Black Dog to his feet.)

BIG 8: One, two, three—lift.

ROB: Hold it, hold it…

SHIRL: Lemme help.

ROB: I got him now.

BIG 8: Ow!

ROB: Sorry, babe. Okay. Okay. Haul him, haul him.

SHIRL: Jesus, Mary, and Joseph…

BIG 8: Git your arm back here. Now. Now! Now!!

(Amazingly enough, he is on his feet. They steady for their final assault on the broom closet.)

BLACK DOG: *(Gravelly and small but audible.)* Give me…beer.

(Shirl screams. They all step back; he falls. Rob leaps on him, hands on his throat. He exerts every muscle in the act of strangulation.)

ROB: Die, damn you. Die, die, die, die, die.

(Shirl screams. Big 8 slaps her. She stops.)

BIG 8: *(Speaks calmly and sweetly. Meanwhile, Rob has scrambled off Black Dog and gone to get the hunting knife left on the island.)*
Shirl, darlin', why don't you go on out there an' give your sweetie pie a great big kiss.
(At this point, Rob re-straddles Black Dog. Black Dog reaches up and grabs his knife hand, and they struggle.)
Uh-huh, uh-huh, welcome him home from his work with a little damn affection.
(Black Dog and Rob roll across the floor.)

SHIRL: *(Panicked and horrified.)* Uh-huh.

BIG 8: Uh-huh. Little kisses and hugs.
(Rob, with a supreme effort, drives the knife into Black Dog's chest. A second time. A third time. Both Big 8 and Shirl scream. Black Dog goes limp. His arm drops.)

BIG 8: Go. GO.

SHIRL: Well, uh-huh, sure, I'll just go right out there.
(Shedevil sits rocking in a chair, singing "What a Friend I Have in Jesus.")
I'll kill you if you don't shut up!
(Exhausted, Rob rolls off the body.)

ROB: Well, he's dead now, by God.

SHIRL: *(To Big 8.)* Does it matter that I'm covered with blood?

BIG 8: *(Smiling both wildly and coquettishly. To Shirl.)* Ummm, well, let's see, I don't know, it just might.

ROB: See, I finished him off.

BIG 8: Shirl, you just sashay on over there to the faucet an' pretty up.

ROB: Dead as a possum on a highway interchange!

BIG 8: *(Shaking him by his shirtfront.)* Will…you…be quiet. *(She goes to the door and calls.)* Baxter, what are you doin' out there, darlin'?

BAXTER: *(Offstage.)* Been meanin' to check my oil.

BIG 8: *(Looking back in.)* Checkin' his oil.

SHIRL: *(Turning.)* How I look?

BIG 8: *(Going over.)* Well, honey…I could just…well…tidy you up.
(Maniacally cleans her.)

ROB: *(To Shedevil.)* Sorry what I said. I'd like to hear the hymn you were singin'.

BIG 8: *(A murderous whisper.)* No, you wouldn't. You wouldn't like to hear that hymn.

(Out the door.) I cain't think on a better thing in this worl' you should
be doing, Baxter.

(Shirl, through washing, fights to bring order to her hair and demeanor.)

Now, Baxter, you stay put, 'cause Shirl, she's comin' out with a surprise.

BAXTER: *(From offstage.)* Surprise!

BIG 8: *(To Shirl.)* Git the hell out there, Shirl.

SHIRL: Do I look all right?

BIG 8: Few drops here an' there. You jes' tell him you got a nosebleed.

SHIRL: My God, Big 8, what the hell are we into?

SHEDEVIL: Murder an' strangulations.

BIG 8: *(To Shirl.)* Go. Go on, baby. Shoo. Go.

(Shirl heads out. Big 8 heads over for where Rob is at work.)

BAXTER: *(From offstage.)* Hi, Honey, I can't hardly wait.

(Shirl pops back in.)

SHIRL: Surprise!

(Rob and Big 8 are getting Black Dog back on his feet.)

BIG 8: I cain't believe yer jokin' now, Shirl.

SHIRL: Surprise. Surprise, goddamnit.

BIG 8: Have you gone flat crazy?

SHIRL: You told Baxter I was bringing him out a surprise.

BIG 8: *(Irritated, straining every muscle.)* Well, bring him out a surprise, Shirl.

SHIRL: Well, what the hell am I s'posed to bring him?

BIG 8: Well, what the hell does the man like?

SHIRL: I don't know.

BIG 8: You got to know, you been datin' him for nine years.

SHIRL: I just don't know.

BIG 8: You *have to know!*

SHIRL: Breasts.

BIG 8: Well, take off yer shirt an' go tell 'im hello.

(Shirl goes out unbuttoning her shirt.)

Shedevil, get over here.

SHEDEVIL: I can't touch him.

ROB: We ain't got the heft to git him in.

SHEDEVIL: Don't make me.

ROB: Baby, darlin' chickadee, I'm yer lovin' man, askin' for some help here.
Give yer ol' baby jes' a little hand here, Sweetiecakes.

BIG 8: You don't git over here, you'll spend the rest of your miserable life in a
maximum security prison.

SHEDEVIL: Okay.

(She comes over.)

ROB: Grab on.

BIG 8: Git him up on his knees.

ROB: Dang.

BIG 8: Pull.

ROB: One, two, three…. Lift!

(They get Black Dog upright.)

Git the door.

(Shedevil opens the broom closet.)

Okay, we got 'er.

(To Shedevil.) You clean.

SHEDEVIL: Do what?

BIG 8: Clean. Clean! My God, you musta cleaned up somethin' in yer miserable life. Clean up!

SHEDEVIL: Okay.

ROB: Gotta get him up.

BIG 8: Oh God, my hand went inside his chest!

ROB: Back him in.

BIG 8: Losin' my grip.

SHEDEVIL: I'm cleanin'.

ROB: Little more. Now. Gonna lift him up an' in.

BIG 8: On three.

BIG 8: One, two, three.

(They all roar with the effort, but they get Black Dog in and slam the door. They are exhausted and bloody and half-crazed with the effort.)

Hot damn! Whooee!

(They embrace.)

ROB: Ain't done nuthin' like that since your horse died in that horse trailer.

(Big 8 starts to laugh.)

You remember that horse trailer?

BIG 8: *(Laughing.)* Do I remember?

ROB: *(Starting to laugh.)* Started pullin' that horse out an' his leg come off.

SHEDEVIL: His leg came off?!

BIG 8: Right in his hand.

SHEDEVIL: That's horrible.

ROB: It was.

BIG 8: It was downright *horrible.*

(All three of them are laughing.)

ROB: I fainted.

BIG 8: He did.

ROB: Bam, right on the ground.

> (They all rock with laughter.)

BIG 8: Wait a minute.

BIG 8: Hold it!

> (The laughter stops.)
>
> Put the stuff in the fridge.
>
> (Mayhem.)

ROB: Don't have time.

BIG 8: Throw it out the back then.

> (More mayhem.)

ROB: You want these ribs?

BIG 8: No, I don't want the ribs!

> (They finish. They look at each other. They're smeared with Black Dog's blood.)
>
> We gotta change!
>
> (The three of them rush upstairs just as Baxter comes in with Shirl, who is buttoning up her shirt. He has his arms affectionately around her.)

BAXTER: (He is a small, balding cop, slightly overweight, maybe 45 years old.) Honey-bunny, baby, you are the everlovin' best.

SHIRL: Thank you, Baxter bow-wow.

BAXTER: I've never, ever, never been welcomed home like that.

SHIRL: I just been thinkin' on you all day.

BAXTER: An' I been thinkin' about you.

SHIRL: You have?

BAXTER: An' *now*, I'm really thinkin' about you!

SHIRL: You naughty thing.

BAXTER: So I want you to sit right over here, an' I want you to listen to me good.

SHIRL: (She sees drops of blood on the island.) You bad ol' policeman, I got both my ears trained on yer mouth.

BAXTER: You a good ol', big ol' girl.

SHIRL: Baxter, you are makin' me giggle an' squirm!

> (She turns and tries to wipe it off with her handkerchief.)

BAXTER: Bee-utiful Shirl, you see before you, in the uniform he is proud to wear…an' I want you to see the 'Merican flag on my breast…

> (Shirl cleans up here and there.)

…on my breast, sweet land o' liberty, a man…

> (Points to himself.)

…man standin' before you…little overweight…a man you know is crippled for procreation 'cause of wounds he received below the waist protectin' the bulk grocery store…this man givin' his life to two things: Shirl Bitahatcher an' justice.

(Shirl sees another drop and wipes.)

Hey, Shirl, don't move around too much or I goin' to forget this.

SHIRL: Sorry, Baxter.

BAXTER: Hardest thing I ever done.

SHIRL: I'm lovin' it.

BAXTER: *(Picking up the thread.)*…an' justice. You could ask a hunnert folks an' they would tell you Baxter Blue, he's a man who does right, couldn't do no wrong.

SHIRL: *(Taking every opportunity to remove blood spots.)* Amen.

BAXTER: Now, I'm standin' on the precipice of a big career, Shirl. Bein' a two-man department, I'm already the number two man.

SHIRL: Uh-huh.

BAXTER: Chief Esperanza, at 300 pounds, he's on the edge of retirement, 'cause he can't make the stairs. That day comes, you wouldn't hafta slaughter cattle no more. A wife ain't meant to come home bloody. *(A pause.)* That ain't a joke on your nosebleed now.

SHIRL: Not taken as such.

BAXTER: You got a hesitancy on me, Shirl…

SHIRL: Now…

BAXTER: You do. You turned me down eighteen months running. *(Improvising.)* I will say I take yer welcome today as a turnin' point. Everbody knows I'm a breast man.

SHIRL: I'm jest gonna lean on the kitchen island here.

BAXTER: Sure thing. *(Looks down at some blood they didn't wipe up, also sees some blood on the broom closet door.)* You got the nosebleed pretty bad.

SHIRL: Get 'em sometime when I'm thinkin' about you.

BAXTER: You're kiddin'?

SHIRL: Huh-uh.

BAXTER: Damn, Shirl, you get a man hot. Listen… *(He pulls a letter out of his back pocket.)* This here's a letter from Big Fork…she's a job offer.

SHIRL: Police?

BAXTER: Cement. Used to work in cement. My daddy was in cement.

SHIRL: *(Glancing at the stairs.)* I remember you tol' me. *(A moment.)* Big Fork's pretty far off.

BAXTER: This here's the moment, girl. We poised on a knife edge. It's either you or cement.

(Big 8 re-enters. A new outfit, clean as a penny. She is followed by Rob, also spotless, and Shedevil, who is wearing a housedress of Big 8's, which is much too big.)

BIG 8: Well, hell, if it ain't Baxter Blue. Good on you.

BAXTER: Uh-huh.

BIG 8: How they hangin'?

(Baxter looks stricken.)

Hell, Baxter, I'm sorry, I jes' allus forget.

BAXTER: Ummm. 'Pology accepted. It ain't "how's a man hangin'," it's does he do right?

ROB: Now that's the damn truth, Baxter. There is good an' there's bad…

BIG 8: Don't git him started. *(Turns to Shedevil.)* Now, this little girl here…

SHEDEVIL: *(Definitely playing a role.)* Susie Pertman.

BAXTER: Perkman?

SHEDEVIL: Pert. Per*t*man. Some folks call me Perky.

BAXTER: Real pleasure, Perky.

(They shake hands.)

SHEDEVIL: *(Chipper.)* I got an artificial hand.

BAXTER: Aw shoot, I'm sorry.

SHEDEVIL: Don't you worry, it's Teflon.

SHIRL: Perky is just visitin'.

SHEDEVIL: Till my hair grows out.

(Everyone laughs.)

BIG 8: Her fiancé is…*(Pause.)*

SHIRL: Well, he's just an ol'…*(Pause.)*

ROB: Friend.

BAXTER: Would you be expectin'? I mean, sorta seems like a maternity frock.

SHEDEVIL: *(Perky.)* Well, I would.

BAXTER: Ain't *nobody* respects the miracle of birth like I do.

SHEDEVIL: *(Curtseying.)* Well, thank you a bunch.

BAXTER: That wouldn't be yer Harley hawg out there, would it, Perky?

SHEDEVIL: Ummmmm, well…

BAXTER: Couldn't help noticin' that big ol' thing when I come in.

BIG 8: B'longs to her fiancé.

ROB: No, it don't.

BIG 8: Yes, it does.

SHIRL: What they mean is…

ROB: In point of fact…

BIG 8: Not to cut it too fine…

SHEDEVIL: It's mine. *(A pause.)*

BAXTER: But he's here, huh?

> *(Black Dog's arm falls out of the closet door.)*

SHEDEVIL: Ummmmmmm…

BIG 8: He sure is an… *(Pause.)*

SHIRL: An' he's just… *(A pause.)*

ROB: Takin' a nap.

BAXTER: Long ride?

SHEDEVIL: Oh, sure…

SHIRL: He's just…

BIG 8: Out like a light.

> *(They chuckle courteously. They are out of conversation.)*

SHIRL: Cuppa?

BIG 8: Coffee?

BAXTER: I can pour me one.

> *(Heads over for the stove. Shirl, Big 8, and Rob all clean up telltale blood.)*

SHEDEVIL: It's so pretty out. Don't you think it's pretty out. I think it's so pretty out.

BAXTER: *(Stopping with the pot in his hand.)* Dang, Shirl, you nosebled on the stove, too.

SHEDEVIL: We could just all go for a walk!

BAXTER: *(Something is confusing him.)* Shirl?

SHIRL: *(Completely taking over.)* You know what, this here is a big day! Uh-huh, it is. Big, big, super big day. *(A nod to Shedevil.)*

BIG 8: *(Picking up.)* Well, what kinda big day is this, Shirl?

SHIRL: *(Moving him away from the stove.)* Well, Baxter here… *(Slaps his shoulder coyly.)*…he is such a cute thang!

BAXTER: What?

SHIRL: Well, he just… *(She fans herself and giggles.)*

BIG 8: *(In the spirit.)* Baxter Blue, you dirty ol' thing, what're you up to?

BAXTER: What?

ROB: Hol' on here. Hol' on jest a dang minute. Shoot, Baxter, you didn't…

SHIRL: He did!

ROB: *(Slapping Baxter on the back.)* Well, you dirty ol' thing…

BIG 8: Did you go an' pop the question on my bes' friend?!

SHIRL: He did.

BIG 8: He did!

ROB: *(Slaps him again.)* You rowdy ol' breast man!

BAXTER: I do that every month.

SHIRL: But!!!

> *(Baxter is so startled he whirls around, almost losing his balance.)*

But there's a big difference this time.

BIG 8: *(Keeping the ball in the air.)* What's the difference this time, Shirl?

SHIRL: The difference this time *is*…I'm gonna say "yes."

> *(Big 8 lets out a scream, throws her hands up in the air and grabs Shirl in an embrace. Rob pounds Baxter on the back.)*

ROB: Ring-a-ding-ding, Mr. Baxter Blue!

BIG 8: *(To Shirl.)* Girl, you are on easy street!

ROB: Hot snookie, Baxter! What you got to say for yourself, son?

BAXTER: I'm just stunned.

BIG 8: *(To Baxter.)* Open me up a hug, you chunky li'l lawman you!

SHEDEVIL: Well, am I in the right place at the right time or what?

ROB: You done the right thang by that boy, Shirl.

SHIRL: I just thank you all potfulls.

ROB: Speech, Baxter, dagnabbit.

BIG 8: Speech, an' no kiddin'.

> *(Big 8, Rob, and Shedevil chant, "Speech, speech, speech." Rob grabs Baxter and sets him up on the butcher block.)*

BAXTER: *(When he's grabbed.)* Whoa, there, hoss!

ROB: I gotcha.

SHIRL: Now, you be careful there.

BAXTER: All right, fer heaven's sake.

> *(He's up.)*

ROB: Let 'er rip, Blue-boy!

> *(They applaud.)*

BAXTER: Well, shoot, I'm damn gratified.

> *(More applause; Rob whistles.)*

Hells bells, I'll give a damn speech, damnit.

ROB: *(Quieting the applause.)* Give that man room ta let loose!

> *(Silence descends.)*

BAXTER: *(Lets out a sort of rooster/coyote call. Waves his hat.)* Gonna be a hot time in the sagebrush tonight!

> *(Applause. Whistles.)*

I love Shirl Bitahatcher, an' I love America! I am the by God wild man of the Wild West. Rip-diddley-ay-do-ring-a-ding-day!

ROB: You tell 'em, wild man!

BAXTER: *(During this speech, Shedevil, taking advantage of the focus on Baxter, slips away, takes the silver buckles, which are still in the kitchen, and puts them in her bag. Shirl notices. Big 8 notices.)*

I am tall as a tornado, noisy as a thunderstorm, hotter than any hell you got in Arizona! EEEYA! From my left hand to my right hand is a by God thousand miles. I'm half man, half mountain lion an' half alligator. I drink me a five gallon jug a' corn whiskey between the time my eyes open an' my feet hit the floor. I eat me Texas for breakfast with the Pacific Ocean for a chaser, an' dine on a thousand head of short horn steers roasted on a slow spit in hell come nightfall. Yowsa bowsa! You lookin' for trouble, I'm Beelzebub in a cotton nightshirt. Yippy-ay-ay-ay-yo, I'm an old cowhand with a wedding band, I'm a gonna do it for sure!

(Rob lets loose a rodeo yell. A pause.)

BIG 8: You gonna talk about Shirl?

BAXTER: *(Laughing embarrassedly.)* Ah hell, I forgot.

(Everybody laughs.)

I'm a family man, Shirl. Been lookin' fer my family ever since I was born. When my sweet Ginny Sue threw herself front of the Amtrak, I didn't think I'd never find true love again.

SHIRL: You poor thang.

BAXTER: But the land à the bald eagle, it took care a me in good time. Brought Shirl down from Laramie an' I been goo-goo since the first day. Hell, I been double goo-goo.

(Laughter.)

She always overlooked my little disability…

SHIRL: Honey, that's nothin'.

BAXTER: Brought me back to the church, keeps me down to six-pack a day an' she allus drops some spareribs by the station. *(He tears up.)* I'm gonna be a good husband, Shirl. Gonna stick with law enforcement. Gonna love, honor, an' obey you, so help me God. *(Quiet.)* I guess tha's all.

(Wild applause.)

ROB: *(Over the top.)* Damn, that was fine ! Y'all the man, Baxter Blue.

BAXTER: Well, I ain't one of your fancy talkers.

SHIRL: *(Really touched.)* You come on over here an' give me a smacker, Baxter.

BAXTER: *(Taking Rob's hand to get down.)* I would purely be honored to do *that*.

(Shirl is standing in front of the broom closet. Baxter comes around where she is.)

BIG 8: All right, you get on in here, sweet thang.

(He is positioned where he can kiss her.)

ROB: *(Dead serious.)* There ain't nothin' beats love.

(There is a tremendous roar and, simultaneously, Black Dog's fist pierces the broom closet door right between Shirl and Baxter. Shirl shrieks with terror and keeps shrieking as she flees.)

BAXTER: Son-of-a-bitch. *(He backs away, unsnapping his service pistol.)*

BIG 8: Take it easy, Baxter.

BAXTER: Son-of-a-bitch!

SHEDEVIL: Oh my God.

(Tremendous shattering and the door of the broom closet falls into the room, revealing…)

BLACK DOG: I kill you and eat your hearts!!

(Baxter empties his pistol into this gory Frankenstein amidst the shrieks and yells of the others. Black Dog continues in Russian as the bullets strike home.) Animals! Vultures! Capitalist whores!

ROB: *(The following lines also overlap during the firing.)* Git out, Big 8!

SHEDEVIL: Oh my God, he's comin'.

BIG 8: Git back, critter!

(After eight shots, Black Dog takes one more step and falls to the floor. Silence descends, except for hard breathing and minor whimpering. We see Big 8's mind work. She takes a step forward.)

Baxter Blue, what the hell have you done?

BAXTER: What?

BIG 8: I jes' cain't believe this.

BAXTER: What?!

SHIRL: *(Pointing at the fallen Black Dog.)* He was jokin'!

ROB: But…

BAXTER: Jokin'?

BIG 8: You goddamned fool, that's her fiancé. *(She points at Shedevil.)*

ROB: But…

SHEDEVIL: *(On it. She breaks down in piteous sobs.)* My poor…

SHIRL: Billy.

SHEDEVIL: …Jimmy.

BAXTER: *(Appalled.)* That's Jimmy?

BIG 8: They came down here on the Harley to git married.

BAXTER: Oh my God.

SHIRL: *(Coming to him.)* Baxter, honey, you went crazy.

BAXTER: But he came blastin' outa that closet. Yellin', sayin' he was gonna eat us.

BIG 8: Completely unarmed, darlin'.

BAXTER: He had an *accent!*

SHIRL: Baby, ain't you s'posed to give a warnin'?

BAXTER: Well, I…

SHEDEVIL: *(Kneeling by Black Dog.)* Jimmy, Jimmy, my darling Jimmy.

BAXTER: But he…

BIG 8: He's a joker, honey. We'd been talkin' on you an' here you come pullin' in, an' Jimmy says "How 'bout I give him a little scare," an' we said, "Okay," 'cause how you love a li'l jokin'.

(Shedevil, crying, runs into the bathroom and closes the door. Shirl goes after her.)

BAXTER: He's unarmed?

BIG 8: *(Gently.)* Look at him.

ROB: Jeminy crickets, what are we gonna do?

BAXTER: I killed him.

BIG 8: Shot him twelve times.

SHIRL: Six times.

BIG 8: Yeah, it was six.

ROB: Hell, that'd kill an elephant.

BAXTER: *(Disoriented.)* I shot an unarmed man playin' a joke.

SHIRL: *(To the bathroom door.)* Please come out, Patti.

SHEDEVIL: *(From inside.)* Perky.

SHIRL: *(To the door.)* Perky, damnit.

BIG 8: We got to do some quick thinkin' here, boy.

BAXTER: *(It hits him.)* I'm a rogue cop.

BIG 8: Wadn't yer fault, Baxter.

SHIRL: *(A murderous whisper.)* Git out here, Perky.

BAXTER: *(Pointing at the body.)* That isn't right. I didn't do right.

(He puts his hands over his face. Shedevil walks out of the bathroom and over to Baxter.)

SHEDEVIL: Mr. Blue?

BAXTER: It's a blot on my badge.

SHEDEVIL: Mr. Blue?

BAXTER: *(Looking at her.)* Perky?

SHEDEVIL: You have to listen to me.

BAXTER: I have to turn myself in.

SHEDEVIL: Hold my hand. *(He does.)* Hold hard. Vladimer was doomed.

BAXTER: His name was Vladimer?

SHEDEVIL: No, but he let me call him that. His family in Kiev used to take him to the basement…

ROB: The basement…

SHEDEVIL: You don't even want to know what they did there. Jimmy had been an alcoholic…

BAXTER: His name was Jimmy but he let you call him Vladimer?

SHEDEVIL: Yes. He was drug addicted, had an eating disorder, he had terrible, terrible problems with depression; it's what made him a jokester. He killed a man, by mistake, on peyote.

BAXTER: As a joke?

SHEDEVIL: Hold my other hand.

(He does.)

He served his time and found his God. Then he disappeared, left everybody, me included, an' was gone for five years.

BAXTER: But…

SHEDEVIL: Vaporized from the face of the earth. I wanted to help him. He wanted to marry me.

BAXTER: So, you're not carryin' his baby?

SHEDEVIL: I am.

BAXTER: He's been gone five years.

SHEDEVIL: He popped in once before.

BAXTER: I see.

SHEDEVIL: The last two weeks have been hell. Every night, he'd beat me.

BAXTER: *(Horrified.)* Beat you?

SHEDEVIL: Then he'd want me to cook home fries.

BAXTER: No?

SHEDEVIL: Then he'd beg me to kill him. Then he'd pull a few jokes.

BAXTER: Holy moley.

SHEDEVIL: Tonight, he'da make me cook home fries again.

BAXTER: Lordy…

SHEDEVIL: I just want to thank you, sir; you give him the peace he'd searched the world for.

BAXTER: I can hardly believe it.

SHEDEVIL: I can only say you did right.

SHIRL: You did right, honey.

ROB: More than that, you did good.

(Baxter breaks down crying. Shirl holds him; the others applaud him.)

BAXTER: Perky.

(He embraces her. Big 8 steps forward.)

BIG 8: I got to point out we got a sichy-ation here.

(People listen up.)

To the world, we got a lawman who's a brutal killer. They gonna rip off his badge…

SHIRL: Rip it off…

BIG 8: Whap him in the banger fifteen to twenty years.

SHIRL: A policeman in prison?

BIG 8: That man will never be able to take a damn shower.

SHIRL: Why can't he take a shower?

BIG 8: I'll explain it to you later.

SHIRL: Okay.

BIG 8: However, seen the other way, it's a act a' compassion.

SHEDEVIL: It is.

BIG 8: Somethin' every one of us in this room shoulda' done.

ROB: 'At's right.

SHIRL: Oh, I see about the shower.

BIG 8: We should have tried an' we didn't.

SHEDEVIL: Should have.

BIG 8: On'y Baxter did right.

ROB: Damn straight.

BIG 8: Now, we know it was Baxter did it...

> (A chorus of "He did," "Did it right here," "Did it in cold blood.")

> ... but we will never, never, never say.

> ("Never, never.")

> You shot him down, but it's family business now.

> (She hugs him.)

BAXTER: By God, I'm honored...I am honored just to be in this home.

ROB: (Raising one arm, fist closed, to the sky.) For Baxter.

SHIRL: For Baxter.

> (The others raise their arms and then, finally, Baxter. They are bound in blood. They look at each other.)

ROB: Now, how we gonna do this?

SHIRL: Well, one good thing, he ain't been seen in five years.

SHEDEVIL: That's right.

ROB: That's right.

BIG 8: His last wish was just to disappear.

> (A pause. They look at each other.)

SHIRL: Well, I can give him some help on that.

BAXTER: How's that, Honeybee?

SHIRL: I got my tools and aprons in the truck.

> (She strides out.)

> (Lights go down on the scene.)

SCENE 2

The lights come up on pure Breughel. Blood is everywhere. What's left of Black Dog is under a tarp on top of the butcher block island. Everyone wears bloody slaughterhouse aprons. They are equipped with well-used hatchets and saws, dripping gore. There are several garbage bags already filled. It is night; the room is full of shadows. A hanging lamp over the island swings back and forth. Shirl, Big 8, and Shedevil are on top of the butcher block, working. Shedevil is standing with an open bag to receive the parts. As the lights come up, Shirl throws something into Shedevil's bag. We don't see exactly, but it reminds us of a foot. Rob is stacking bags and cleaning. Baxter sits away from this scene, his head in his hands. Everyone's face and hands are smeared with blood, except Baxter's. Shirl is sawing. Big 8 is hacking right through the tarp with an ax. A radio on the counter is tuned to a country station.

BIG 8: Hell, I like a little music while I work.

SHIRL: On the last leg now.

SHEDEVIL: Thwack!

ROB: I'm stackin' 'em up over here.

SHIRL: How you doin', Baxter honey?

BAXTER: Lord, dear Lord, give me strength.

SHIRL: Lemme finish up here, Big 8.

BIG 8: *(Rolling off the butcher block.)* Hard on the sciatica. I got to get me some Tylenol.

SHIRL: Shoot. *(Whack!)* I can do this. *(Whack!)* Twelve hours at a go. *(Whack, whack, whack!)* I believe that should just about do 'er. First one of those I ever butchered. *(Getting off the island. To Shedevil.)* Bring that bag around here, will you, sweetie?
(Shedevil brings a black bag to the other side. Shirl pulls the tarp off, leans forward and, with her forearms, sweeps the last of the remains into Shedevil's bag.)
Okey-dokey hokey-pokey.

ROB: Here we go.

SHIRL: *(She looks around at her companions.)* Hey, I could use me some snacks.
(Baxter runs out the front door.)
Shoulda give him a Dramamine.

BIG 8: Work up a damn thirst.

SHIRL: Shedevil, whack us out a couple of ice waters, will ya?
(Shedevil goes to the fridge.)

I did a couple more of these, I'd be nigh onto gettin' it right.

(Baxter appears in the door.)

How you doin', Sweetpea?

BAXTER: Little mite queasy.

SHIRL: *(Reassuring.)* I was every bit of that when I started in slaughterin'. You just got to realize the nation's got to eat.

BIG 8: Or somethin'.

SHIRL: *(Gets it.)* Or somethin'.

BAXTER: I just…

BIG 8: Speak up, Baxter boy.

BAXTER: I just…see, I'm just wantin' to thank everybody.

BIG 8: Like they say on TV, "It takes a village." *(Gives Baxter a pat.)* Now, we got to have a little pow-wow here.

(Shedevil passes around ice water.)

SHIRL: *(Having checked the cupboards.)* Chex-Mix anybody's peckish.

(Rob leans on the island. Shedevil hops up and sits. The overhead lamp creates an odd spectacle. All except Baxter are in the slaughter aprons provided by Shirl.)

ROB: Got a couple root beers left.

(It has the atmosphere of a lunch-break at an abattoir.)

SHIRL: *(To Big 8.)* Little Thing, you still got my ol' cover-up from our pajama party? *(Touches Baxter's arm.)* A boy don't like to see his honey in her work things.

BIG 8: Top of the stairs.

(Shirl goes.)

Now, you listen up here, Baxter. We done our part, now it's up to you.

BAXTER: Yes, ma'am.

BIG 8: Don't call me ma'am. Time to take the garbage out, Baxter. Stick those bags in yer cruiser, honor poor ol' Jimmy's desire to disappear.

ROB: Got to stick him where the sun don't shine, boy.

BAXTER: I don't know…

SHEDEVIL: You can do it, Mr. Blue.

BAXTER: City dump's out.

ROB: How come?

BAXTER: Dogs.

SHIRL: How 'bout your attic?

(Shirl reappears in a robe. She also brings one for Big 8.)

BAXTER: Mama goes through my things. There is an old cistern in the basement of the police station.

ROB: See there.

BAXTER: Nobody goes down there.

BIG 8: Hey!

BAXTER: What?

SHIRL: Big 8's sayin' we don't want to know, baby.

BAXTER: Oh. But nobody does go down…

BIG 8: *(Finger to her lips.)* Shhh.

BAXTER: I git it.

SHIRL: *(Pecks him on the cheek.)* Snuggle bunny, you might want to load up.

BAXTER: Okey-dokey. *(Goes for a load of bags.)* I think it's gonna work out.
(Heads for door.) I'll tell you one thing. *(Turns to face them.)* I got friends.

ROB: You do.

SHIRL: That's right.

BAXTER: Gonna take me a couple of loads.

SHIRL: Don't drop nothin'.
(He exits.)

BIG 8: Well, it's been real interestin' for a Monday. Did pretty good, though.

SHIRL: *(Offers Big 8 a cover-up.)* Sis, we did real good.
(Big 8, Rob, and Shedevil take off the slaughterhouse aprons. They get piled with the trash bags for Baxter to take out. Big 8 puts on the cover-up, taking off soiled clothes, if necessary.)

BIG 8: *(To Shedevil.)* Your real name Perky?

SHEDEVIL: Yeah, right.

BIG 8: Plus you ain't got an artificial hand, huh?

SHEDEVIL: Hell no.

ROB: So Black Dog didn't cut if off.

SHEDEVIL: Duh.

BIG 8 You got you a real talent for deception.

SHEDEVIL: Like you don't?

ROB: Well, it worked out, didn't it? Worked out for the best. See, the good guys…

BIG 8: *(Baxter re-enters for more bags.)* Rob Bob?

ROB: Well, it did.

BIG 8: Put a plug in it, would ya?

SHIRL: *(Pointing.)* You got a little toe stickin' out the bag there.

BAXTER: Oh my God.

SHIRL: *(Pushing the finger back in with her finger.)* This little piggy went to market.

BAXTER: Oh my God.

(She pecks him on the cheek.)

SHIRL: All set now, sugar pie?

BAXTER: *(As he exits.)* What am I doin'?

ROB: *(To Big 8, who is washing up. He puts on his shirt.)* Hey, Big 8?

BIG 8: *(A little cranky.)* What?

ROB: You know there's eleven Hoppy pitchers where the hero an' the girl ride out, you know, end of the pitcher?

BIG 8: Nine.

ROB: No, there's eleven.

SHIRL: *(Warningly.)* Rob Bob.

ROB: I wondered could I borry the loan of a couple of horses.

BIG 8: Where you headed, Rob Bob?

ROB: Well…

BIG 8: Go on, I ain't gonna be mad.

ROB: Figgered we'd go up to the cabin. No offense meant.

BIG 8: No offense taken.

ROB: Practice up, an' we might git hitched 'fore rodeo season.

SHIRL: *(Looks at Big 8.)* Oh my.

BIG 8: You up for that, Shedevil?

SHEDEVIL: Whatever.

BIG 8: What the hell's your name, girl?

SHEDEVIL: *(Staring directly at her.)* My name is get-outta-my-face, yo.

(A moment, then Big 8 looks over at Rob.)

BIG 8: You still goin' for "Top Cowboy," right?

ROB: Girl, I'm bringin' you back the buckle.

BIG 8: *(Looking at Shedevil.)* Yeah, I got me some fine buckles.

SHIRL: Speakin' of buckles…

BIG 8: Put a sock in it, Shirl.

ROB: *(To Big 8.)* That's a solemn promise.

BIG 8: Well, that's all right then.

SHIRL: It is?

BIG 8: It's all right.

ROB: Gollee! Give me a hug, 8.

BIG 8: Not in front of your fiancée.

ROB: Oh yeah. Say now, end of the pitcher it's usual the hero would pick out a little somethin' on the guitar.

BIG 8: It's pretty late, Rob Bob.

ROB: Couple of choruses of "Tumblin' Tumbleweeds"?

SHIRL: We got work real early.

ROB: *(Disappointed.)* Well, okay then.

BIG 8: *(To Shirl.)* Girlfrien', tomorrow mornin' I can skip the spareribs.
(Shirl chuckles.)
Shedevil, seems like a pretty girl allus gits good luck, don't it? Got a good man fer yer hubby, got a bad man off yer trail, an' you don't have to listen to Lucifer Lee singin' "I Did it My Way." My hat's off to you, darlin'.
(Baxter is taking another load out.)
Git outta here, younguns, I got housework to do.

ROB: We got to do the kiss.

SHIRL: We might could skip the kiss.

ROB: Dude, you can't skip the final kiss.

BIG 8: *(Shirl starts to speak; Big 8 stops her with a gesture.)* Cowboy, you the most traditional sumbitch I ever saw.
(Baxter returns. They all look at Rob and Shedevil.)

ROB: Stand up straight, Shedevil. We gonna ride the trails together.
(He kisses her sweetly on the lips.)

BAXTER: What's goin' on?

SHIRL: Don't even start to think.

BAXTER: But, she's affianced.

BIG 8: He's kinda dead, Baxter.

BAXTER: *(Looks at the bag he's picked up.)* Well, that's true.

SHIRL: Git that las' load out of here, Honeypot.
(Baxter goes.)

ROB: Better git our stuff.
(He runs upstairs for his saddle and bag. Shedevil crosses to get her bag.)

SHIRL: I'll help you tidy up.

BIG 8: Purely appreciate that.
(They go to get out cleaning materials. Rob returns with his gear.)

ROB: Big 8?

BIG 8: *(Turning.)* Yeah.

ROB: You got the spirit of the cowboy code, Big 8.

BIG 8: Uh-huh.
(He moves to embrace her. She forestalls him.)
Better say yer last words.

ROB: Huh?

BIG 8: Like Hoppy.

ROB: Oh, Jeez…holy moley… *(Goes and tosses his gear out the broken door.)*
Darn-a-doodle, I almost forgot that. *(Turns.)* Lemme see. Ummm. Bad

guy died. Good guy got the girl. Town's safe, an' justice triumphed. How's that?

BIG 8: Real good.

ROB: Guess me and the schoolmarm better mount up.

SHEDEVIL: Big 8?

BIG 8: Yeah.

SHEDEVIL: Y'all a bunch of schizoid murderin' misfits, an' you treated me bad as a stray dog while you done unspeakable horrors, but all in all I had a pretty good time.

BIG 8: Uh-huh.

SHEDEVIL: Thwack, kaboom.

BIG 8: Same to you, darlin'.

ROB: Let's mount up.

BIG 8: *(Rob and Shedevil start to go.)* Hey, Rob Bob?

ROB: Yes, ma'am.

BIG 8: Don't the hero carry his bride across the threshold?

ROB: Ain't that comin' in?

BIG 8: Well, you only got the goin' out.

ROB: Dang, I hadn't thought a' that.

BIG 8: You almost did.

(Rob picks Shedevil up in his arms.)

ROB: All right now! Here we go. Ow!

BIG 8: What is it, darlin'?

ROB: Somethin' popped in my back.

BIG 8: Wouldn't be nuthin' serious.

SHEDEVIL: You drop me, you're toast.

ROB: Ow.

BIG 8: You carry her on out.

ROB See you on down the trail. *(As he goes.)* Ow. Dang, that hurts. Ow. *(His voice disappears in the night.)* Dang. Oh my goodness. Ow. Shoot! *(Shirl and Big 8 watch them disappear into the world beyond.)*

BIG 8: They're a pair, ain't they?

SHIRL: Did you pop that boy's back on purpose?

BIG 8: Oh, I don't know.

SHIRL: *(Eyes narrowed.)* What the hell you doin'?

BIG 8: What?

SHIRL: That girl absconded with your buckles.

BIG 8: I know.

SHIRL: I know you know.

BIG 8: Just a little weddin' present.

SHIRL: Uh-huh.

BIG 8: I got a big heart Shirl.

(Big 8 starts to clean. Shirl stares at her.)

You gonna take Baxter?

SHIRL: To the cleaners maybe.

BIG 8: Shirl?!

SHIRL: What he'll have in the police basement, hey, I'm goin' shoppin'.

BAXTER: *(Entering.)* I got him all in the cruiser.

SHIRL: You go along, sugar pie. I'm gonna hep Sis tidy.

(He stands there.)

Baxter?

(He stands.)

What is it, Baxter?

BAXTER: I have forced my sweet beloved to dismember a human body, and with these hands I have carried slimy black plastic bags filled with dripping body parts, and now, by the dark of night, will stuff them in a basement cistern at the center of the temple of justice, and then, depraved, will go on livin' as part of the human community though I have become homicidal pond scum always seein' blood, blood, blood on my hands, branded forever with the mark of Cain, forsaken by my church and country, wanderin' like a wraith the secondary roads of Wyoming, giving out speeding tickets. The only upside is for the last three hours since I killed poor Jimmy, I been nonstop hard as a rock.

SHIRL: *(Pleased and amazed.)* Well, I'll be home real soon, Baxter.

BAXTER: The Lord works in mysterious ways.

SHIRL: You betcha.

(He raises a hand in benediction and exits.)

SHIRL: Hard day for you, Mama?

BIG 8: Seen better. Got its recompenses.

SHIRL: *(As they clean.)* Now what recompenses would those be, sister mine?

(Big 8 reaches in a drawer and tosses two rubber-banded stacks of bills onto the butcher block.)

SHIRL: Well, goodness gracious.

BIG 8: You recall Black Dog come lookin' for his cocaine money?

SHIRL: How'd you git it, girl?

BIG 8: Oh, I found a spare minute.

SHIRL: You cute ol' thing. She didn't notice, huh?

BIG 8: There was a lot goin' on.

SHIRL: Won't she miss it?

BIG 8: I don't believe she wants no further ado with us. Whatta ya' think?

(They smile and clean.)

SHIRL: How much would that be, sister mine?

BIG 8: Maybe nine thousand.

SHIRL: Six for the mortgage an' three for me?

BIG 8: I could see that.

SHIRL: *(Sticks out her hand.)* Sold American.

(They shake. From outside, we hear Rob's cry, "Hi yo, Silver, away!" Hoofbeats drum, moving away into silence.)

BIG 8: That boy is shameless!

(They clean.)

SHIRL: Did he hurt his back bad?

BIG 8: He did, yes.

SHIRL: Damn shame.

BIG 8: Damn shame.

(They clean.)

You think we're bad girls, Sis?

SHIRL: Littlebit, we're just doin' what we can.

BIG 8: Okay then.

SHIRL: You gonna miss the lovin'?

BIG 8: Gettin' harder to come by.

SHIRL: Damn truth.

(A beautiful young cowboy in full garb appears in the doorway.)

DONNIE: 'Scuse me.

(They see him.)

BIG 8: Thank you Jesus.

DONNIE: Woulda knocked but there's the lack of a door.

BIG 8: Uh-huh.

DONNIE: My name would be Memphis Donnie Pride.

BIG 8: Oh yeah. I believe I heard you're a pretty good roper?

DONNIE: *(Radiant smile.)* Ever onc't in a while.

BIG 8: Broke up, huh?

DONNIE: Doctors said I was flat done.

BIG 8: Doctors, huh?

DONNIE: Yes, ma'am.

BIG 8: Don't call me ma'am, Donnie Pride.

DONNIE: But you the legendary Big 8.

BIG 8: Gettin' more legendary by the minute.

DONNIE: Can you do 'er?

BIG 8: Cowboy, you take a seat on the porch. Little bit I'll be out to lay some hands on you.

DONNIE: Much obliged. I can't hardly wait.

(Tips his hat. Exits.)

SHIRL: He can't hardly wait.

(They salute. Lights fade.)
(Black out.)

END OF PLAY

The Deal

from BACK STORY

Based on characters
created by Joan Ackermann

A dramatic anthology by
Joan Ackermann, Courtney Baron, Neena Beber, Constance Congdon, Jon Klein, Shirley Lauro, Craig Lucas, Eduardo Machado, Donald Margulies, Jane Martin, Susan Miller, John Olive, Tanya Palmer, David Rambo, Edwin Sanchez, Adele Edling Shank, Mayo Simon, and Val Smith

ORIGINAL PRODUCTION

Back Story was commissioned by Actors Theatre of Louisville and premiered at the Humana Festival of New American Plays in March 2000. It was directed by Pascaline Bellegarde, Aimée Hayes, Dano Madden, Meredith McDonough, and Sullivan Canaday White with the following cast:

Ethan . . . . Phil Bolin, Cary Calebs, Patrick
                                                                Dall'Occhio, Jeff Jenkins, Tom Johnson,
                                                                Cabe McCarty, Tom Moglia, Stephen Sislen,
                                                                Mark Watson, Zach Welsheimer, Travis York
Ainsley . . . . Shawna Joy Anderson, Molly M.
                                                                Binder, Rachel Burttram, Christy Collier,
                                                                Samantha Desz, Melody G. Fenster, Aimeé
                                                                Kleisner, Kimberly Megna, Holly W. Sims,
                                                                Heather Springsteen, Jessica Wortham

and with the following production staff:

Scenic Designer . . . . Paul Owen
Costume Designer . . . . Kevin McLeod
Lighting Designer. . . . . Greg Sullivan
Sound Designer . . . . Darron L. West
Properties Designer . . . . Mark Walston
Stage Manager . . . . Amber D. Martin
Dramaturgs. . . . . Michael Bigelow Dixon & Amy Wegener
Assistant Dramaturg. . . . . Kerry Mulvaney

CHARACTERS

ETHAN BELCHER
AINSLEY BELCHER

THE DEAL

Ainsley sits at a kitchen table with nine glass-bottled beers on it.

AINSLEY: I never drank nine beers before. I feel strangely free. Ethan, bring me my toe out of the refrigerator, will you? I like to see my toe when I'm drunk.

(He brings the toe. It's in a ziplock sandwich bag.)

Thanks. Two and a half years old, an' I cut this baby clean off with a snow shovel the night Momma went to the hospital to have you. You ingrate. One of a thousand sacrifices, baby brother. If ol' Reuben hadn't a come along drunk as a lord, I might have bled to death, but, more importantly, I would never, never have played the oboe. Did you know Reuben played with the Boston Symphony Orchestra for thirty years? That old drunk, who would have thought it. He's got crystal pure tone. You play a duet with Reuben, you downright feel fucked. He's eighty-one years old come November.

(She opens the ziplock and dumps the toe into her hand.)

They sewed this baby on an' it lasted fourteen years till it snapped off that time I fell when I was doing cross-country. I believe the moral to be that you can't put something broken back together. Not in the long run. This has proved true in all three of my romantic relationships. In each one, we split an' then came back together an' then broke off forever. The toe knows.

(She puts it back in the bag.)

I wonder how it came to be that I'm a supporting role even in my own life. I mean I thought I'd star in my life, but it hasn't worked out that way. You're the star of my life, brother mine. Whatever I am it's in relation to you. Second oboe. You know people hear about my toe before they hear about me? I meet 'em an' they say, "Oh, sure, you're the one keeps her toe in the refrigerator." Second fiddle to my own body parts. At what point, Ethan, is it determined in your own life whether you are to be a first chair or just a general all-purpose oboist? I believe it was when you were born, Ethan, and I wasn't allowed to go to the hospital. I was not…among the chosen, though I did, however, achieve self-mutilation with the snow shovel. Well, "They also serve who only bleed and wait," right? I believe I'll put my claim to fame back in the freezer compartment and fix you some dinner. What, dearest Ethan, would you like for dinner? I was once offered admission to the Boston Conservatory of Music, and though our family mythology would have it that I gave it up on your behalf, my sad, wild brother, I actually declined on the basis that it was a hell of a lot of money just to come out playing second oboe. It seemed a…pretension to be expensively trained to be ordinary. Oh, it's best to know who you are…or so they tell you.

• • •

Beauty

CHARACTERS

CARLA
BETHANY

BEAUTY

An apartment. Minimalist set. A young woman, Carla, on the phone.

CARLA: In love with me? You're in love with me? Could you describe yourself again? Uh-huh. Uh-huh. And you spoke to me? *(A knock at the door.)* Listen, I always hate to interrupt a marriage proposal, but…could you possibly hold that thought? *(Puts phone down and goes to door. Bethany, the same age as Carla and a friend, is there. She carries the sort of Mideastern lamp we know of from Aladdin.)*

BETHANY: Thank God you were home. I mean, you're not going to believe this!

CARLA: Somebody on the phone. *(Goes back to it.)*

BETHANY: I mean, I just had a beach urge, so I told them at work my uncle was dying…

CARLA: *(Motions to Bethany for quiet.)* And you were the one in the leather jacket with the tattoo? What was the tattoo? *(Carla again asks Bethany, who is gesturing wildly that she should hang up, to cool it.)* Look, a screaming eagle from shoulder to shoulder, maybe. There were a lot of people in the bar.

BETHANY: *(Gesturing and mouthing.)* I have to get back to work.

CARLA: *(On phone.)* See, the thing is, I'm probably not going to marry someone I can't remember…particularly when I don't drink. Sorry. Sorry. Sorry. *(She hangs up.)* Madness.

BETHANY: So I ran out to the beach…

CARLA: This was some guy I never met who apparently offered me a beer…

BETHANY: …low tide and this… *(The lamp.)* …was just sitting there, lying there…

CARLA: …and he tracks me down…

BETHANY: …on the beach, and I lift this lid thing…

CARLA: …and seriously proposes marriage.

BETHANY: …and a genie comes out.

CARLA: I mean, that's twice in a…what?

BETHANY: A genie comes out of this thing.

CARLA: A genie?

BETHANY: I'm not kidding, the whole Disney kind of thing, swirling smoke, and then this twenty-foot-high, see-through guy in like an Arabian out-fit.

CARLA: Very funny.

BETHANY: Yes, funny, but twenty feet high! I look up and down the beach, I'm alone. I don't have my pepper spray or my hand alarm. You know me, when I'm petrified I joke. I say his voice is too high for Robin Williams, and he says he's a castrati. Naturally. Who else would I meet?

CARLA: What's a castrati?

BETHANY: You know…

(The appropriate gesture.)

CARLA: Bethany, dear one, I have three modeling calls. I am meeting Ralph Lauren!

BETHANY: Okay, good. Ralph Lauren. Look, I am not kidding!

CARLA: You're not kidding what?!

BETHANY: There is a genie in this thingamajig.

CARLA: Uh-huh. I'll be back around eight.

BETHANY: And he offered me *wishes!*

CARLA: Is this some elaborate practical joke because it's my birthday?

BETHANY: No, happy birthday, but I'm like crazed because I'm on this deserted beach with a twenty-foot-high, see-through genie, so like sarcastically…you know how I need a new car…I said fine, gimme 25,000 dollars…

CARLA: On the beach with the genie?

BETHANY: Yeah, right, exactly, and it rains down out of the sky.

CARLA: Oh sure.

BETHANY: *(Pulling a wad out of her purse.)* Count it, those are thousands. I lost one in the surf.

(Carla sees the top bill. Looks at Bethany, who nods encouragement. Carla thumbs through them.)

CARLA: These look real.

BETHANY: Yeah.

CARLA: And they rained down out of the sky?

BETHANY: Yeah.

CARLA: You've been really strange lately, are you dealing?

BETHANY: Dealing what, I've even given up chocolate.

CARLA: Let me see the genie.

BETHANY: Wait, wait.

CARLA: Bethany, I don't have time to screw around. Let me see the genie or let me go on my appointments.

BETHANY: Wait! So I pick up the money…see, there's sand on the money… and I'm like nuts so I say, you know, "Okay, look, ummm, big guy, my uncle is in the hospital" …because as you know when I said to the people at work my uncle was dying, I was on one level telling the truth although it had nothing to do with the beach, but he was in Intensive Care after the accident, and that's on my mind, so I say, okay, Genie, heal my uncle…which is like impossible given he was hit by two trucks, and the genie says, "Yes, Master"…like they're supposed to say, and he goes into this like kind of whirlwind, kicking up sand and stuff, and I'm like, "Oh my God!" and the air clears, and he bows, you know, and says, "It is done, Master," and I say, "Okay, whatever-you-are, I'm calling on my cell phone," and I get it out and I get this doctor who is like dumbstruck who says my uncle came to, walked out of Intensive Care and left the hospital! I'm not kidding, Carla.

CARLA: On your mother's grave?

BETHANY: On my mother's grave.

(They look at each other.)

CARLA: Let me see the genie.

BETHANY: No, no, look, that's the whole thing…I was just, like, reacting, you know, responding, and that's already two wishes…although I'm really pleased about my uncle, the $25,000 thing, I could have asked for $10 million, and there is only one wish left.

CARLA: So ask for $10 million.

BETHANY: I don't think so. I don't think so. I mean, I gotta focus in here. Do you have a sparkling water?

CARLA: No. Bethany, I'm missing Ralph Lauren now. Very possibly my one chance to go from catalogue model to the very, very big time, so, if you are joking, stop joking.

BETHANY: Not joking. See, see, the thing is, I know what I want. In my guts. Yes. Underneath my entire bitch of a life is this unspoken, ferocious, all-consuming urge…

CARLA: *(Trying to get her to move this along.)* Ferocious, all-consuming urge…

BETHANY: I want to be like you.

CARLA: Me?

BETHANY: Yes.

CARLA: Half the time you don't even like me.

BETHANY: Jealous. The ogre of jealousy.

CARLA: You're the one with the $40,000 job straight out of school. You're the one who has published short stories. I'm the one hanging on by her fingernails in modeling. The one who has creeps calling her on the phone. The one who had to have a nose job.

BETHANY: I want to be beautiful.

CARLA: You are beautiful.

BETHANY: Carla, I'm not beautiful.

CARLA: You have charm. You have personality. You know perfectly well you're pretty.

BETHANY: "Pretty," see, that's it. Pretty is the minor leagues of beautiful. Pretty is what people discover about you after they know you. Beautiful is what knocks them out across the room. Pretty, you get called a couple of times a year; *beautiful* is twenty-four hours a day.

CARLA: Yeah? So?

BETHANY: So?! We're talking *beauty* here. Don't say "So?" Beauty is the real deal. You are the center of any moment of your life. People stare. Men flock. I've seen you get offered discounts on makeup for no reason. Parents treat beautiful children better. Studies show your income goes up. You can have sex anytime you want it. Men have to know me. That takes up to a year. I'm continually horny.

CARLA: Bethany, I don't even like sex. I can't have a conversation without men coming on to me. I have no privacy. I get hassled on the street. They start pressuring me from the beginning. Half the time, it never occurs to them to start with a conversation. Smart guys like you. You've had three long-term relationships, and you're only twenty-three. I haven't had one. The good guys, the smart guys are scared to death of me. I'm surrounded by male bimbos who think a preposition is when you go to school away from home. I have no woman friends except you. I don't even want to talk about this!

BETHANY: I knew you'd say something like this. See, you're "in the club" so you can say this. It's the way beauty functions as an elite. You're trying to keep it all for yourself.

CARLA: I'm trying to tell you it's no picnic.

BETHANY: But it's what everybody wants. It's the nasty secret at large in the world. It's the unspoken tidal desire in every room and on every street. It's the unspoken, the soundless whisper…millions upon millions of people longing hopelessly and forever to stop being whatever they are and be beautiful, but the difference between those ardent multitudes and me is that I have a goddamn genie and one more wish!

CARLA: Well, it's not what I want. This is me, Carla. I have never read a whole book. Page six, I can't remember page four. The last thing I read was *The*

Complete Idiot's Guide to WordPerfect. I leave dinner parties right after the dessert because I'm out of conversation. You know the dumb blond joke about the application where it says, "Sign here," she put Sagittarius? I've done that. Only beautiful guys approach me, and that's because they want to borrow my eye shadow. I barely exist outside a mirror! You don't want to *be me.*

BETHANY: None of you tell the truth. That's why you have no friends. We can all see you're just trying to make us feel better because we aren't in your league. This only proves to me it should be my third wish. Money can only buy things. Beauty makes you the center of the universe.

(Bethany picks up the lamp.)

CARLA: Don't do it. Bethany, don't wish it! I am telling you you'll regret it.

(Bethany lifts the lid. There is a tremendous crash, and the lights go out. Then they flicker and come back up, revealing Bethany and Carla on the floor where they have been thrown by the explosion. We don't realize it at first, but they have exchanged places.)

CARLA/BETHANY: Oh God.

BETHANY/CARLA: Oh God.

CARLA/BETHANY: Am I bleeding? Am I dying?

BETHANY/CARLA: I'm so dizzy. You're not bleeding.

CARLA/BETHANY: Neither are you.

BETHANY/CARLA: I feel so weird.

CARLA/BETHANY: Me too. I feel... *(Looking at her hands.)* Oh, my God, I'm wearing your jewelry. I'm wearing your nail polish.

BETHANY/CARLA: I know I'm over here, but I can see myself over there.

CARLA/BETHANY: I'm wearing your dress. I have your legs!!

BETHANY/CARLA: These aren't my shoes. I can't meet Ralph Lauren wearing these shoes!

CARLA/BETHANY: I wanted to be beautiful, but I didn't want to be you.

BETHANY/CARLA: Thanks a lot!!

CARLA/BETHANY: I've got to go. I want to pick someone out and get laid.

BETHANY/CARLA: You can't just walk out of here in my body!

CARLA/BETHANY: Wait a minute. Wait a minute. What's eleven eighteenths of 1,726?

BETHANY/CARLA: Why?

CARLA/BETHANY: I'm a public accountant. I want to know if you have my brain.

BETHANY/CARLA: One hundred thirty-two and a half.

CARLA/BETHANY: You have my brain.

BETHANY/CARLA: What shade of Rubenstein lipstick does Cindy Crawford wear with teal blue?

CARLA/BETHANY: Raging Storm.

BETHANY/CARLA: You have my brain. You poor bastard.

CARLA/BETHANY: I don't care. Don't you see?

BETHANY/CARLA: See what?

CARLA/BETHANY: We both have the one thing, the one and only thing everybody wants.

BETHANY/CARLA: What is that?

CARLA/BETHANY: It's better than beauty for me; it's better than brains for you.

BETHANY/CARLA: What? What?!

CARLA/BETHANY: Different problems.

(Blackout.)

END OF PLAY

Tattoo

CHARACTERS

LINK
JENNY
JONES
VLADIMIR
WILLIAM

TATTOO

Three women in their twenties sit on chairs facing a door upstage. Link (short for Linchovna) is dressed in black slacks, has short blond hair, several earrings, and all ten fingers adorned with rings. Jenny is dressed in a suit as a young advertising account executive might for a date. Jones is more in the girly-girl vein with curly hair and Laura Ashley style. She is a graduate student who works also as a waitress.

JENNY: What time is it?

JONES: *(Very Southern.)* 7:45.

JENNY: Where is this guy?

LINK: *(A Russian accent.)* He will come. He is sister's ex-husband. Very reliable person. He will come.

JONES: But...like if they both... I mean what do we do if, you know, they both...

LINK: Very reliable.

JONES: I am sweating like a shot-putter.

JENNY: Calm down. Breathe. *(Knock.)* See.

JONES: But what if it's...

LINK: Is Vladimir. Very Russian knock. Okay? I get.

JONES: But if it's William, do we...

LINK: Only Russian is knocking so deliberate as this. You sit, I do. *(She goes to the door.)* Ah. *(Russian.)* Ooh m^{ie}yáh b ^{ih}ll pree-páh-dok syáird-tsuh. Tih uh-púz-dah-vá-yesh. *(You gave me a heart attack. You are late.)*

VLADIMIR: *(Russian.)* Ahv-tóe-booss pree-shóal púhz-dnuh. Yah lóohch-shuh dyéluhl shtaw smúg. *(Bus was late. I did the best I could.)* *(He enters. He is big, very big, and bearded and tattooed. He has a bag with him much like an old-fashioned doctor bag.)* (K)huh-ruh-sháw, éh-tut ch^{ie}l-uh-v^{ie}k gdyeh aown. *(Okay, this guy he is where?)*

JONES: My God, he's speaking Russian.

LINK: He *is* Russian. All Russians are coming to your country, get ready. *(Russian.)* Aown n^{i}ee yesh-cháw n^{i}ee pree-yéh-(k)hull. Ee-dée zhdoo féh-toy k^{w}óm-nah-tuh. *(He hasn't arrived. Go in that room and wait.)*

VLADIMIR: *(Russian.)* (K) huh-ruh-sháw nᵃoᵂ ooh mⁱᵉn-yáh svee-dáh-nyuh chᴵée-ez chahss. Éh-tuh dvair? *(Okay, but in one hour I have an appointment. That door?)*

(Vladimir heads toward the other room.)

LINK: *(Russian.)* Da. *(Yes.)*

JENNY: What did you tell him?

LINK: Be ready. We will tell him when. Call him in.

JONES: Is this really a good idea? Is this really, really, really a good idea?

JENNY: We need closure. He needs closure. There is going to be closure.

(A knock on the door.)

JONES: *(Whispering.)* Oh my God. Oh my God it's him. I have a good idea. You guys do this. You'll be better at this than me. I'll just…oh my God, can I do this?

LINK: Sit down. Not to vacillate. We do this. *(They arrange themselves on the chairs.)* Okay. Very calm. Very good. This is no more than result of his actions. We are a living logic for him. Breathing. Breathing. Good. Okay. We begin. *(Another knock.)* I am liking this.

(She opens the door. The man outside, William, immediately grabs her and pulls her into a passionate kiss. After it has gone on for a while, he has the sense of being watched. He removes his lips from Link and sees the seated women.)

WILLIAM: Oh shit.

JENNY: Hello, William.

JONES: Hi.

LINK: *(Still in his arms.)* Hello, William.

WILLIAM: *(Trying to recover.)* All right, all right, this is really…an intrusion. This is really second-rate is what it is. I cannot believe…have I ever gone through your purses, have I ever gone through…

JENNY: You were going to say "our drawers"?

WILLIAM: No, no, I wasn't, Jenny, I wasn't going to say "your drawers." I was pointing out that there are issues of privacy, that there are questions of trust… *(Realizes he is still embracing Link.)* Oh. Excuse me. *(He releases her.)* I was so…

JENNY: Fucked up.

WILLIAM: No, not fucked up, Jenny, taken aback. Yes. Completely taken aback that you…

JENNY: Knew each other.

WILLIAM: No, I didn't say…you are putting, unfairly, words in my mouth. Look

Jenny, if you are looking for the negative, you will find the negative. If you insist something is shoddy, it will look shoddy to you.

JONES: My daddy will come down here and eat your lunch!

WILLIAM: Jones, will you for once in your life wait to start crying until there is something to cry about?

JONES: You slept with me at 6 A.M. this morning!

WILLIAM: Well, yes I did, Jones. I did that. Well, actually, it was around 6:15.

JENNY: So that was the early meeting?

WILLIAM: Well no, I mean yes, there was an early meeting…

JONES: You said you had to see me. You said you were wracked with desire.

LINK: Wracked with desire?

JENNY: You said that to me at lunch.

WILLIAM: Okay, hold it…

JENNY: It's why I went into the trees with you in the park.

LINK: Wracked with desire, yes, it's very charming.

WILLIAM: Excuse me…

LINK: In the trees his methodology is what?

JENNY: Kissed my neck.

JONES: That's it! That's what he does! He goes for your goddamn neck like an attack dog! And here I was thinking that was because he was wracked with desire!

LINK: Then hand goes up leg. He is then unbuttons the blouse…

JONES: Then he starts saying "please," he says "please" over and over and over! Please, please, please!

LINK: Is like puppy.

WILLIAM: All right, goddammit, I concede the point!

JENNY: He concedes the point.

WILLIAM: If the point is that I am having more than one relationship, you can get off that point because nobody is arguing with you!

JENNY: Oh good.

WILLIAM: We can calm down!

JENNY: Fine.

JONES: You made love to me at 6 AM this morning! You called me your little tuna melt!

JENNY: Tuna melt?

LINK: What is tuna melt?

JENNY: You took me behind the trees at noon.

LINK: And tonight you will teach me *Kama Sutra*.

WILLIAM: This isn't about sex. This is about something way more profound than sex.

JENNY: Oh good, because I thought it *was* about sex.

WILLIAM: Well, it isn't, Jenny it's about…

JENNY: Screwing like a rabbit.

WILLIAM: No.

JENNY: Completely indiscriminate sex.

LINK: Altogether impersonal.

JENNY: Wildly dysfunctional.

JONES: He called me his tuna melt.

JENNY: Okay, Jones, that adds a dollop of romance.

WILLIAM: You may not recognize this but it's about *passion*. It is a frank admission that complex personalities have complex needs, and that…

JENNY: Point of order.

WILLIAM: Each of those needs finds passionate fulfillment…

JENNY: Point of order.

WILLIAM: What?

JENNY: You are the complex personality in question?

WILLIAM: Yes, I am.

JENNY: Just trying to keep up.

WILLIAM: Now each one of you is very different.

JENNY: We are very different.

WILLIAM: And in each case a different part of me responds. I don't give the same thing, I don't get the same thing. The me that is with each of you could not respond to the others. That self is faithful and would never betray you. You wouldn't want that part of me you don't have, and were I not as complex as I am there wouldn't have been enough of each part of me for you to relate to, to care about, in fact, to love.

(There is a long, stunned pause.)

JONES: What the *hell* is he talking about?

LINK: He has many souls.

JENNY: He da three-souled man.

WILLIAM: Go ahead, Jenny, make fun of what you don't understand. You are a wonderful person, a very talented advertising account executive, but you have a demeaningly reductive view of life. That is one of the reasons your spirit has sought me out. You want to be carried into deeper water.

JENNY: Well I will admit that it's getting pretty deep.

WILLIAM: Now I'm not saying there aren't issues here. Matters of the heart, intimacies that I want to discuss with you alone, Jenny, and you too Jones, of course I meant you, too.

JONES: Okay now, I want to get down and talk some Georgia talk here…you know, get right on down in the red dirt here…and what I got on my mind is "am I *is* or am I *ain't* your tuna melt?"

WILLIAM: I am what you need me to be, Jones. *(Link locks the door.)* What are you doing, Link?

LINK: I am making here old-fashioned totalitarian state.

JENNY: *(Moving one chair away from the others.)* Sit down, William.

WILLIAM: I see no reason to sit down.

JENNY: Bill, do you remember when we very recently began seriously to make our wedding plans?

WILLIAM: Yes, I do.

JENNY: Do you remember saying you wanted a really big wedding?

WILLIAM: Yes I do.

JENNY: And I said, "Honey, I just don't know that many people," and you said, "Sweetie, I could list two hundred family, friends, and business associates right now." And I bet you ten dollars and, by golly, you sat right down and did it!

LINK: He has good organizational memory, to do *this* he had to have such a memory.

JENNY: *(Taking a paper out of her briefcase.)* Now, Bill, this is the account of your activities today that I plan to fax to that list if you don't sit down. *(He glances over the letter and sits down.)* I know it's a little heavy on sexual specifics, but you have such a remarkably individual style I thought it made good reading.

JONES: I am never dressing up like that again at 6 AM!

WILLIAM: What precisely is it that you want?

LINK: Ah.

JENNY: Ah.

JONES: Ah.

JENNY: What precisely? Well, we want you to meet someone.

LINK: *(Russian)* Vlah-dée-meer, vuh-(k)huh-dée! Puh-ráh rahbᵃoʷ-táhts. *(Vladimir, come in! It is time to go to work.)* *(Vladimir enters.)* Vladimir, I am wanting you to meet interesting person William. William, this is interesting person Vladimir.

(Vladimir clicks his heels and bows slightly.)

WILLIAM: If you are planning to kill me or harm me, I would like it to be clearly understood that I am a lawyer, my friends are lawyers, my mother is a lawyer, my brother Don is a *ferocious* lawyer, and you will pay. P-A-Y. Pay.

LINK: I like this, William, this is very dramatic, but in this time we don't kill you. This is very funny idea though. You make good Russian joke. Wait, one moment, I tell Vladimir.

(In Russian, Link communicates William's fear. Vladimir laughs and slaps William on the back.)

JENNY: Okay, so it's "the lady and the tiger." Behind two doors, the choice is yours. Here's the deal. I will fax the aforementioned document to the aforementioned list, or Vladimir will tattoo on your butt our version of what you did today.

(Jenny hands William another piece of paper.)

WILLIAM: What?!

JONES: Signed.

JENNY: And dated.

WILLIAM: You are kidding.

JENNY: Take a good look at Vladimir. Does he look like he's kidding?

(Vladimir opens his bag, takes out a small towel, and begins laying out the tools of his trade.)

LINK: In Russia, this man is thoracic surgeon, but in America he is tattoo artist. Such is fate of Russian people. *(Russian.)* N'ee pláhts, moy droohg. *(Do not weep, my friend.)*

(He wipes his eyes.)

WILLIAM: *(Still holding the paper.)* I am supposed to go through life with this tattooed on my butt?

JENNY: William, like many pharmaceuticals, you need a warning label.

JONES: But they can take a tattoo off.

LINK: Not with Russian inks.

WILLIAM: I cannot believe this is happening to me!

JENNY: So you choose the fax?

WILLIAM: You know perfectly well that would ruin my career.

JENNY: Well, see now, we just seem to be on the horns of a dilemma.

JONES: Your career or your rear.

LINK: The lady…

JONES: Or your skinny white butt.

WILLIAM: How the hell did the three of you find out about each other?

LINK: Vladimir is also private detective.

WILLIAM: *(To Link.)* And what made you think you needed a private detective?

LINK: Because, my darling, I am Russian.

JENNY: So what'll it be, Billy?

WILLIAM: Can I have just a goddamn minute here?

JONES: I'm gonna wash your mouth out with soap.

LINK: Man must come to terms with tragic fate. Is good. Okay, while you think, Vladimir will sing you song of suffering and transfiguration from Ukraine. *(Vladimir does; it has no words but great feeling.)* And I will read you *Kama Sutra.*

WILLIAM: Oh God.

LINK: You say tonight our souls, our bodies will become one through *Kama Sutra.* This I don't want to miss.

(Link begins reading the first few sentences of the Kama Sutra, *"Man, the period of whose life is one hundred years, should practise Dharma, Artha, and Kama at different times and in such a manner that they may harmonize together and not clash in any way. He should acquire learning in his childhood, in his youth, and middle age he should attend to Artha and Kama, and in his old age he should perform Dharma, and thus seek to gain Moksha, i.e., release from further transmigration." Vladimir sings more softly and prepares, the women watch. William fumes and puts his head in his hands. Lights out.)*

END OF PLAY

Barefoot Woman
in a Red Dress

This monologue was written, along with *White Elephants,* on commission for *Heaven and Hell (on Earth): A Divine Comedy.*

BAREFOOT WOMAN
IN A RED DRESS

A young woman in a red dress on a bare stage with bare feet. As the lights come up, the stands, looking at her feet. A moment. She looks up and sees the audience.

CLAIRE: Oh.

You're looking at me.

I'm going to do my dance for you now.

(She does. And very nicely too. She obviously has had training. As she dances, she speaks.)

You've probably noticed I'm naked.

Some of you are imagining me with clothes on.

Whatever.

We can do what we want here.

Till we run out.

(She dances for a moment in silence. Then, still dancing, speaks again.)

As you see …

It's flat all the way to the horizon.

And empty.

No Danish furniture or geologic formations.

No flics.

No sex.

No shopping.

Those who dance, dance separately.

We have only what we can do and what we know.

Which is pretty scary.

The big finish.

(She dances beautifully. She finishes.)

That's the end of my dance.

(Silence.)

Now I just stand here.

(She does.)

I don't I know any poetry.

My singing was the despair of the Midwest.

I play field hockey. But there's no equipment.

I don't do imitations.

(Silence.)

Thank God you're just other people who don't know what to do.

And not an audience.

Imagine having to watch me for eternity.

And vice versa.

(A pause.)

Even at these prices.

Especially naked.

Now, there's something that gets old.

If I had known I would be thrown back on my own resources, I would have become a more interesting person.

Learned an instrument.

As it is, I think I'll lie down.

(She does.)

The hardest thing is …

We don't have to sleep

Or eat.

We can watch each other.

(She watches the audience carefully.)

Please don't take this the wrong way, but

you're not particularly worth watching.

We all should have worked on it.

(She lies still, looking back at her feet. Then she looks up.)

I wonder what made me think I was a self?

Probably the SATs.

(Silence.)

I really can't tell if I'm being punished or beatified.

(A pause.)

I know one thing.

It's not

eternal

rest.

What I think is

We're fucked.

• • •

White Elephants

from HEAVEN AND HELL (ON EARTH):
A DIVINE COMEDY

A comedic anthology by Robert Alexander, Jenny Lyn Bader, Elizabeth Dewberry, Deborah Lynn Frockt, Rebecca Gilman, Keith Glover, Hilly Hicks, Jr., Karen Hines, Michael Kassin, Jane Martin, William Mastrosimone, Guillermo Reyes, Sarah Schulman, Richard Strand, Alice Truan, Elizabeth Wong.

HUMANA FESTIVAL PRODUCTION:

White Elephants, part of *Heaven and Hell (On Earth): A Divine Comedy,* was commissioned by Actors Theatre of Louisville and premiered at the Humana Festival of New American Plays in March 2001. It was directed by Sullivan Canaday White and Meredith McDonough with the following cast:

Giselle . . . . .Nastaran Ahmadi

WHITE ELEPHANTS

GISELLE: Good morning, and to all our cherubim and seraphim inductees, we would like to welcome you to Republican Heaven. If you'll all just flap over here and hover for a minute or two, I'll give you the introductory. First of all, you'll be pleased to know liberals don't go to heaven; it's music we want around here—not whining. You may have noticed there are no black people here; that's not racism—that's interior design. Actually, we do have African Americans, but anyone who is black and Republican has to be so crazy we keep them in a separate space. This isn't about Apartheid; this is about mental health. After the period of acclimatization, many of you will become guardian angels. This means you look after people on earth who make more than $250,000 annually. They'll be up here with us eventually, and we don't want them damaged or scratched. Obviously, most harpists come from high-income families, plus seeing as we're here together for eternity, we prefer you've gone to cotillion. And, as we say here in heaven, it's about manners, manners, manners. Dress code: ties for the gentlemen; ankle-length skirts for the ladies. Please socialize, but remember our house rules: no free needle exchange; no condoms (angels practice abstinence); and definitely no abortion. Pick up your tax rebates on the table to the left, and remember, your heirs will not be paying estate taxes. Hey, if this isn't heaven, what the hell is, huh? You'll notice the banners, the ice cream cake, the party poppers—that's just our endless preparations for Strom and Jessie. All right, seraphim and cherubim, let's mingle, fox-trot, dove hunt, and swap stories about Tuscany. One final thought about our timing and good fortune—you don't have to be down there during a Republican presidency. Joking.

• • •